Marie Curie
A Quest for Light

Facebook: **facebook.com/idwpublishing**
Twitter: **@idwpublishing**
YouTube: **youtube.com/idwpublishing**
Instagram: **@idwpublishing**

ISBN: 978-1-68405-837-2   24 23 22 21   1 2 3 4

Cover Art by
Anna Błaszczyk

Written by
**Frances Andreasen Østerfelt
and Anja Cetti Andersen**

Illustrated by
Anna Błaszczyk

Danish Edition Edited by
**Carsten Søndergaard
and Pernille Arvedsen**

Translated from Danish by
Frances Andreasen Østerfelt

English Edition Edited by
Justin Eisinger

Nachie Marsham, Publisher
Blake Kobashigawa, VP of Sales
Tara McCrillis, VP Publishing Operations
John Barber, Editor-in-Chief
Mark Doyle, Editorial Director, Originals
Justin Eisinger, Editorial Director, Graphic Novels and Collections
Scott Dunbier, Director, Special Projects
Mark Irwin, Editorial Director, Consumer Products Mgr
Joe Hughes, Director, Talent Relations
Anna Morrow, Sr. Marketing Director
Alexandra Hargett, Book & Mass Market Sales Director
Keith Davidson, Senior Manager, PR
Topher Alford, Sr Digital Marketing Manager
Shauna Monteforte, Sr. Director of Manufacturing Operations
Nathan Widick, Sr. Art Director, Head of Design
Neil Uyetake, Sr. Art Director Design & Production
Shawn Lee, Art Director Design & Production
Jack Rivera, Art Director, Marketing

Ted Adams and Robbie Robbins, IDW Founders

The authors wish to express their gratitude to Renaud Huynh and Marité
Amrani of Musée Curie in Paris, and Małgorzata Marciniak of fra Muzeum Marii Skłodowskiej-Curie (Marie Curie museum in Warsaw) for their
generous sharing of knowledge as well as Muzeum Warszawy (Warsaw
Historical Museum) for photographic material from the Warsaw of Marie's
childhood.

Special thanks to Marie and Pierre Curie's granddaughter, professor in
nuclear physics Hélène Langevin-Joliot, for generously sharing insights
into the lives of her grandparents.

Thanks to Danish Arts Foundation (Statens Kunstfond) for their support
and Bikuben-fonden for travel support.

Published with support from the Danish Arts Foundation.

K:
Danish Arts
Foundation

FOREWORD

Marie Curie was born Marya Skłodowska in Poland in 1867. She dedicated her life to science and research and became the first female professor at the Sorbonne University in Paris, and the first female member of the Royal Danish Scientific Society.

Marie Curie was an extraordinary person whose research was groundbreaking in medical science, for treatment and diagnosis. As a lone woman in a scientific world peopled exclusively by males, she was primus motor in the discovery of new elements and legendary in demonstrating the radioactive properties of specific elements. These discoveries were not only vital in scientific evolution, but also instrumental in Marie Curie becoming the first woman to be awarded a Nobel Prize; and the first — and to date the only — person to be awarded two Nobel Prizes in two different scientific categories: the first in physics, the second in chemistry.

Marie grew up in a country where women were forbidden a higher education; but she yearned to learn more. She wanted to understand nature and its laws, to know why things were how they were. It was her impassioned drive and willpower that brought her to France, where she got her education and met the love of her life, the physicist Pierre Curie.

With this graphic novel we want to tell the story about the woman, Marie Curie, who against all odds achieved unique international fame. And with Marie Curie's life as an example, will remind the readers how rich the world could be if equal opportunities existed for everyone — irrespective of gender, race, or nationality.

Frances Andreasen Østerfelt
and Anja C. Andersen

Chapter 1

1867-1884

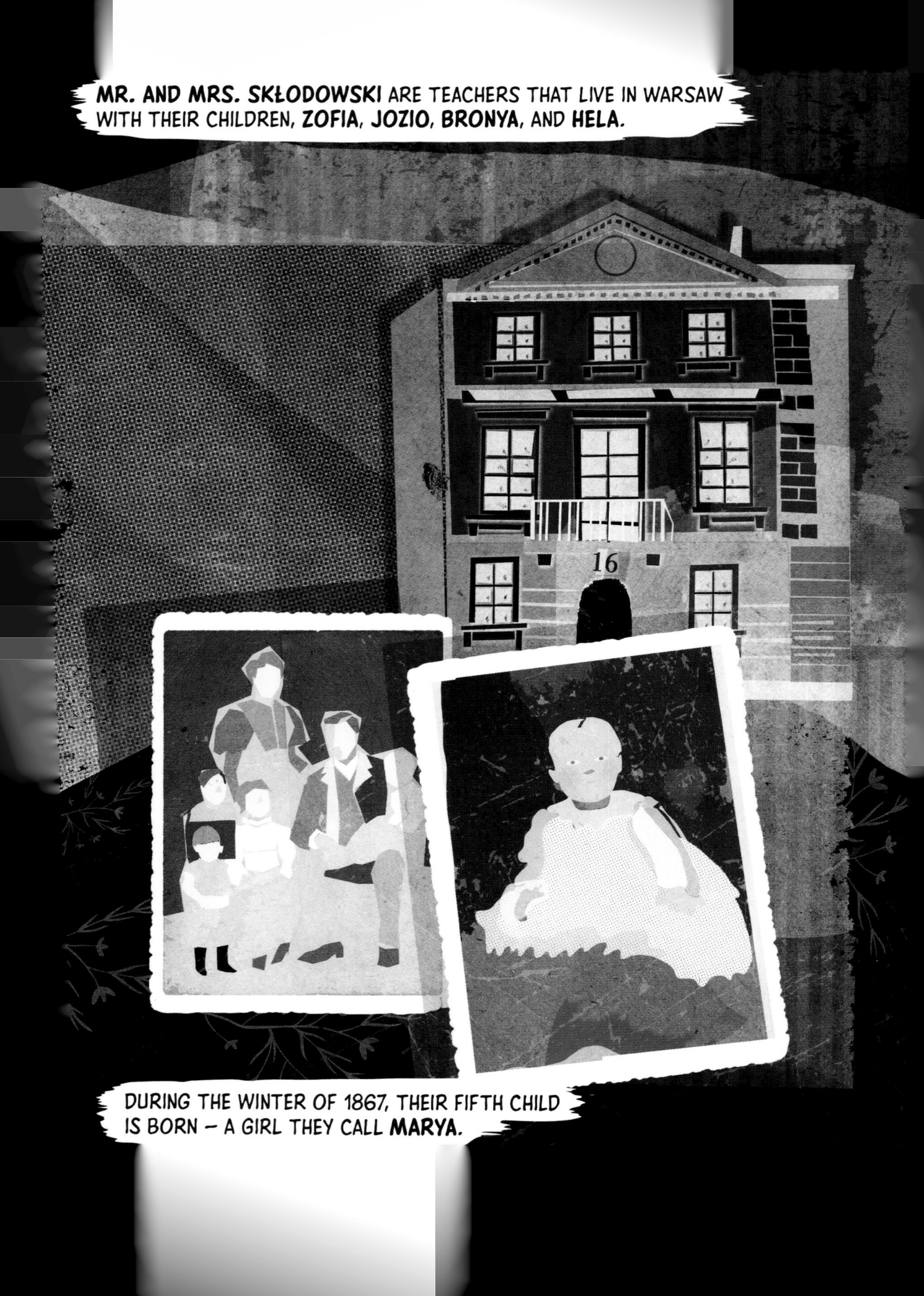
MR. AND MRS. SKŁODOWSKI ARE TEACHERS THAT LIVE IN WARSAW WITH THEIR CHILDREN, ZOFIA, JOZIO, BRONYA, AND HELA.
16
DURING THE WINTER OF 1867, THEIR FIFTH CHILD IS BORN — A GIRL THEY CALL MARYA.

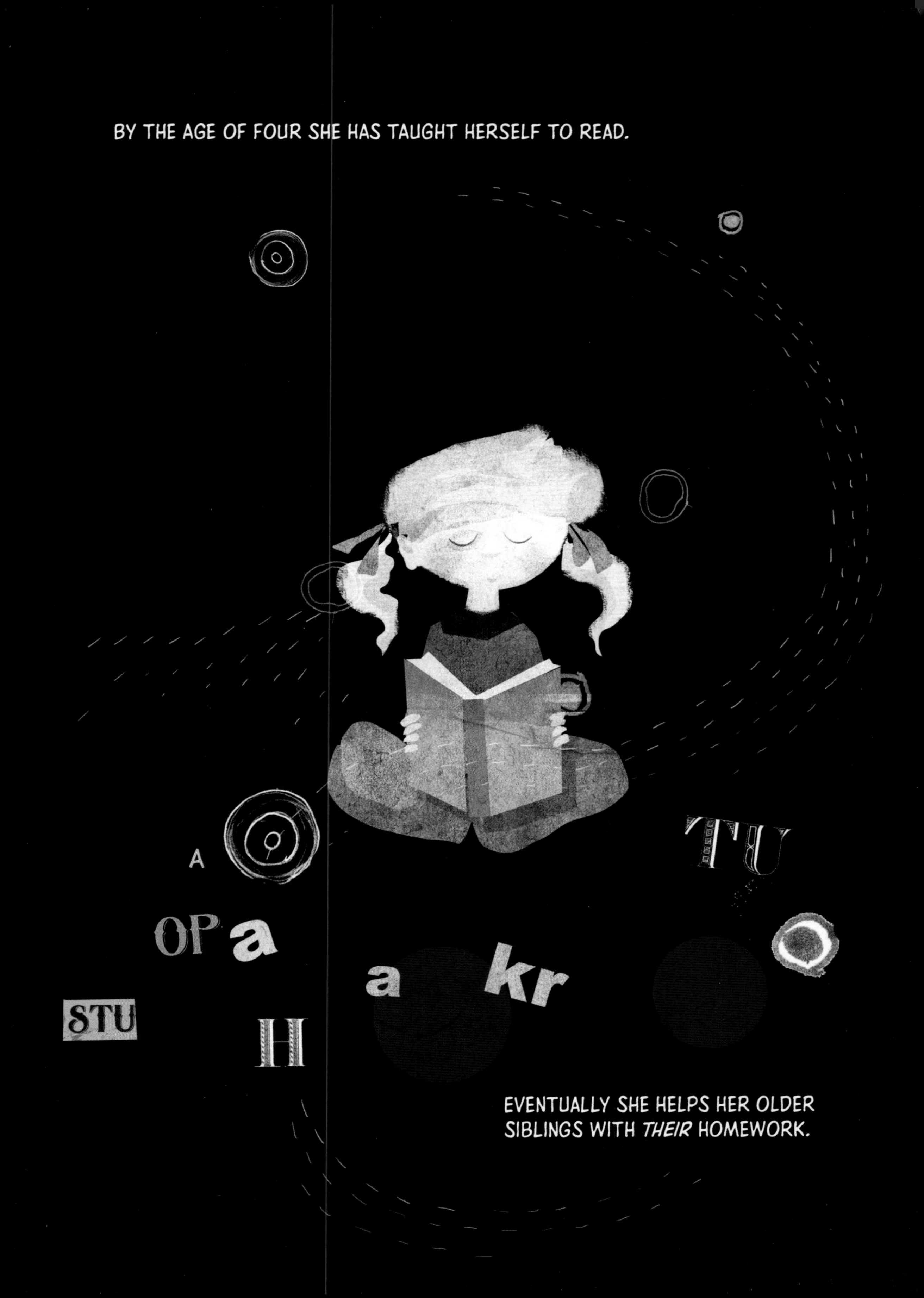
BY THE AGE OF FOUR SHE HAS TAUGHT HERSELF TO READ.
EVENTUALLY SHE HELPS HER OLDER SIBLINGS WITH *THEIR* HOMEWORK.

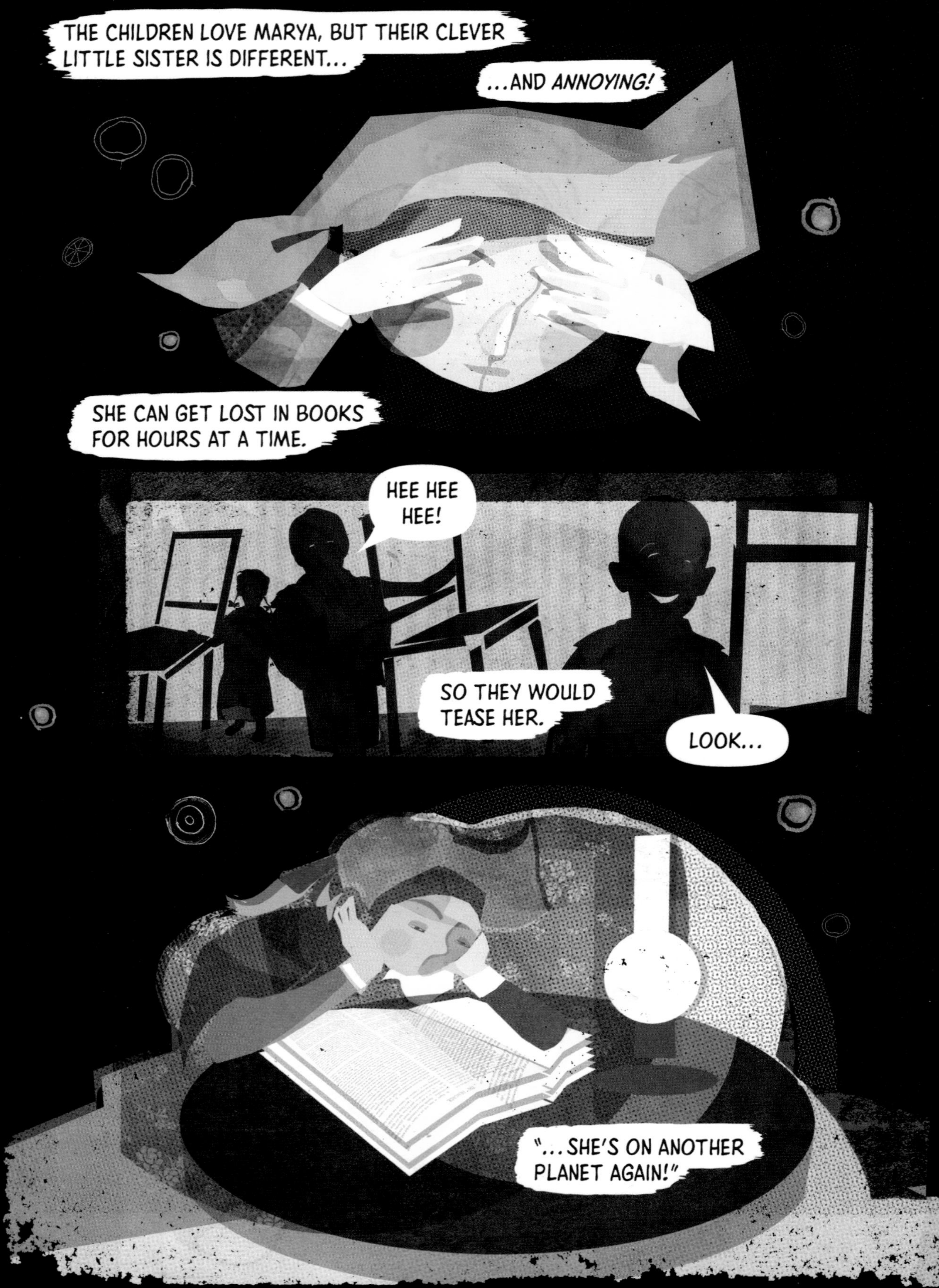
THE CHILDREN LOVE MARYA, BUT THEIR CLEVER LITTLE SISTER IS DIFFERENT...
...AND *ANNOYING!*
SHE CAN GET LOST IN BOOKS FOR HOURS AT A TIME.
HEE HEE HEE!
SO THEY WOULD TEASE HER.
LOOK...
"...SHE'S ON ANOTHER PLANET AGAIN!"

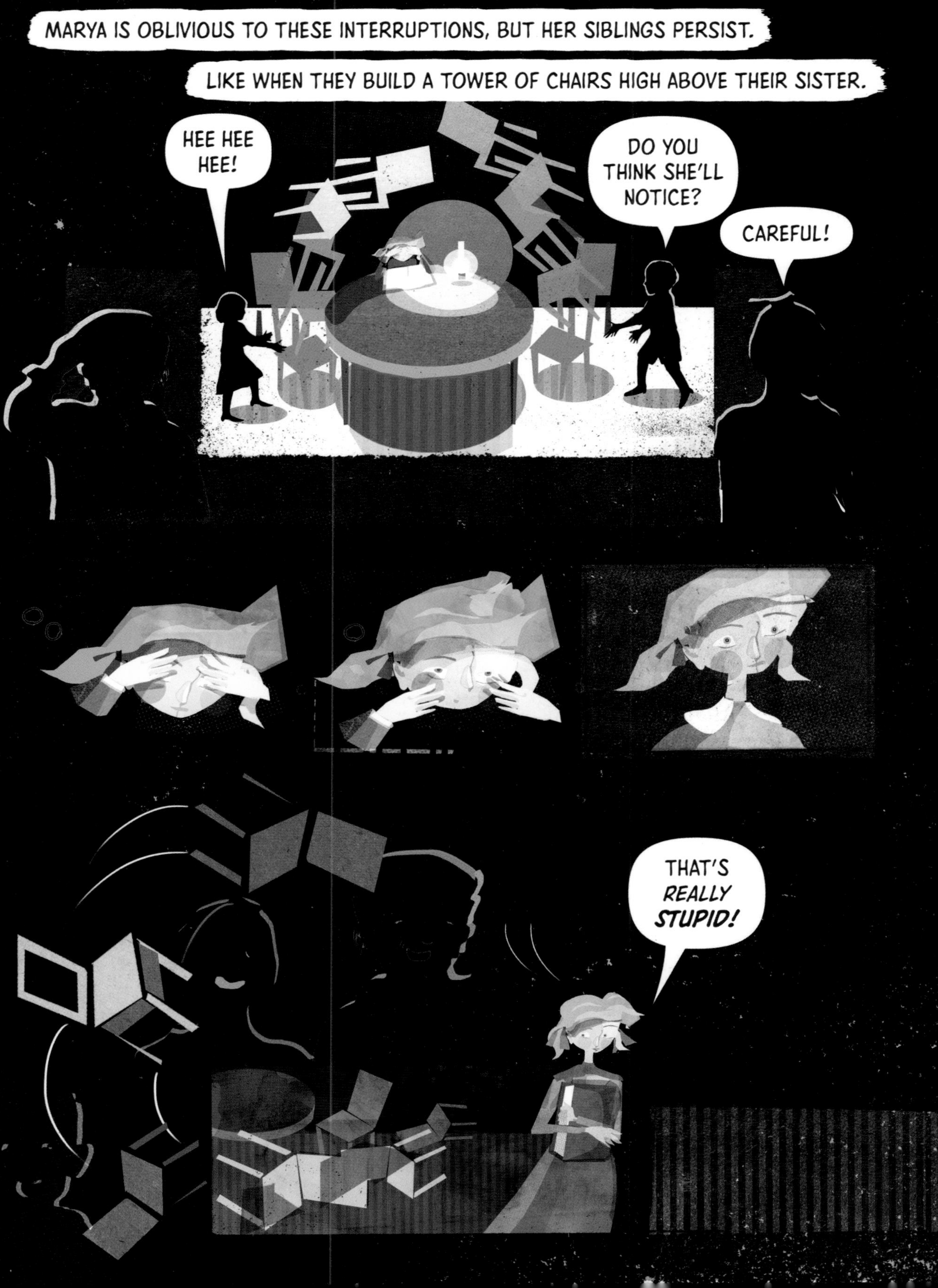
MARYA IS OBLIVIOUS TO THESE INTERRUPTIONS, BUT HER SIBLINGS PERSIST.
LIKE WHEN THEY BUILD A TOWER OF CHAIRS HIGH ABOVE THEIR SISTER.
HEE HEE HEE!
DO YOU THINK SHE'LL NOTICE?
CAREFUL!
THAT'S REALLY STUPID!

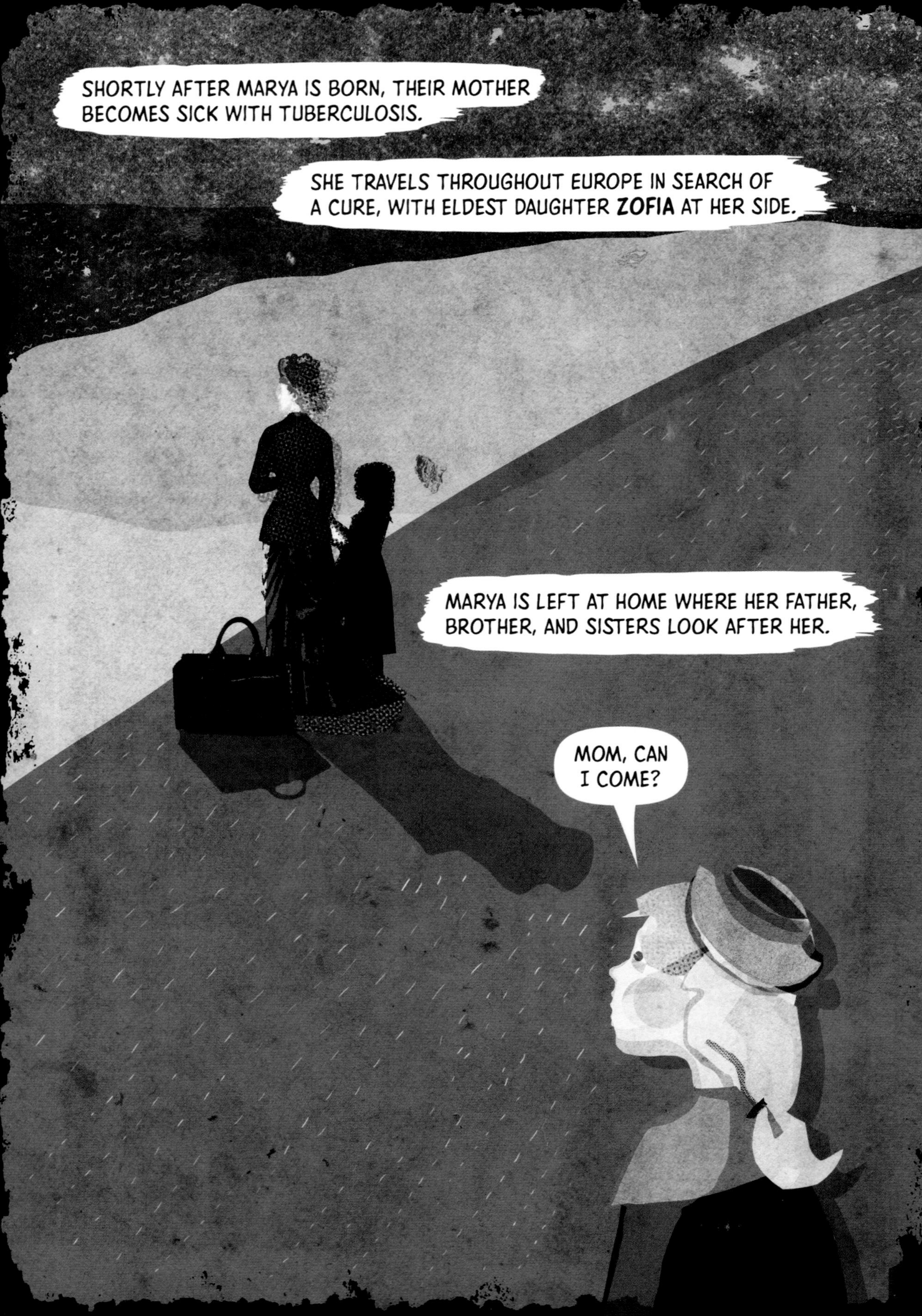
SHORTLY AFTER MARYA IS BORN, THEIR MOTHER BECOMES SICK WITH TUBERCULOSIS.
SHE TRAVELS THROUGHOUT EUROPE IN SEARCH OF A CURE, WITH ELDEST DAUGHTER ZOFIA AT HER SIDE.
MARYA IS LEFT AT HOME WHERE HER FATHER, BROTHER, AND SISTERS LOOK AFTER HER.
MOM, CAN I COME?

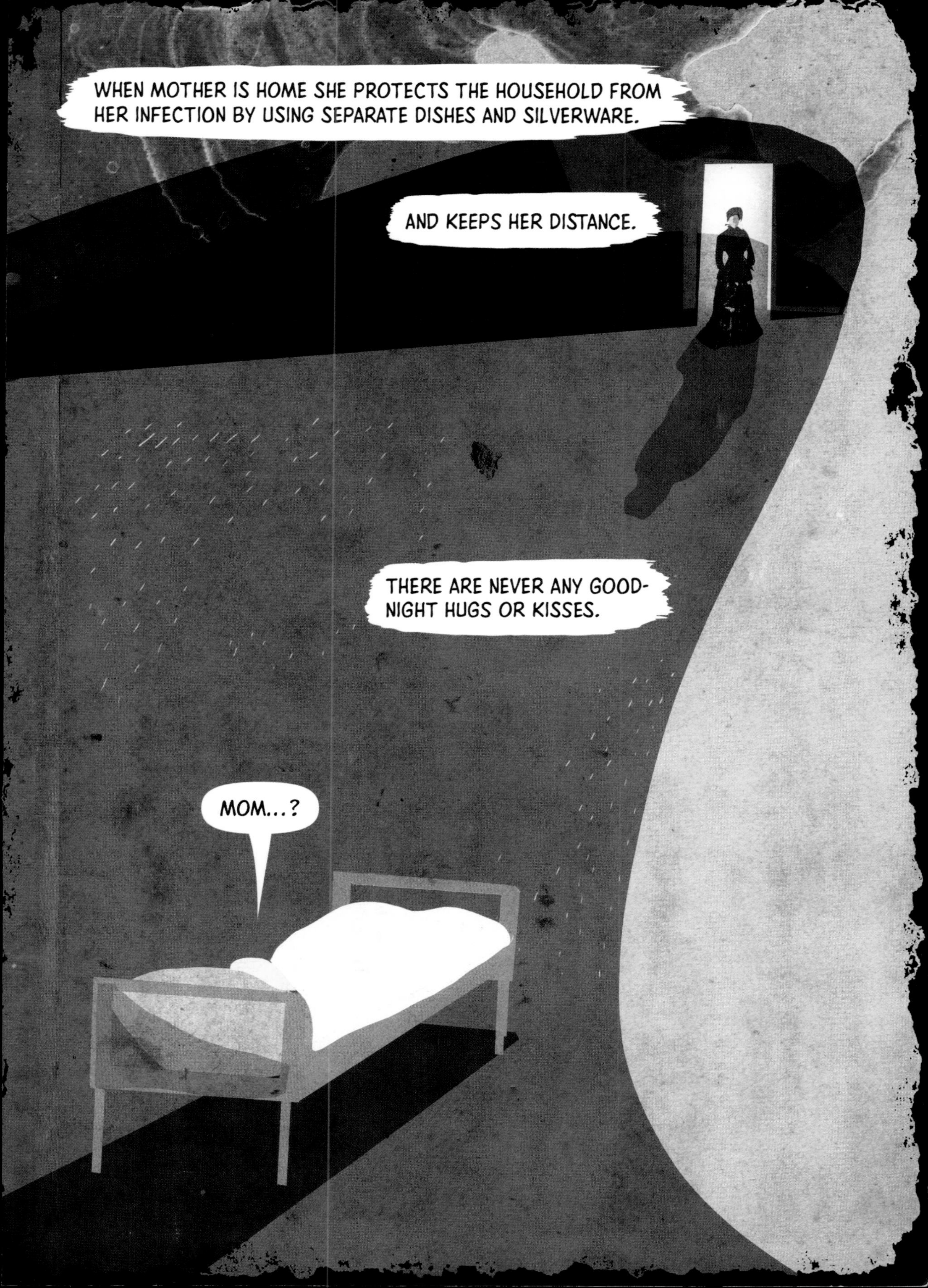
WHEN MOTHER IS HOME SHE PROTECTS THE HOUSEHOLD FROM HER INFECTION BY USING SEPARATE DISHES AND SILVERWARE.
AND KEEPS HER DISTANCE.
THERE ARE NEVER ANY GOOD-NIGHT HUGS OR KISSES.
MOM...?

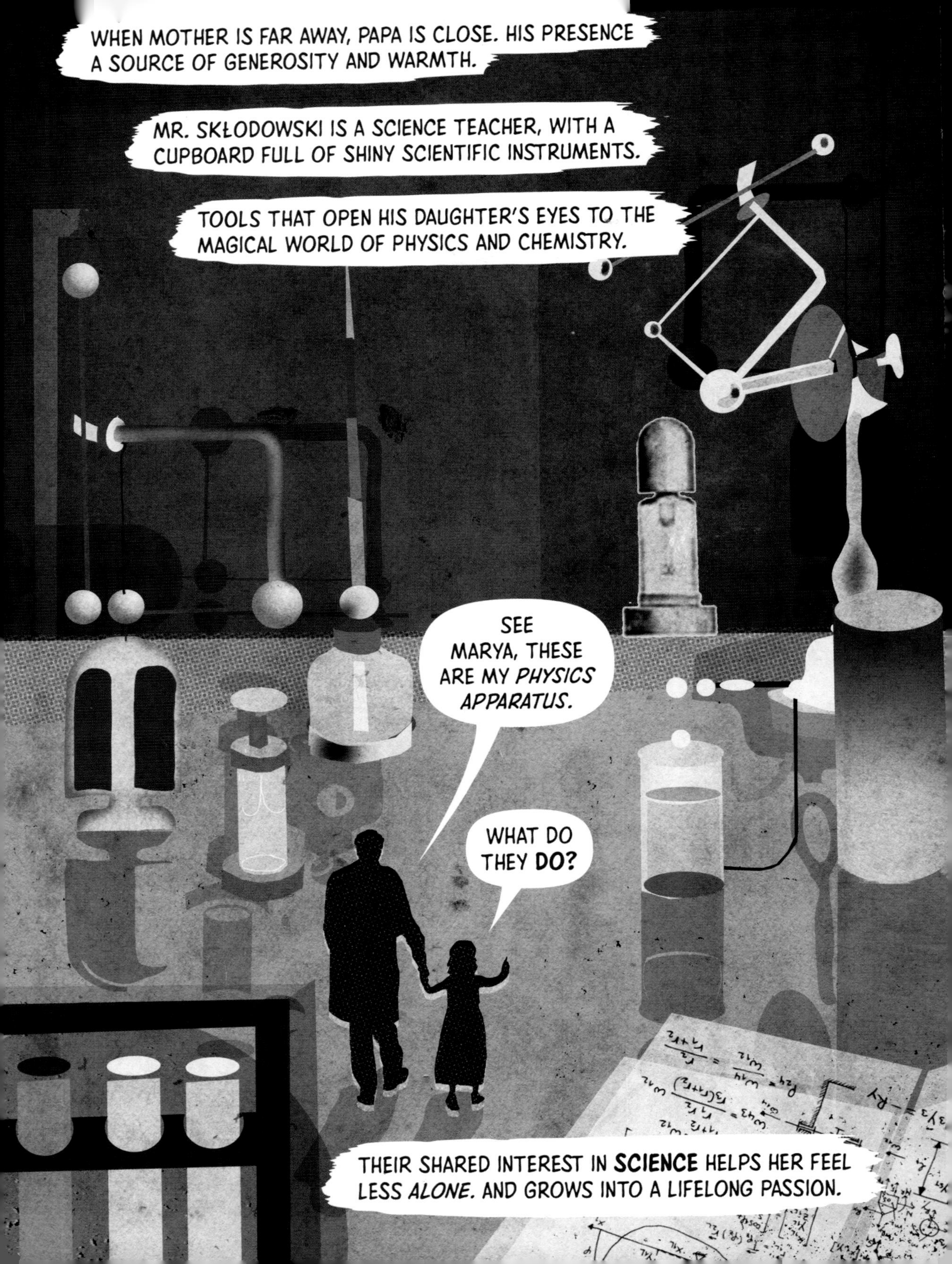

WHEN MOTHER IS FAR AWAY, PAPA IS CLOSE. HIS PRESENCE A SOURCE OF GENEROSITY AND WARMTH.
MR. SKŁODOWSKI IS A SCIENCE TEACHER, WITH A CUPBOARD FULL OF SHINY SCIENTIFIC INSTRUMENTS.
TOOLS THAT OPEN HIS DAUGHTER'S EYES TO THE MAGICAL WORLD OF PHYSICS AND CHEMISTRY.
SEE MARYA, THESE ARE MY *PHYSICS APPARATUS*.
WHAT DO THEY **DO?**
THEIR SHARED INTEREST IN **SCIENCE** HELPS HER FEEL LESS *ALONE*. AND GROWS INTO A LIFELONG PASSION.

IN 1867, POLAND IS CUT UP LIKE A PIE AND OCCUPIED BY THREE MIGHTY POWERS: **AUSTRIA**, **PRUSSIA**, AND **RUSSIA**.

RUSSIA RULES OVER WARSAW.

MOSCOW

BERLIN

WARSAW

GERMAN EMPIRE

RUSSIAN EMPIRE

VIENNA

BUDAPEST

THE POLISH LANGUAGE IS **OUTLAWED**.

ТПРОВОÐНИКЪТѵРНОШО

КАСПФЕҒ₿   L KLOPFERÐ   ПФЕФЕРБЕРГЬ П   PFEFERBERGJ

EVEN SIGNS IN SHOP WINDOWS ARE IN RUSSIAN.

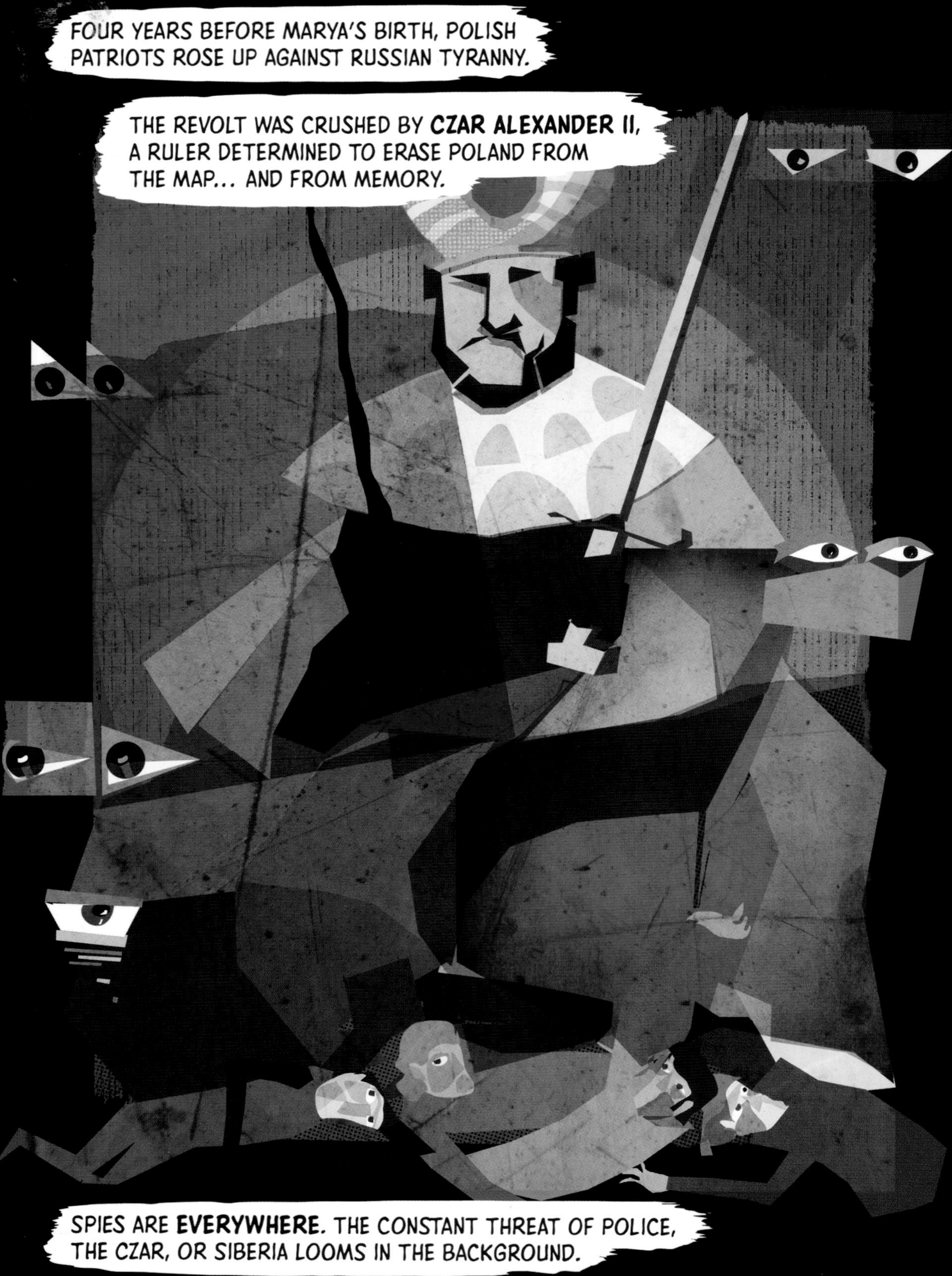
FOUR YEARS BEFORE MARYA'S BIRTH, POLISH PATRIOTS ROSE UP AGAINST RUSSIAN TYRANNY.
THE REVOLT WAS CRUSHED BY **CZAR ALEXANDER II**, A RULER DETERMINED TO ERASE POLAND FROM THE MAP... AND FROM MEMORY.
SPIES ARE **EVERYWHERE**. THE CONSTANT THREAT OF POLICE, THE CZAR, OR SIBERIA LOOMS IN THE BACKGROUND.

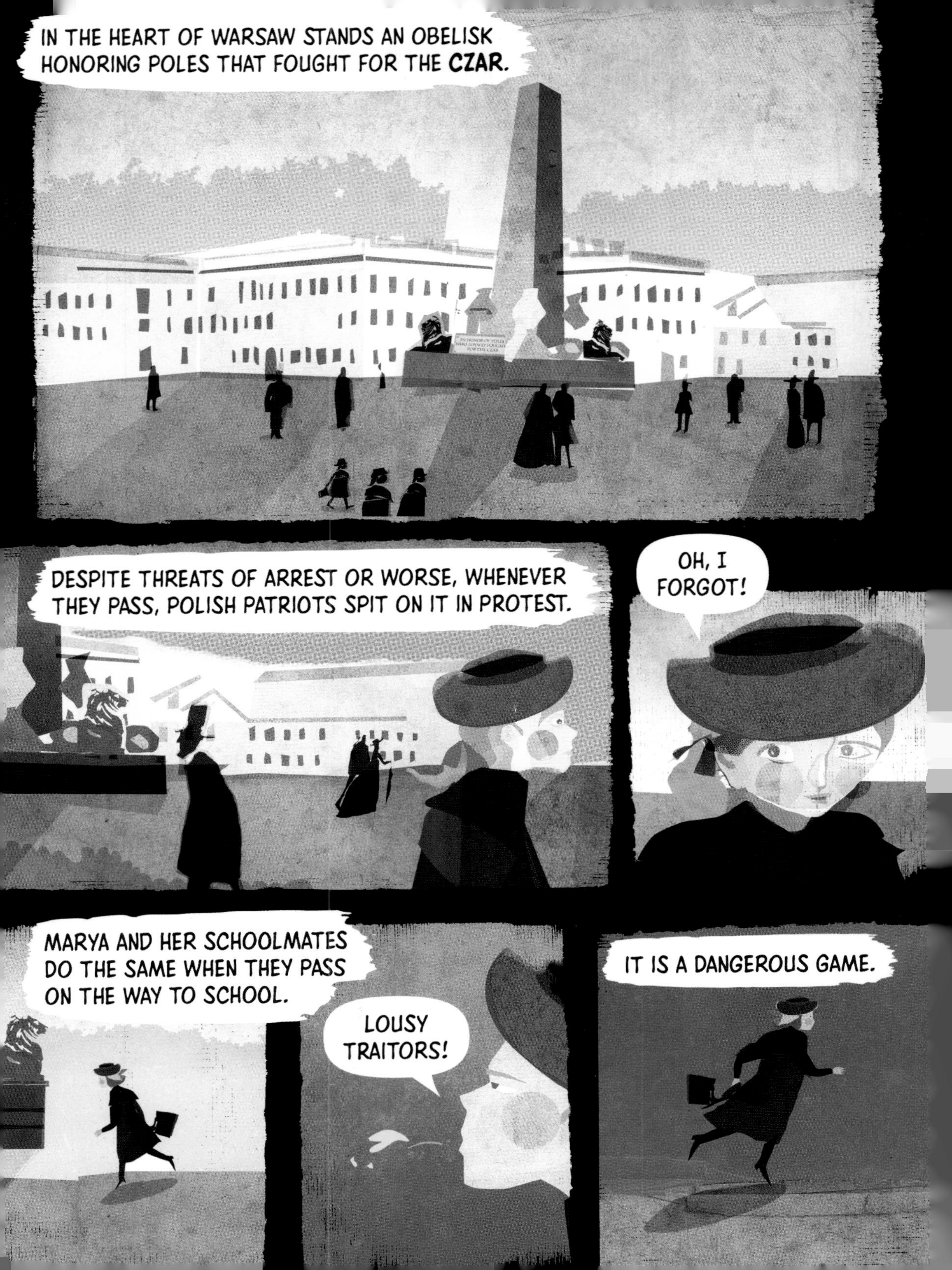
IN THE HEART OF WARSAW STANDS AN OBELISK HONORING POLES THAT FOUGHT FOR THE **CZAR**.
DESPITE THREATS OF ARREST OR WORSE, WHENEVER THEY PASS, POLISH PATRIOTS SPIT ON IT IN PROTEST.
OH, I FORGOT!
MARYA AND HER SCHOOLMATES DO THE SAME WHEN THEY PASS ON THE WAY TO SCHOOL.
LOUSY TRAITORS!
IT IS A DANGEROUS GAME.

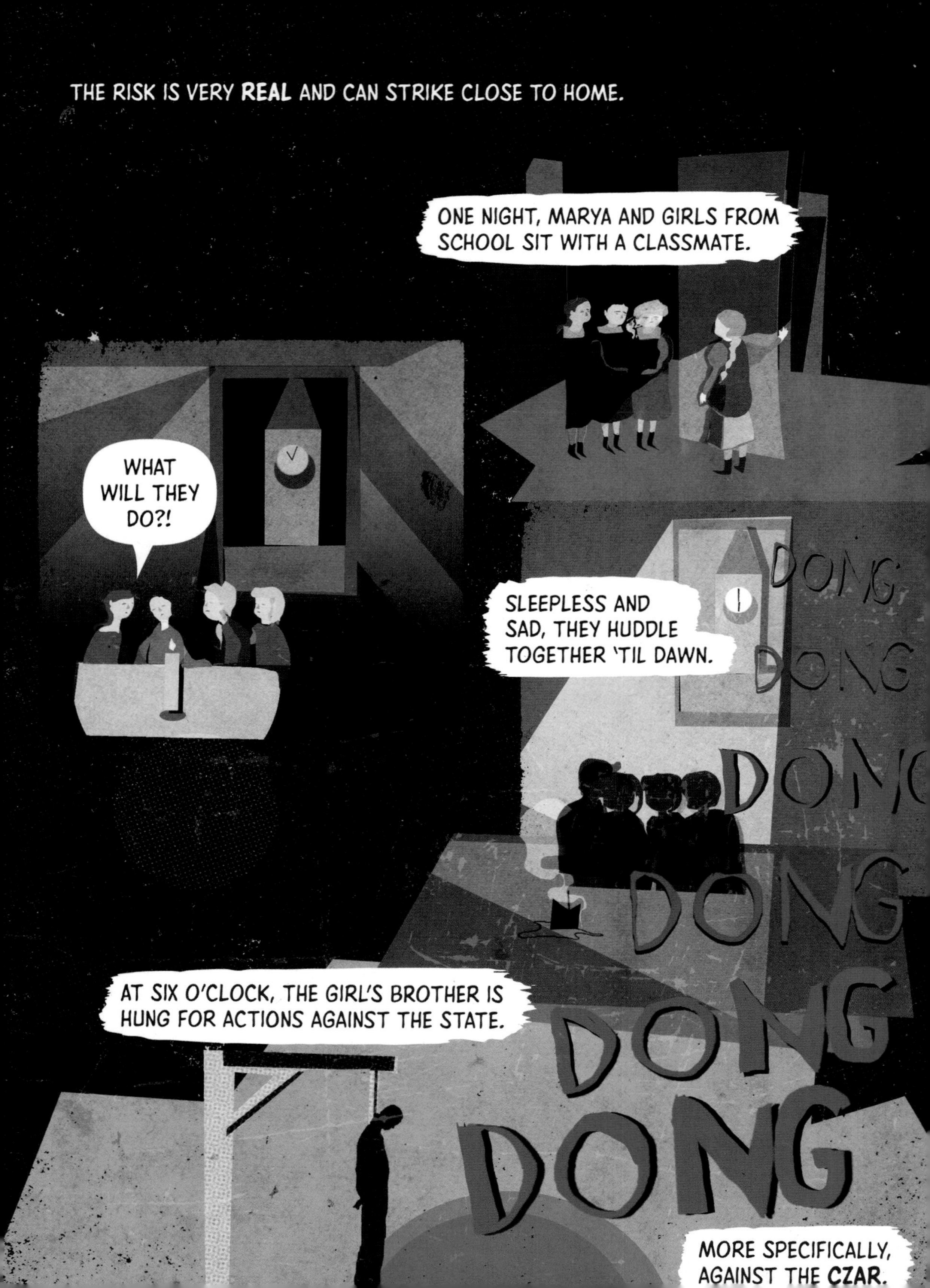
THE RISK IS VERY REAL AND CAN STRIKE CLOSE TO HOME.
ONE NIGHT, MARYA AND GIRLS FROM SCHOOL SIT WITH A CLASSMATE.
WHAT WILL THEY DO?!
SLEEPLESS AND SAD, THEY HUDDLE TOGETHER 'TIL DAWN.
DONG
DONG
DONG
DONG
DONG
DONG
AT SIX O'CLOCK, THE GIRL'S BROTHER IS HUNG FOR ACTIONS AGAINST THE STATE.
MORE SPECIFICALLY, AGAINST THE CZAR.

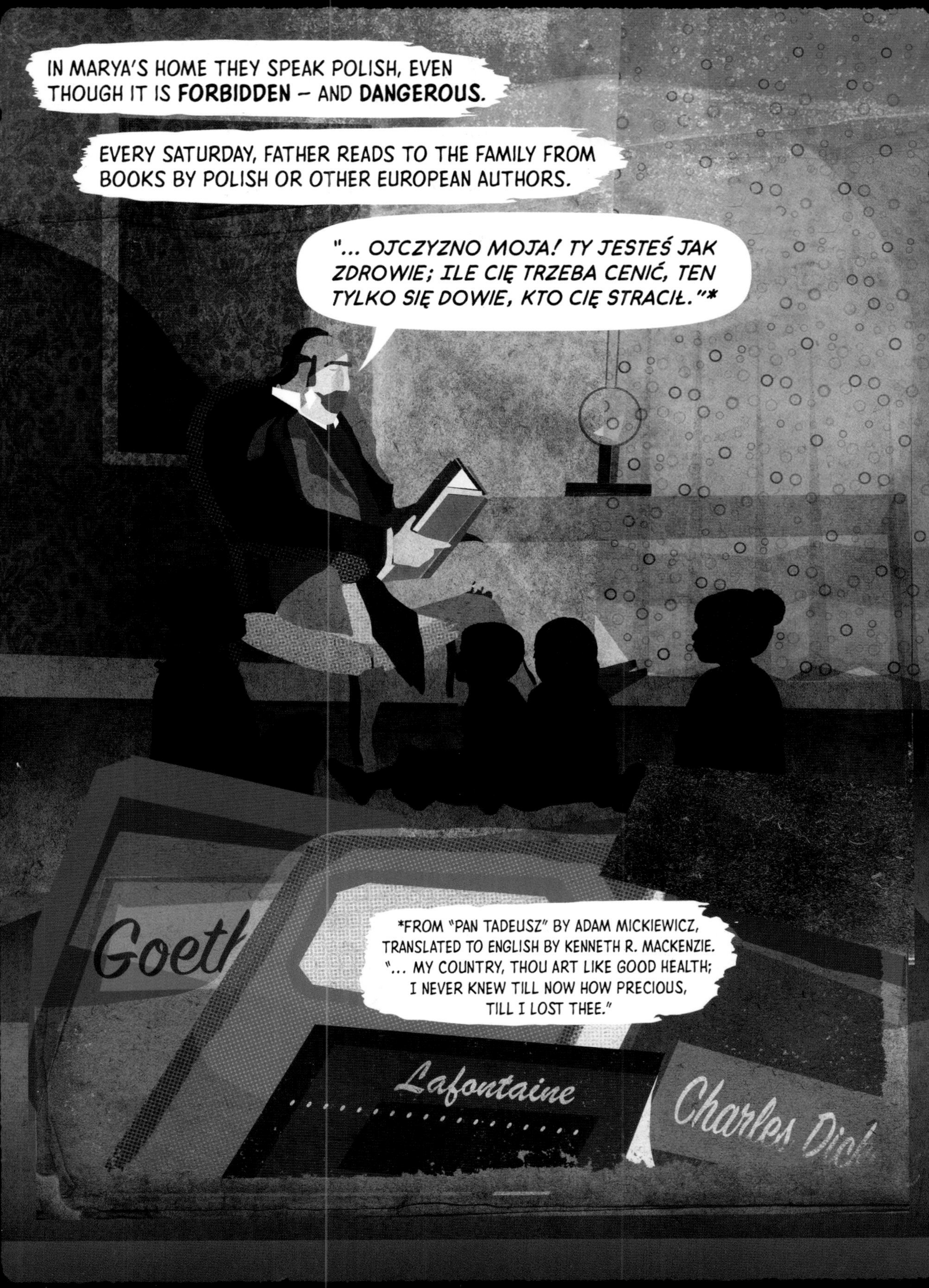
IN MARYA'S HOME THEY SPEAK POLISH, EVEN THOUGH IT IS **FORBIDDEN** – AND **DANGEROUS.**
EVERY SATURDAY, FATHER READS TO THE FAMILY FROM BOOKS BY POLISH OR OTHER EUROPEAN AUTHORS.
"... OJCZYZNO MOJA! TY JESTEŚ JAK ZDROWIE; ILE CIĘ TRZEBA CENIĆ, TEN TYLKO SIĘ DOWIE, KTO CIĘ STRACIŁ."*
Goeth
*FROM "PAN TADEUSZ" BY ADAM MICKIEWICZ, TRANSLATED TO ENGLISH BY KENNETH R. MACKENZIE. "... MY COUNTRY, THOU ART LIKE GOOD HEALTH; I NEVER KNEW TILL NOW HOW PRECIOUS, TILL I LOST THEE."
Lafontaine
Charles Dick

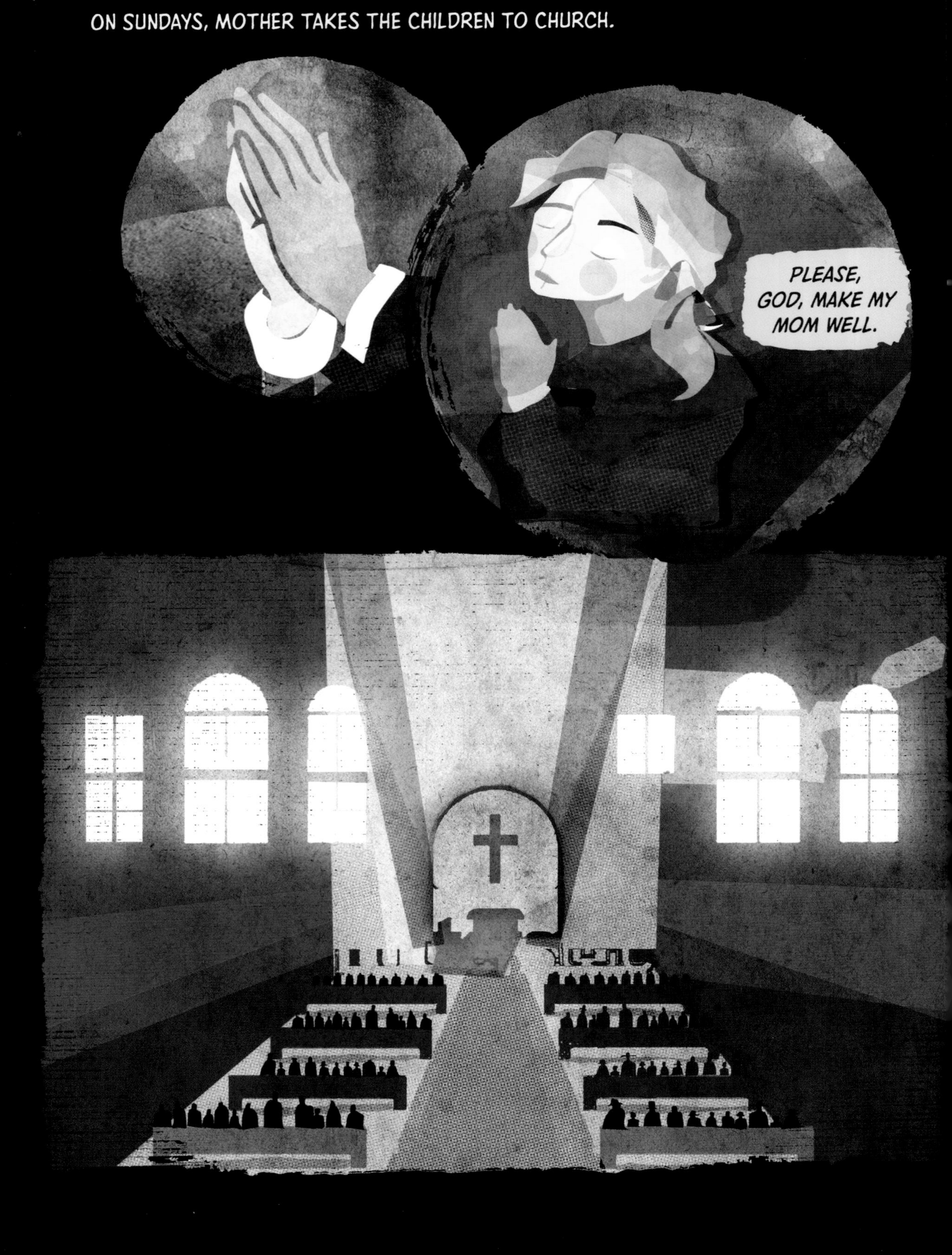
ON SUNDAYS, MOTHER TAKES THE CHILDREN TO CHURCH.
PLEASE, GOD, MAKE MY MOM WELL.

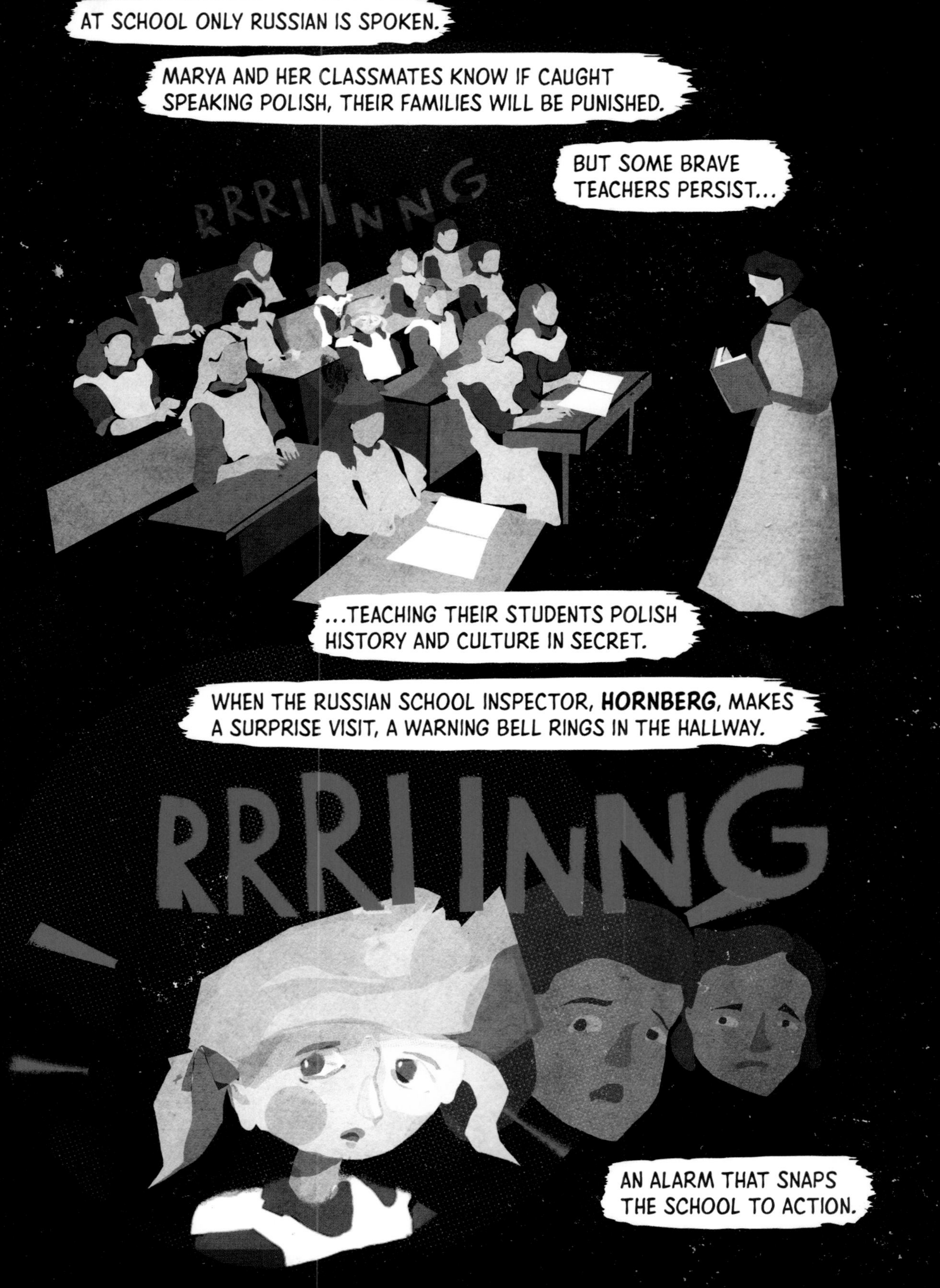
AT SCHOOL ONLY RUSSIAN IS SPOKEN.
MARYA AND HER CLASSMATES KNOW IF CAUGHT SPEAKING POLISH, THEIR FAMILIES WILL BE PUNISHED.
BUT SOME BRAVE TEACHERS PERSIST...
RRRIINNG
...TEACHING THEIR STUDENTS POLISH HISTORY AND CULTURE IN SECRET.
WHEN THE RUSSIAN SCHOOL INSPECTOR, HORNBERG, MAKES A SURPRISE VISIT, A WARNING BELL RINGS IN THE HALLWAY.
RRRIINNG
AN ALARM THAT SNAPS THE SCHOOL TO ACTION.

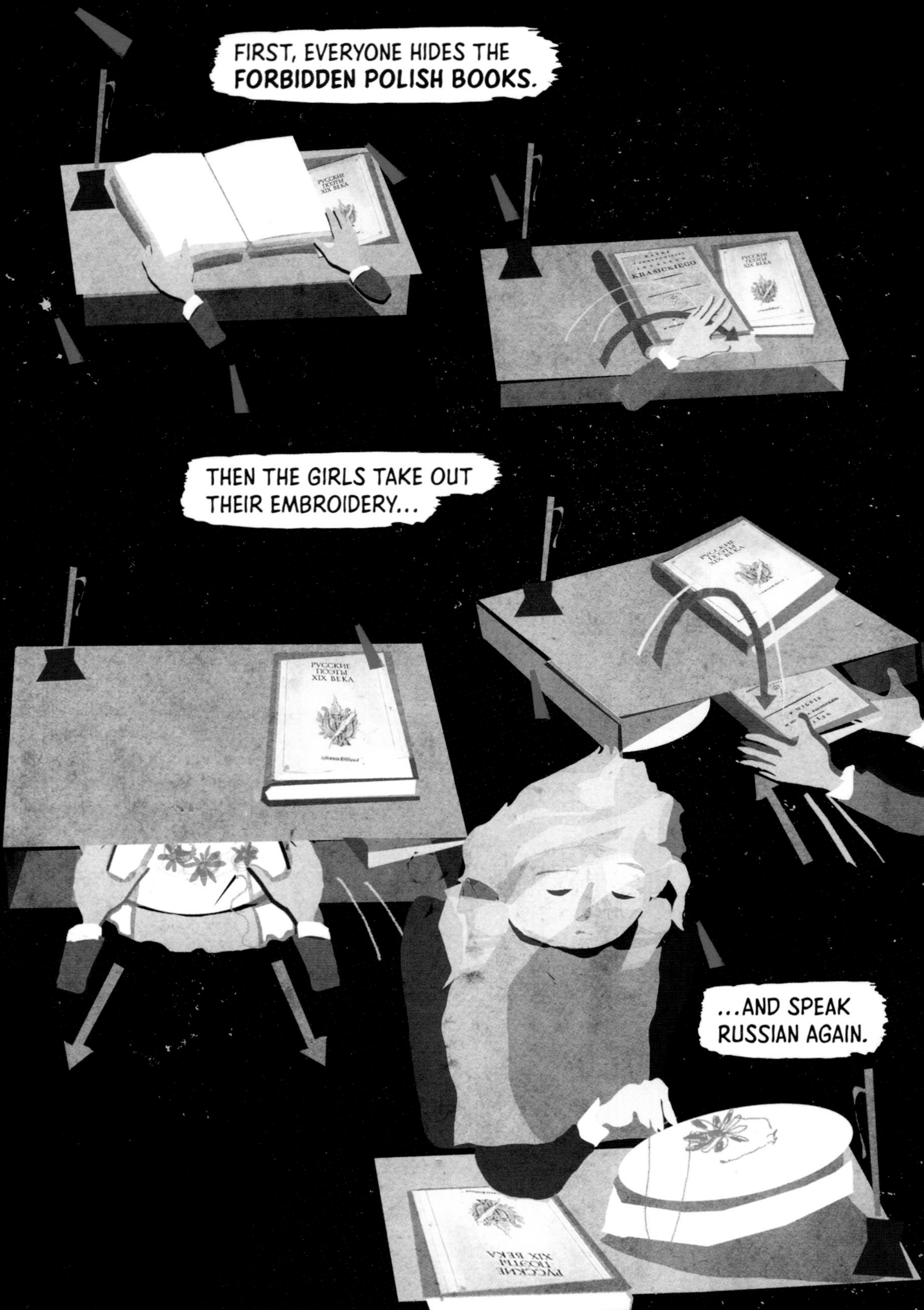

FIRST, EVERYONE HIDES THE FORBIDDEN POLISH BOOKS.
РУССКИЕ ПОЭТЫ XIX ВЕКА
KRASICKIEGO
РУССКИЕ ПОЭТЫ XIX ВЕКА
THEN THE GIRLS TAKE OUT THEIR EMBROIDERY...
РУССКИЕ ПОЭТЫ XIX ВЕКА
РУССКИЕ ПОЭТЫ XIX ВЕКА
...AND SPEAK RUSSIAN AGAIN.
РУССКИЕ ПОЭТЫ XIX ВЕКА

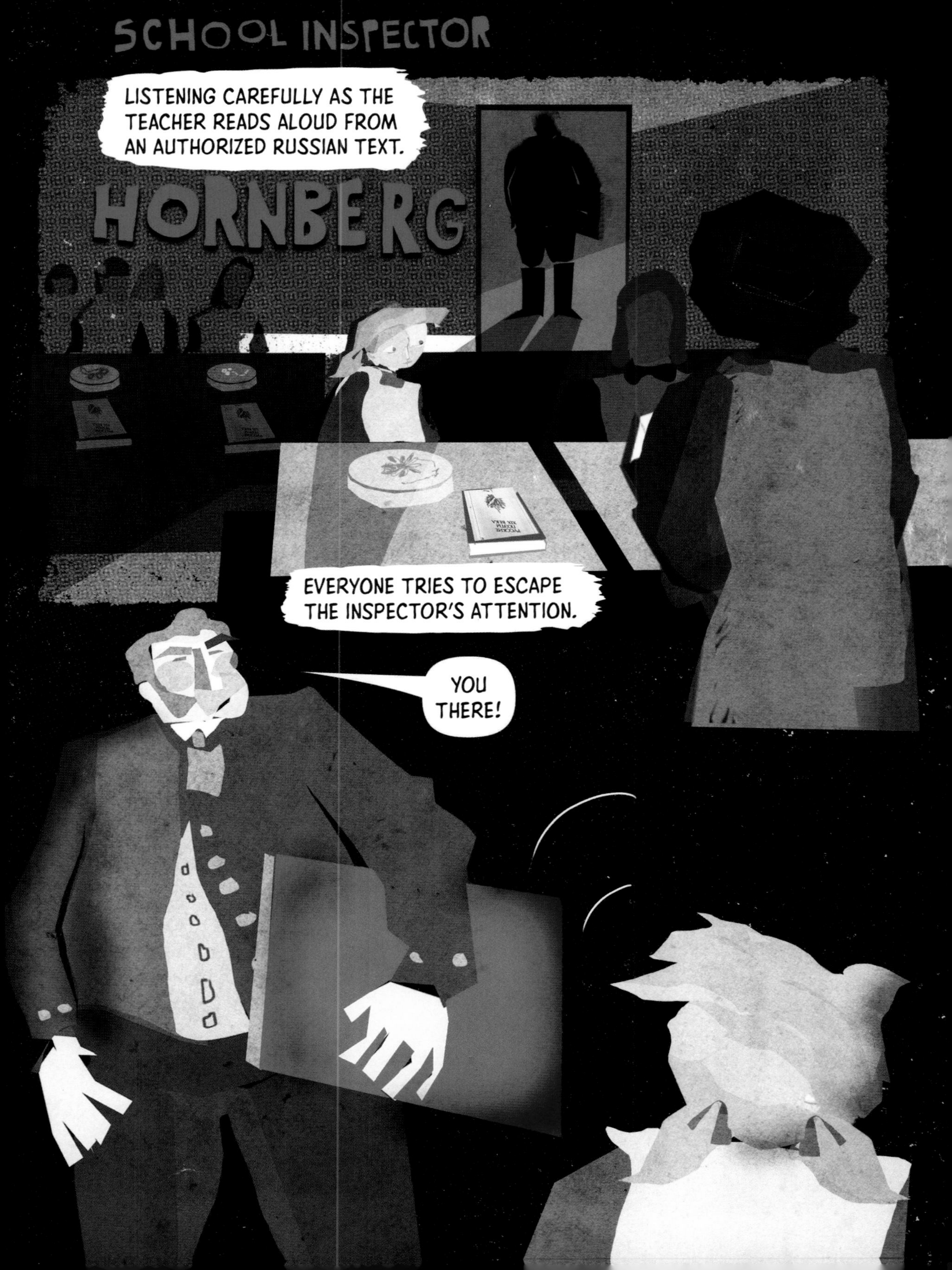
SCHOOL INSPECTOR
LISTENING CAREFULLY AS THE TEACHER READS ALOUD FROM AN AUTHORIZED RUSSIAN TEXT.
HORNBERG
EVERYONE TRIES TO ESCAPE THE INSPECTOR'S ATTENTION.
YOU THERE!

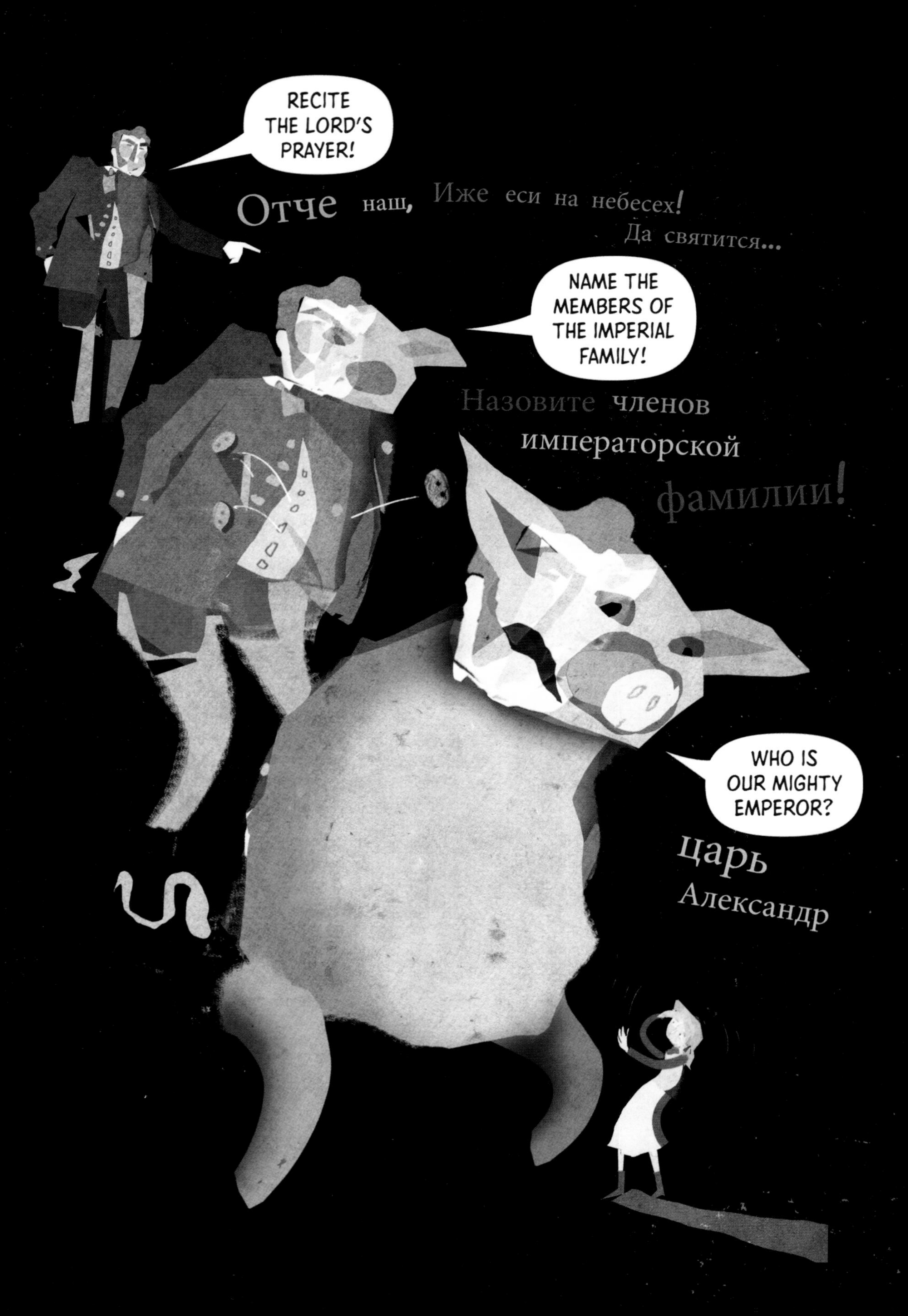
RECITE THE LORD'S PRAYER!
Отче наш, Иже еси на небесех! Да святится...
NAME THE MEMBERS OF THE IMPERIAL FAMILY!
Назовите членов императорской фамилии!
WHO IS OUR MIGHTY EMPEROR?
царь Александр

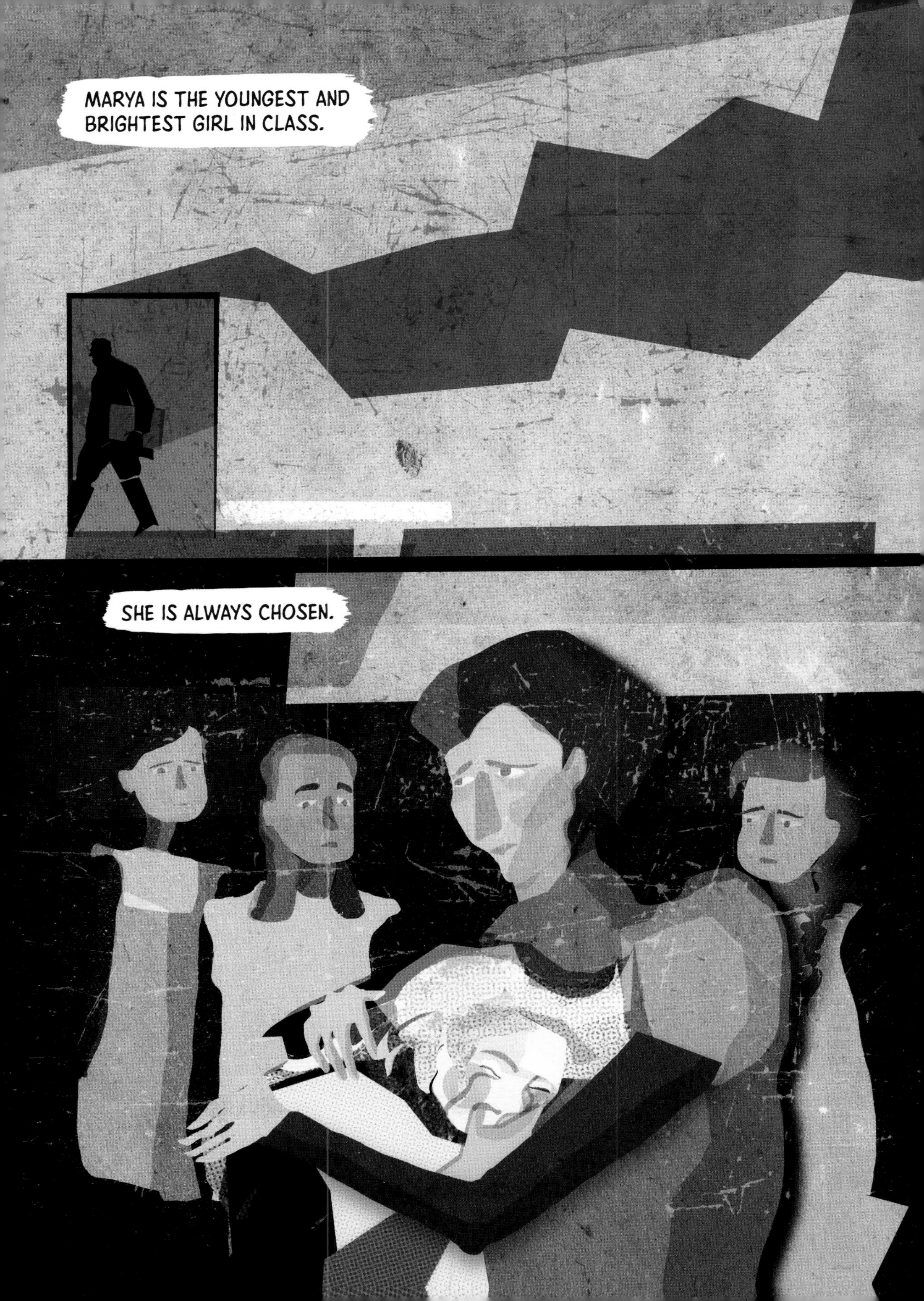
MARYA IS THE YOUNGEST AND BRIGHTEST GIRL IN CLASS.
SHE IS ALWAYS CHOSEN.

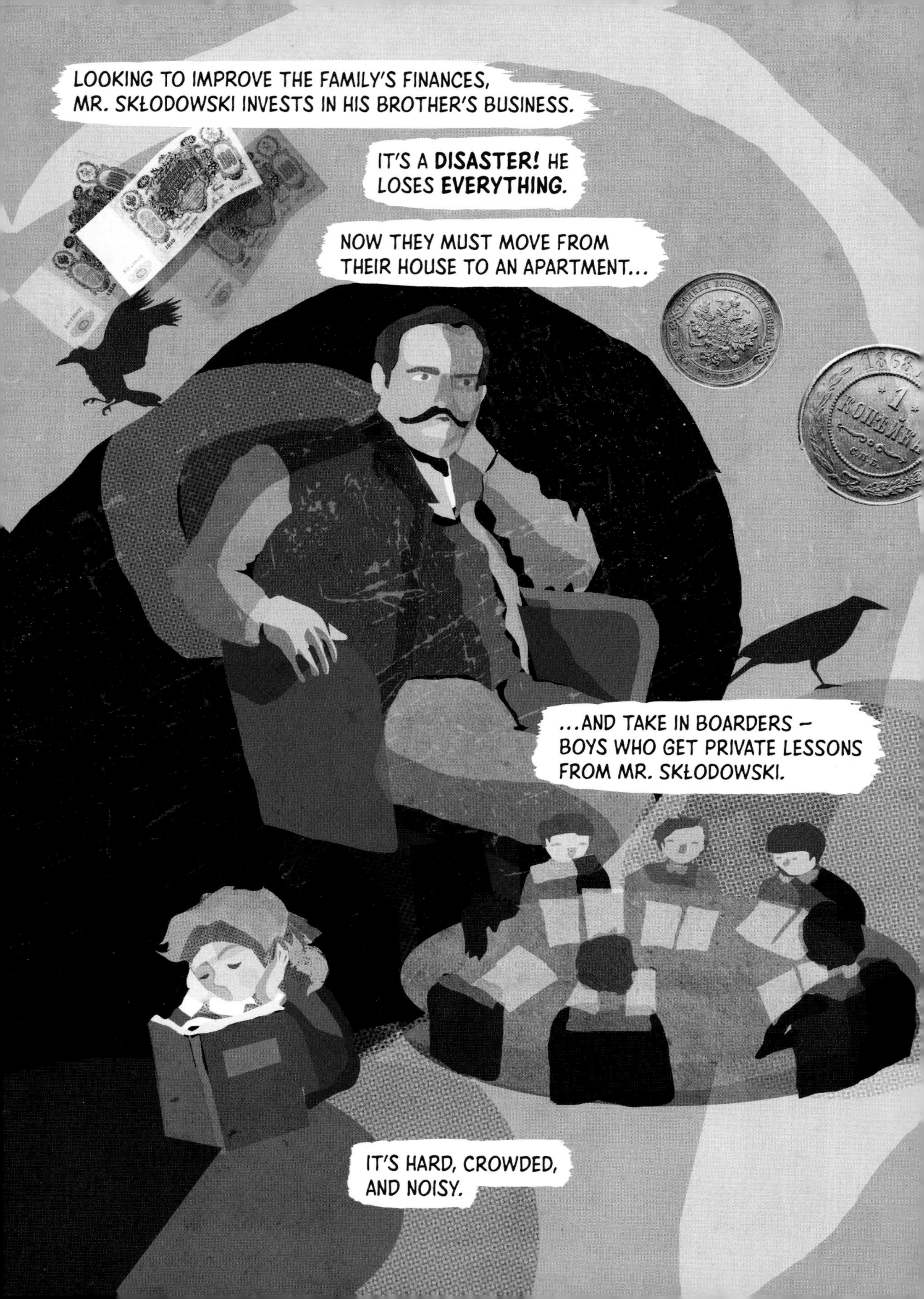
LOOKING TO IMPROVE THE FAMILY'S FINANCES, MR. SKŁODOWSKI INVESTS IN HIS BROTHER'S BUSINESS.
IT'S A **DISASTER!** HE LOSES **EVERYTHING.**
NOW THEY MUST MOVE FROM THEIR HOUSE TO AN APARTMENT...
...AND TAKE IN BOARDERS – BOYS WHO GET PRIVATE LESSONS FROM MR. SKŁODOWSKI.
IT'S HARD, CROWDED, AND NOISY.

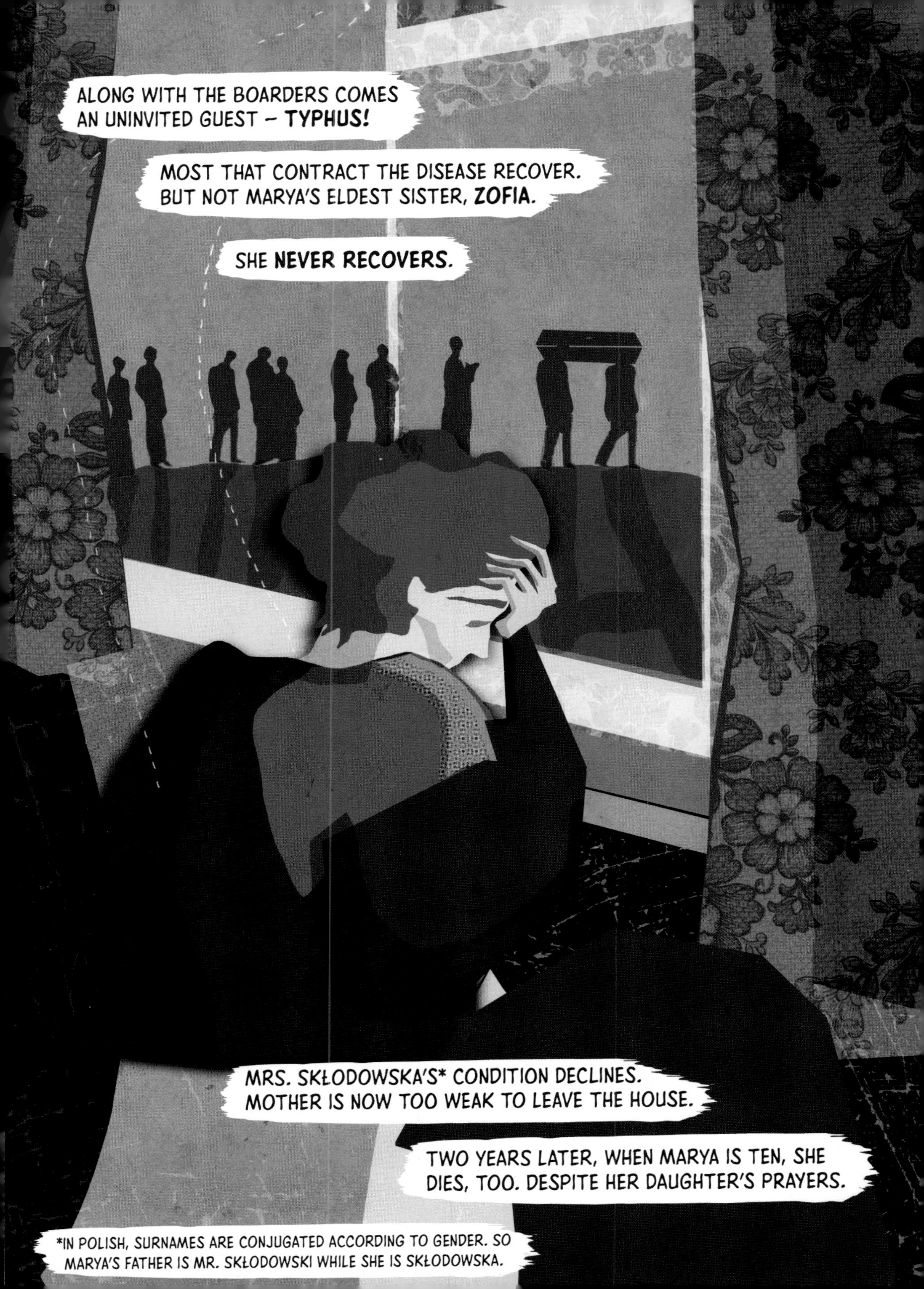
ALONG WITH THE BOARDERS COMES AN UNINVITED GUEST – TYPHUS!
MOST THAT CONTRACT THE DISEASE RECOVER. BUT NOT MARYA'S ELDEST SISTER, ZOFIA.
SHE NEVER RECOVERS.
MRS. SKŁODOWSKA'S* CONDITION DECLINES. MOTHER IS NOW TOO WEAK TO LEAVE THE HOUSE.
TWO YEARS LATER, WHEN MARYA IS TEN, SHE DIES, TOO. DESPITE HER DAUGHTER'S PRAYERS.
*IN POLISH, SURNAMES ARE CONJUGATED ACCORDING TO GENDER. SO MARYA'S FATHER IS MR. SKŁODOWSKI WHILE SHE IS SKŁODOWSKA.

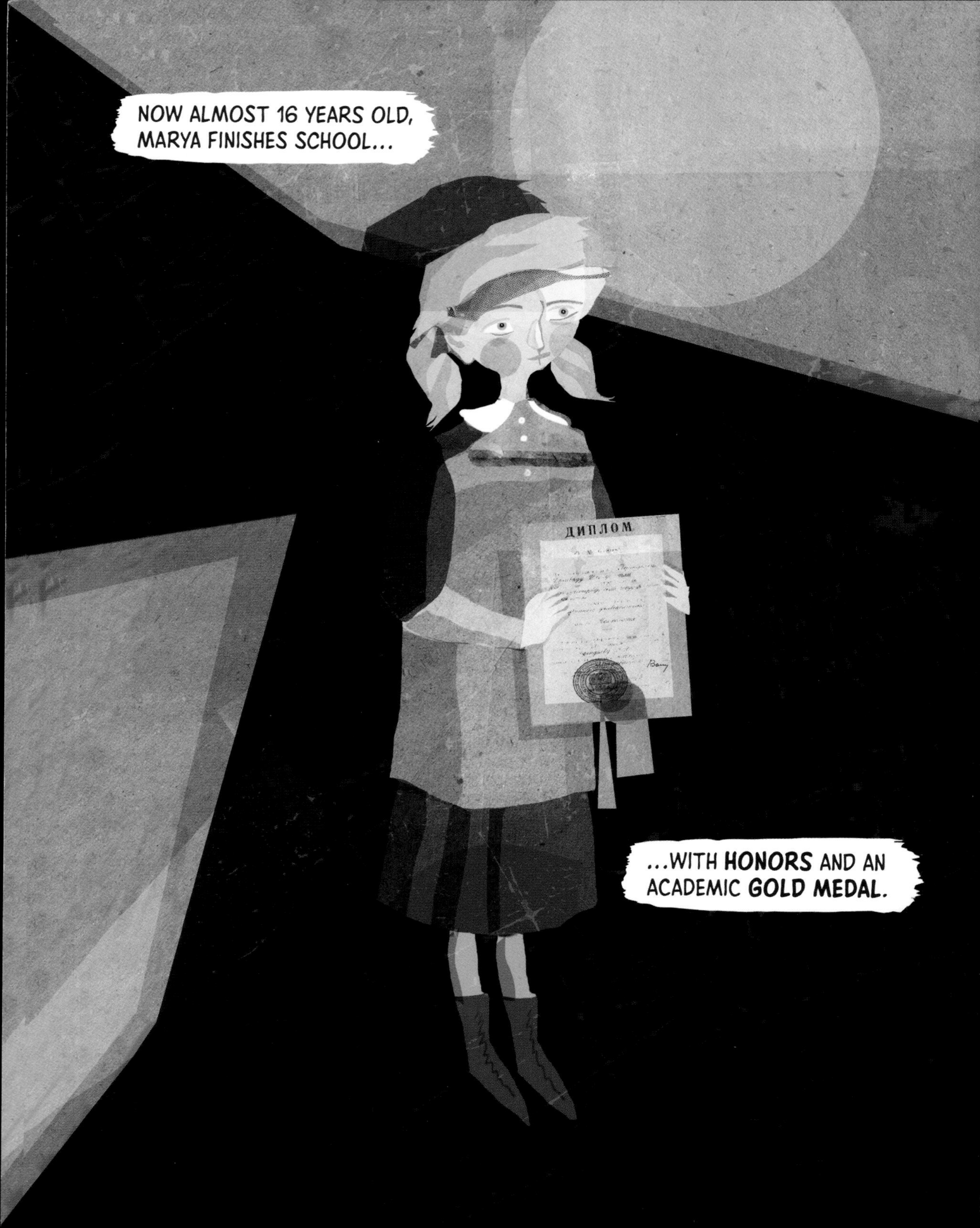
NOW ALMOST 16 YEARS OLD, MARYA FINISHES SCHOOL...
ДИПЛОМ
...WITH **HONORS** AND AN ACADEMIC **GOLD MEDAL**.

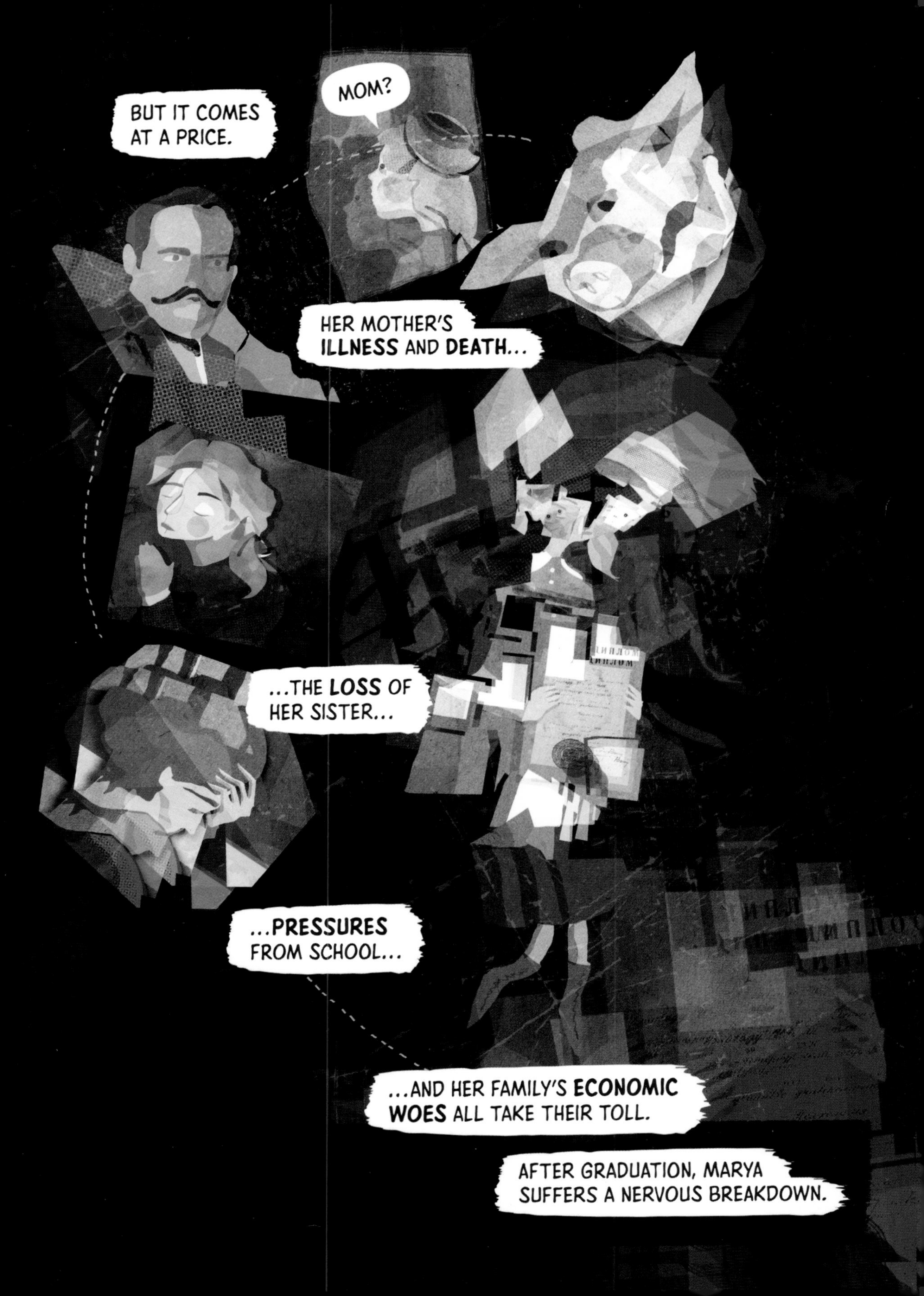
BUT IT COMES AT A PRICE.
MOM?
HER MOTHER'S ILLNESS AND DEATH...
...THE LOSS OF HER SISTER...
...PRESSURES FROM SCHOOL...
...AND HER FAMILY'S ECONOMIC WOES ALL TAKE THEIR TOLL.
AFTER GRADUATION, MARYA SUFFERS A NERVOUS BREAKDOWN.

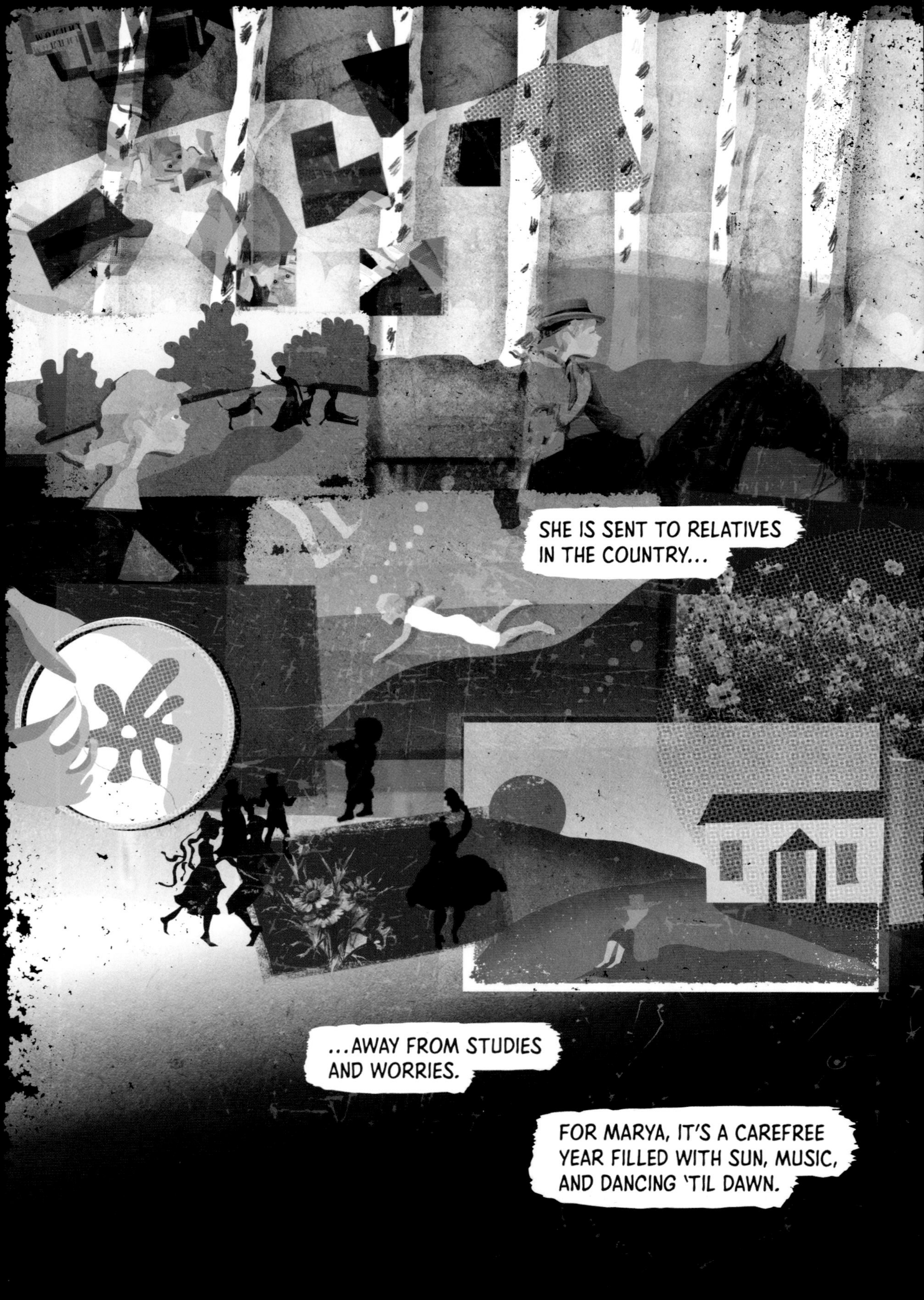
SHE IS SENT TO RELATIVES IN THE COUNTRY...
...AWAY FROM STUDIES AND WORRIES.
FOR MARYA, IT'S A CAREFREE YEAR FILLED WITH SUN, MUSIC, AND DANCING 'TIL DAWN.

Chapter 2

1884-1891

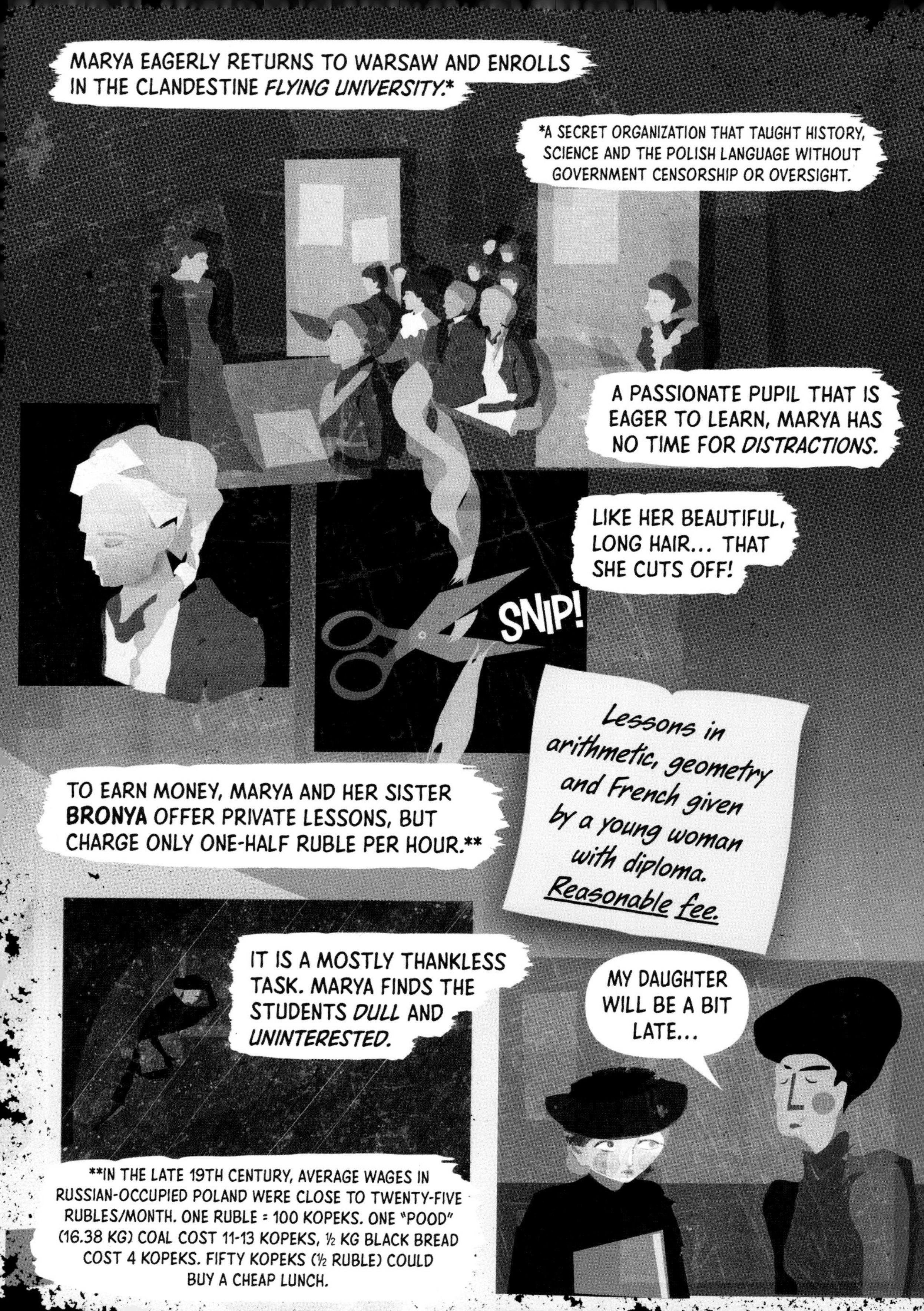
MARYA EAGERLY RETURNS TO WARSAW AND ENROLLS IN THE CLANDESTINE *FLYING UNIVERSITY.**
*A SECRET ORGANIZATION THAT TAUGHT HISTORY, SCIENCE AND THE POLISH LANGUAGE WITHOUT GOVERNMENT CENSORSHIP OR OVERSIGHT.
A PASSIONATE PUPIL THAT IS EAGER TO LEARN, MARYA HAS NO TIME FOR *DISTRACTIONS.*
LIKE HER BEAUTIFUL, LONG HAIR... THAT SHE CUTS OFF!
SNIP!
TO EARN MONEY, MARYA AND HER SISTER **BRONYA** OFFER PRIVATE LESSONS, BUT CHARGE ONLY ONE-HALF RUBLE PER HOUR.**
Lessons in arithmetic, geometry and French given by a young woman with diploma. Reasonable fee.
IT IS A MOSTLY THANKLESS TASK. MARYA FINDS THE STUDENTS *DULL* AND *UNINTERESTED.*
MY DAUGHTER WILL BE A BIT LATE...
**IN THE LATE 19TH CENTURY, AVERAGE WAGES IN RUSSIAN-OCCUPIED POLAND WERE CLOSE TO TWENTY-FIVE RUBLES/MONTH. ONE RUBLE = 100 KOPEKS. ONE "POOD" (16.38 KG) COAL COST 11-13 KOPEKS, ½ KG BLACK BREAD COST 4 KOPEKS. FIFTY KOPEKS (½ RUBLE) COULD BUY A CHEAP LUNCH.

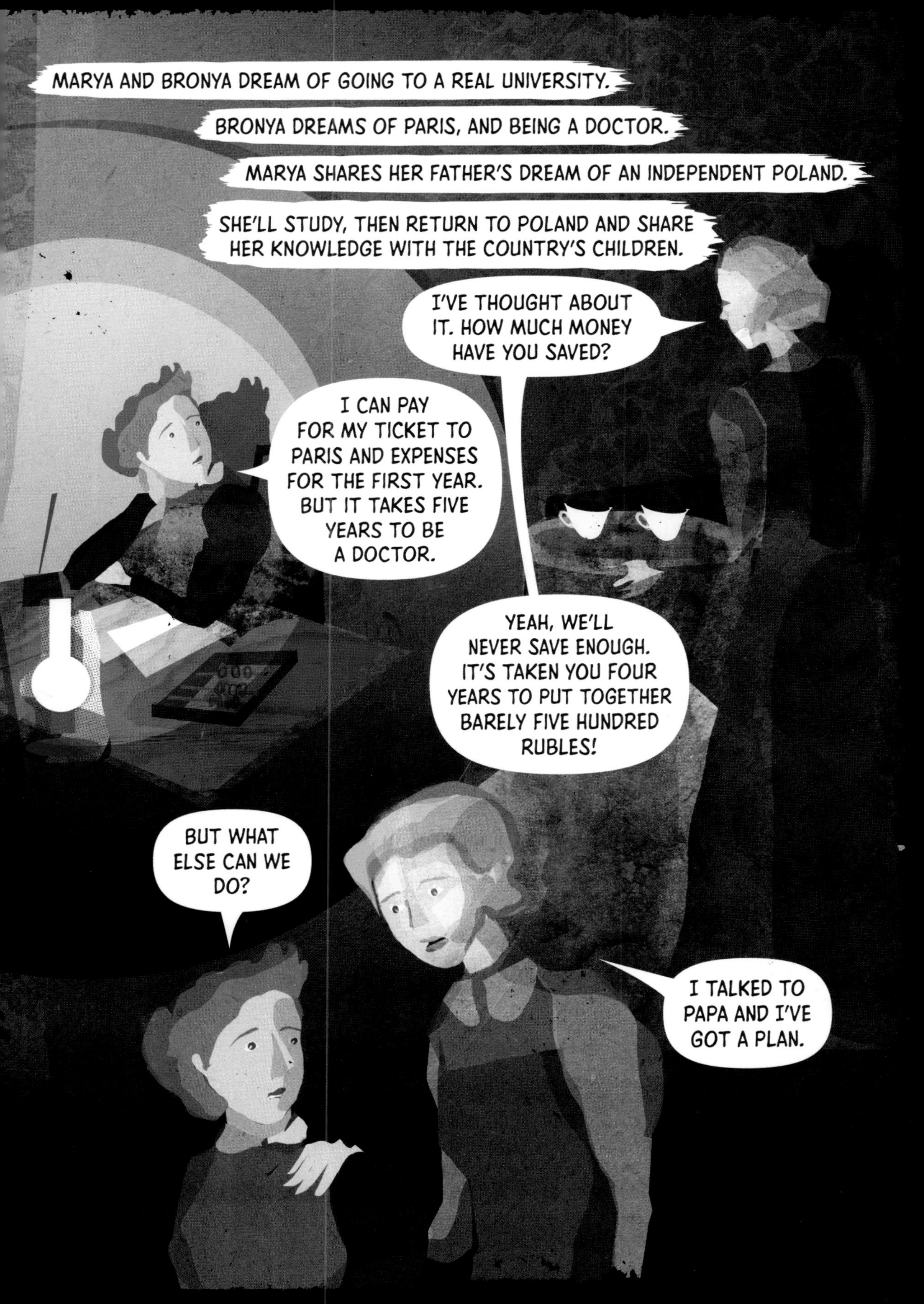
MARYA AND BRONYA DREAM OF GOING TO A REAL UNIVERSITY.
BRONYA DREAMS OF PARIS, AND BEING A DOCTOR.
MARYA SHARES HER FATHER'S DREAM OF AN INDEPENDENT POLAND.
SHE'LL STUDY, THEN RETURN TO POLAND AND SHARE HER KNOWLEDGE WITH THE COUNTRY'S CHILDREN.
I'VE THOUGHT ABOUT IT. HOW MUCH MONEY HAVE YOU SAVED?
I CAN PAY FOR MY TICKET TO PARIS AND EXPENSES FOR THE FIRST YEAR. BUT IT TAKES FIVE YEARS TO BE A DOCTOR.
YEAH, WE'LL NEVER SAVE ENOUGH. IT'S TAKEN YOU FOUR YEARS TO PUT TOGETHER BARELY FIVE HUNDRED RUBLES!
BUT WHAT ELSE CAN WE DO?
I TALKED TO PAPA AND I'VE GOT A PLAN.

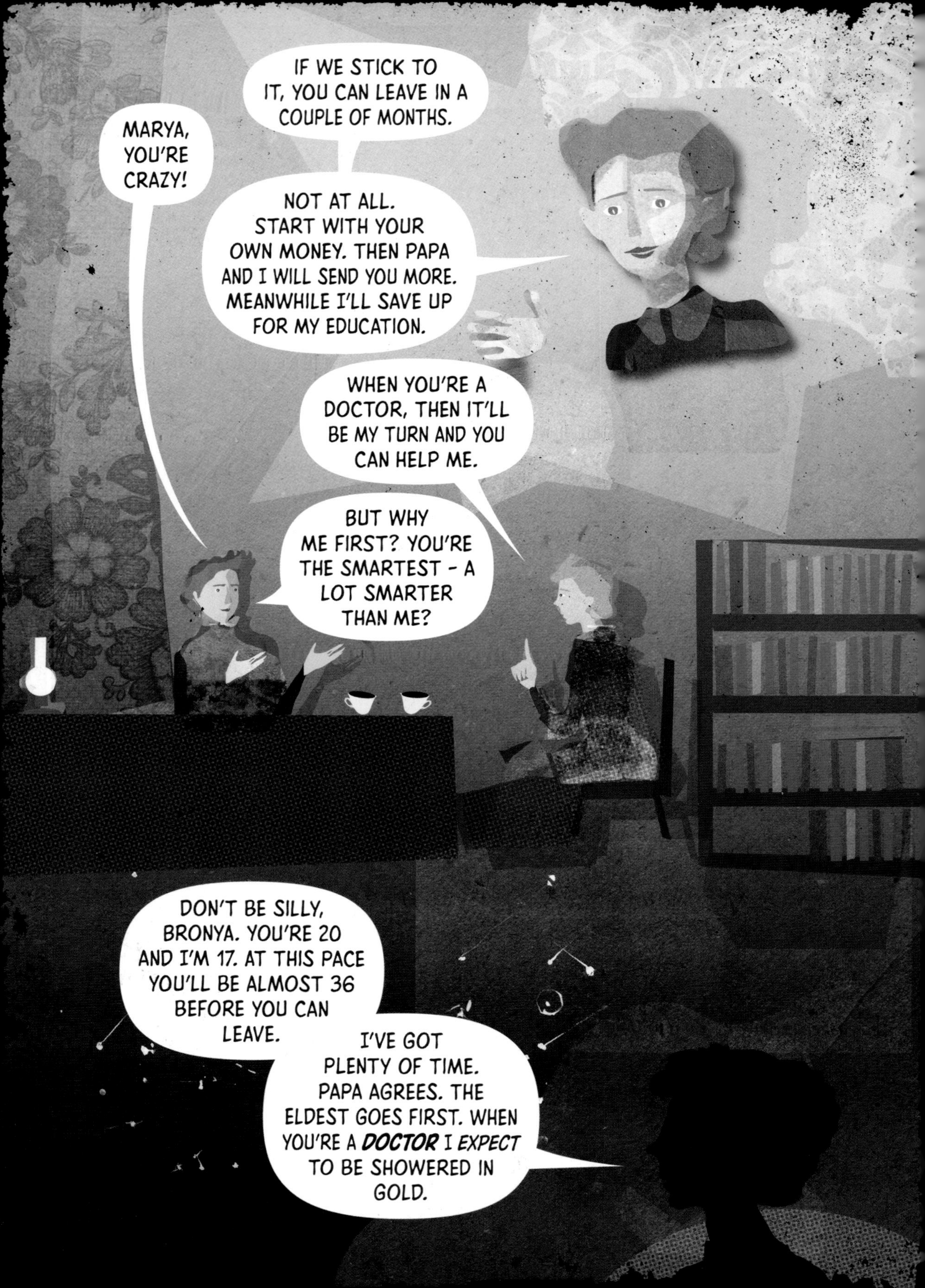
IF WE STICK TO IT, YOU CAN LEAVE IN A COUPLE OF MONTHS.
MARYA, YOU'RE CRAZY!
NOT AT ALL. START WITH YOUR OWN MONEY. THEN PAPA AND I WILL SEND YOU MORE. MEANWHILE I'LL SAVE UP FOR MY EDUCATION.
WHEN YOU'RE A DOCTOR, THEN IT'LL BE MY TURN AND YOU CAN HELP ME.
BUT WHY ME FIRST? YOU'RE THE SMARTEST - A LOT SMARTER THAN ME?
DON'T BE SILLY, BRONYA. YOU'RE 20 AND I'M 17. AT THIS PACE YOU'LL BE ALMOST 36 BEFORE YOU CAN LEAVE.
I'VE GOT PLENTY OF TIME. PAPA AGREES. THE ELDEST GOES FIRST. WHEN YOU'RE A ***DOCTOR*** I *EXPECT* TO BE SHOWERED IN GOLD.

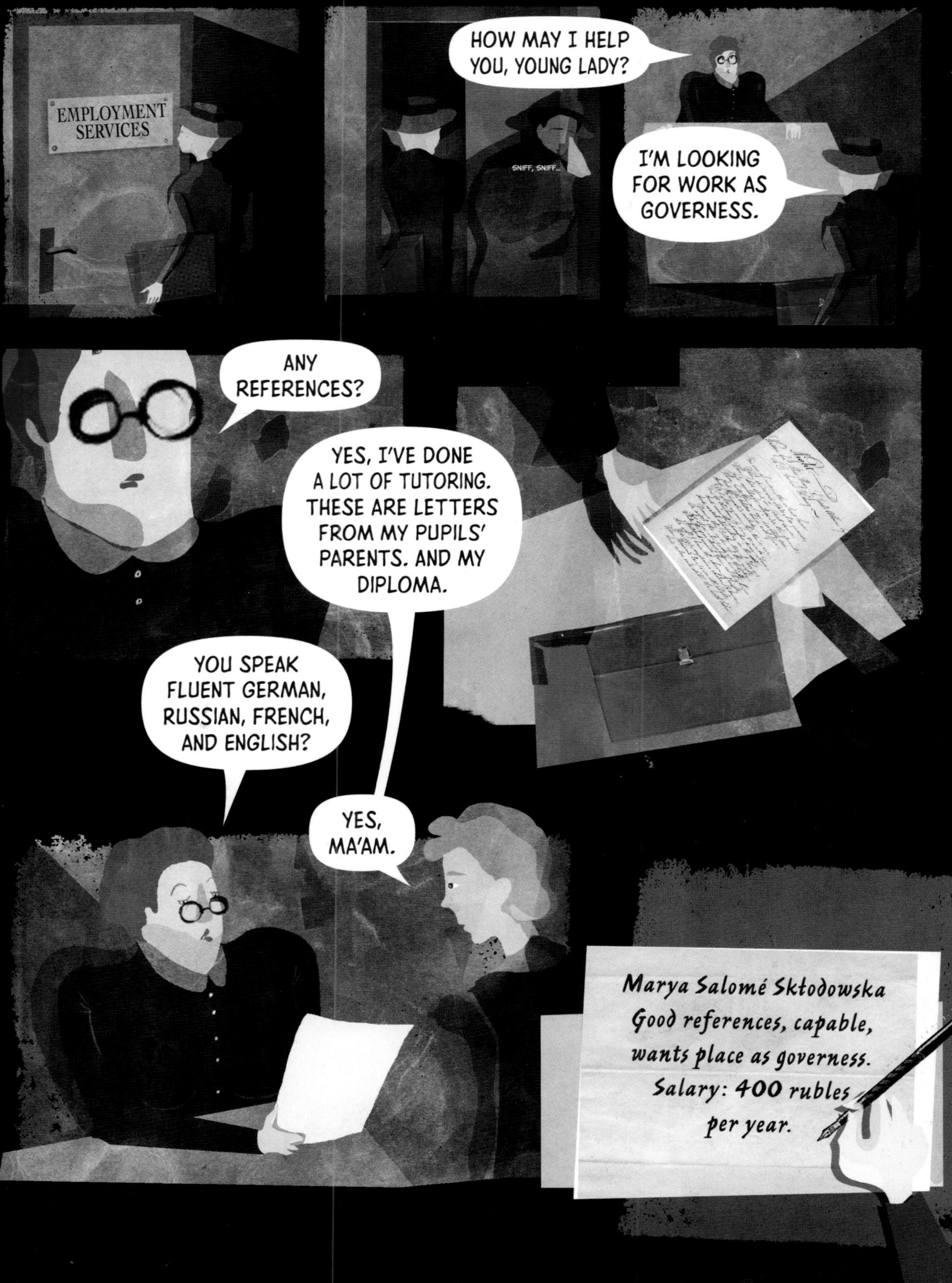
EMPLOYMENT SERVICES
SNIFF, SNIFF...
HOW MAY I HELP YOU, YOUNG LADY?
I'M LOOKING FOR WORK AS GOVERNESS.
ANY REFERENCES?
YES, I'VE DONE A LOT OF TUTORING. THESE ARE LETTERS FROM MY PUPILS' PARENTS. AND MY DIPLOMA.
YOU SPEAK FLUENT GERMAN, RUSSIAN, FRENCH, AND ENGLISH?
YES, MA'AM.
Marya Salomé Skłodowska
Good references, capable,
wants place as governess.
Salary: 400 rubles
per year.

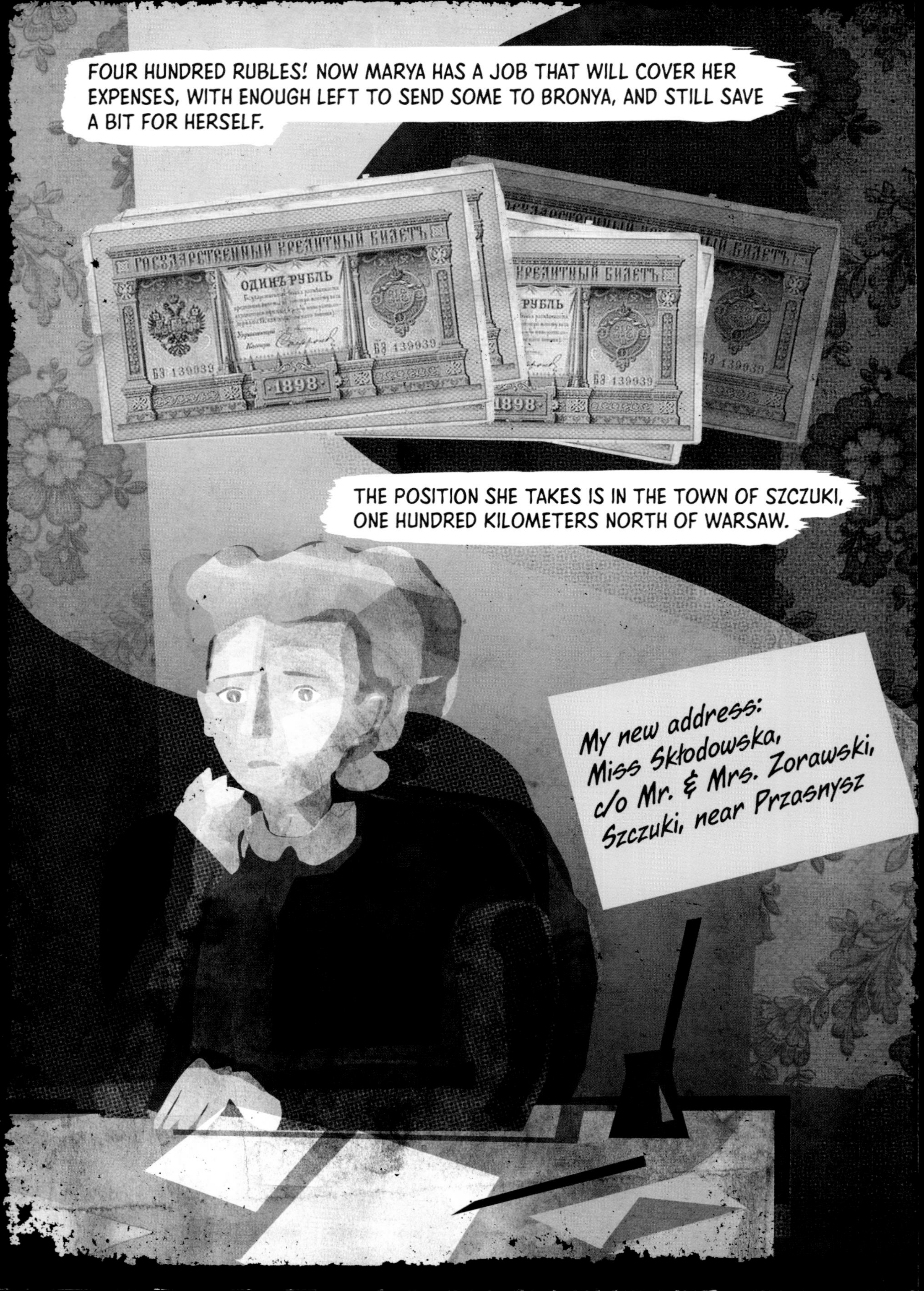
FOUR HUNDRED RUBLES! NOW MARYA HAS A JOB THAT WILL COVER HER EXPENSES, WITH ENOUGH LEFT TO SEND SOME TO BRONYA, AND STILL SAVE A BIT FOR HERSELF.
THE POSITION SHE TAKES IS IN THE TOWN OF SZCZUKI, ONE HUNDRED KILOMETERS NORTH OF WARSAW.
My new address: Miss Skłodowska, c/o Mr. & Mrs. Zorawski, Szczuki, near Przasnysz

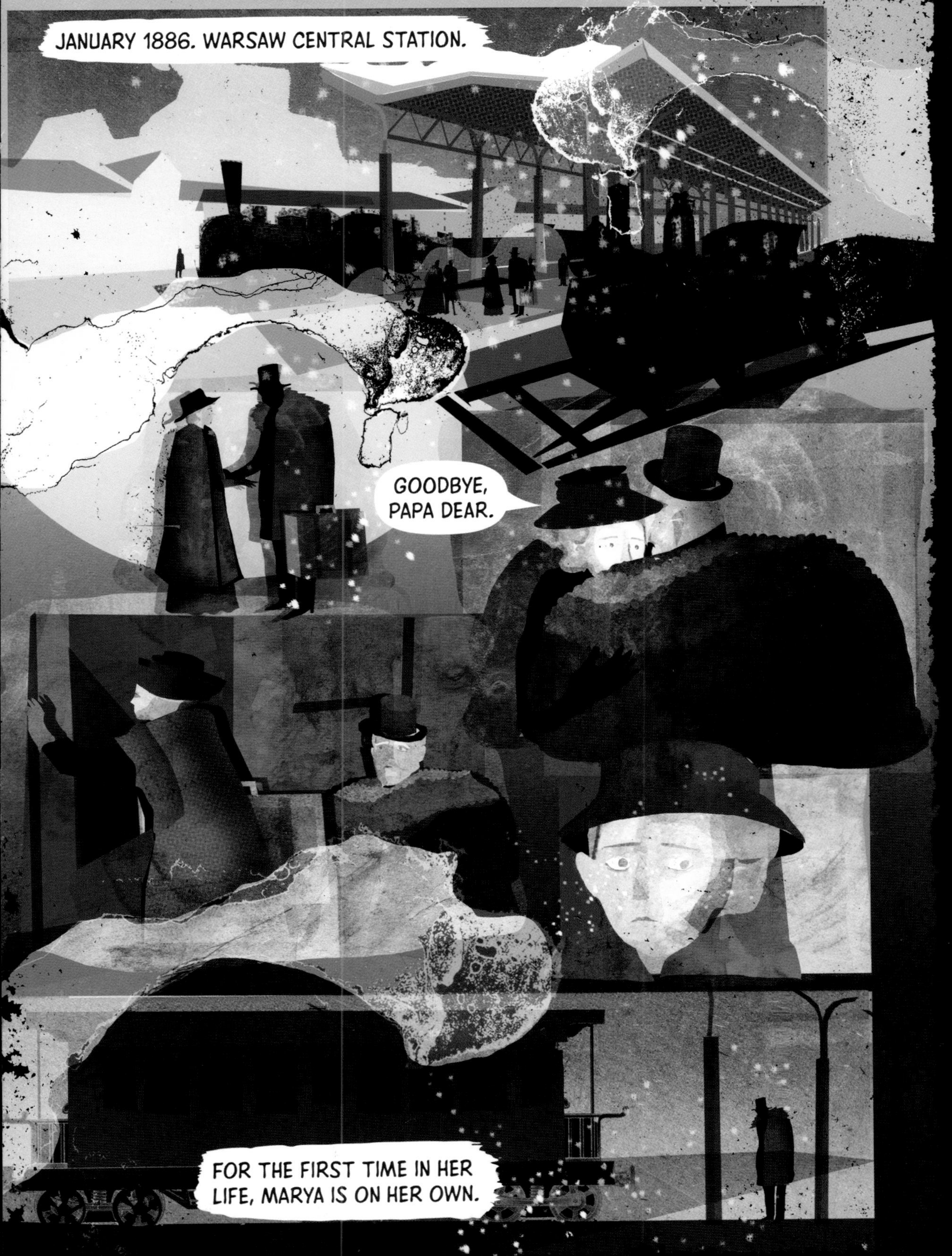
JANUARY 1886. WARSAW CENTRAL STATION.
GOODBYE, PAPA DEAR.
FOR THE FIRST TIME IN HER LIFE, MARYA IS ON HER OWN.

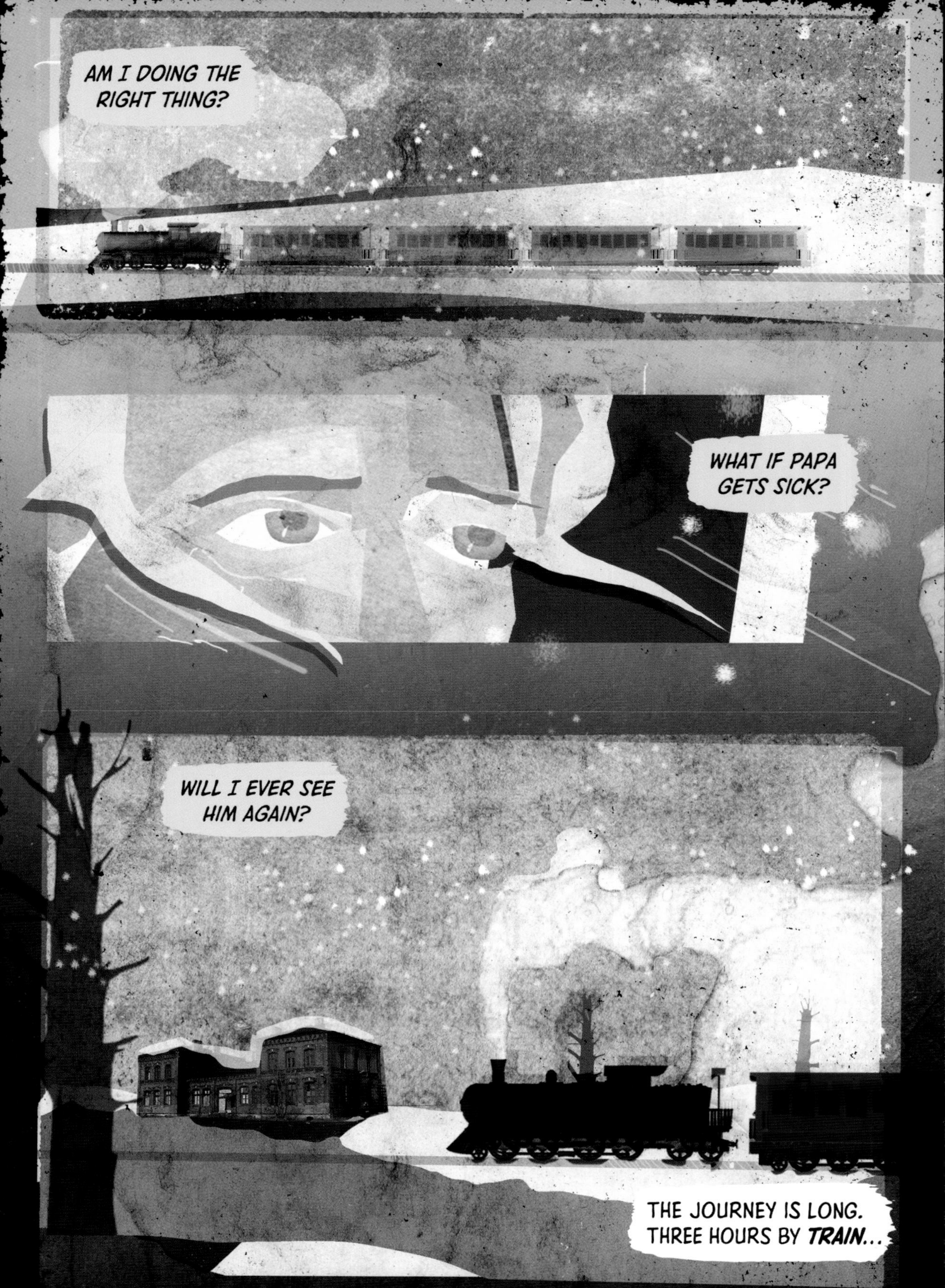
AM I DOING THE RIGHT THING?
WHAT IF PAPA GETS SICK?
WILL I EVER SEE HIM AGAIN?
THE JOURNEY IS LONG. THREE HOURS BY TRAIN...

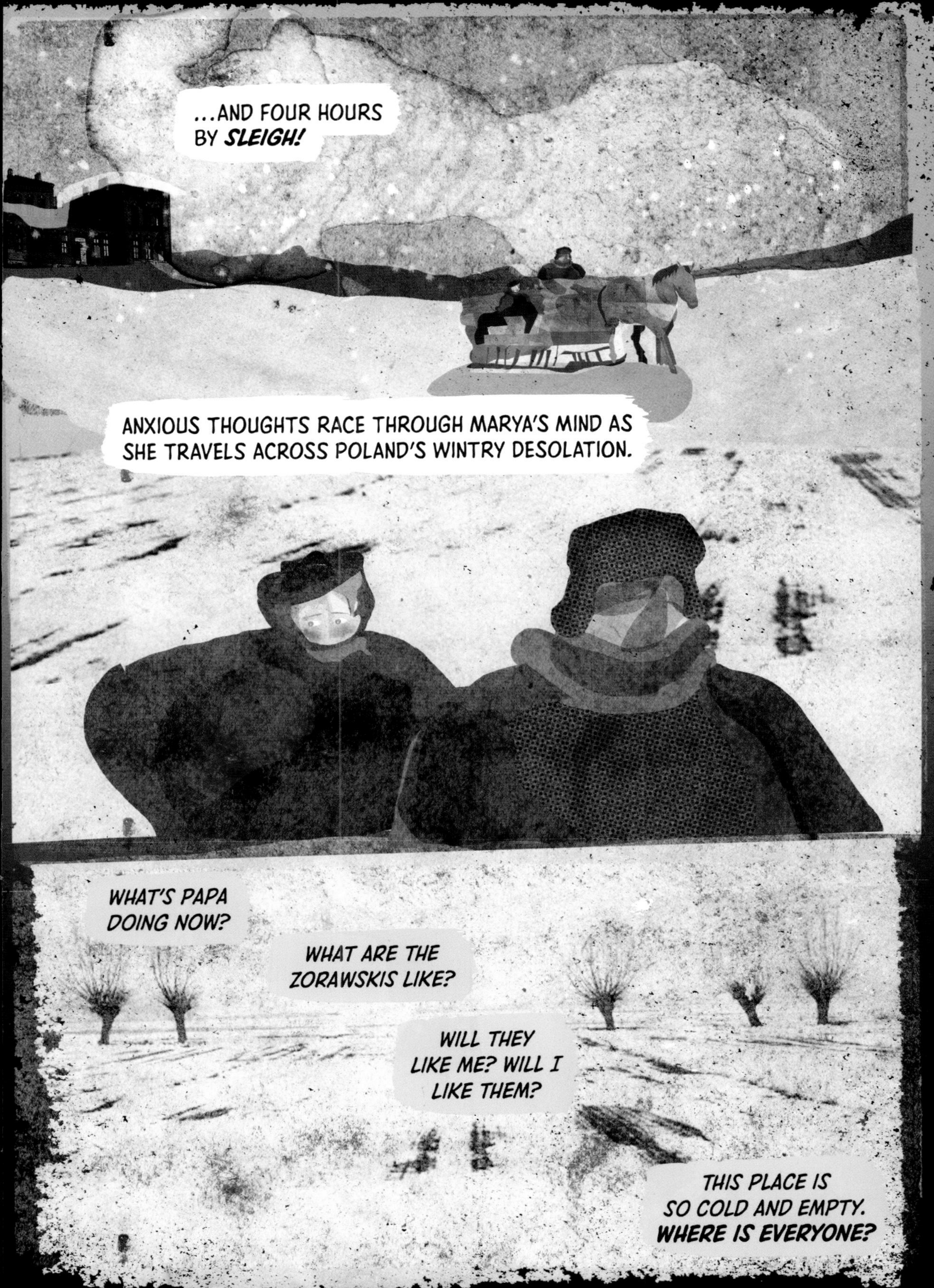
...AND FOUR HOURS BY SLEIGH!
ANXIOUS THOUGHTS RACE THROUGH MARYA'S MIND AS SHE TRAVELS ACROSS POLAND'S WINTRY DESOLATION.
WHAT'S PAPA DOING NOW?
WHAT ARE THE ZORAWSKIS LIKE?
WILL THEY LIKE ME? WILL I LIKE THEM?
THIS PLACE IS SO COLD AND EMPTY. WHERE IS EVERYONE?

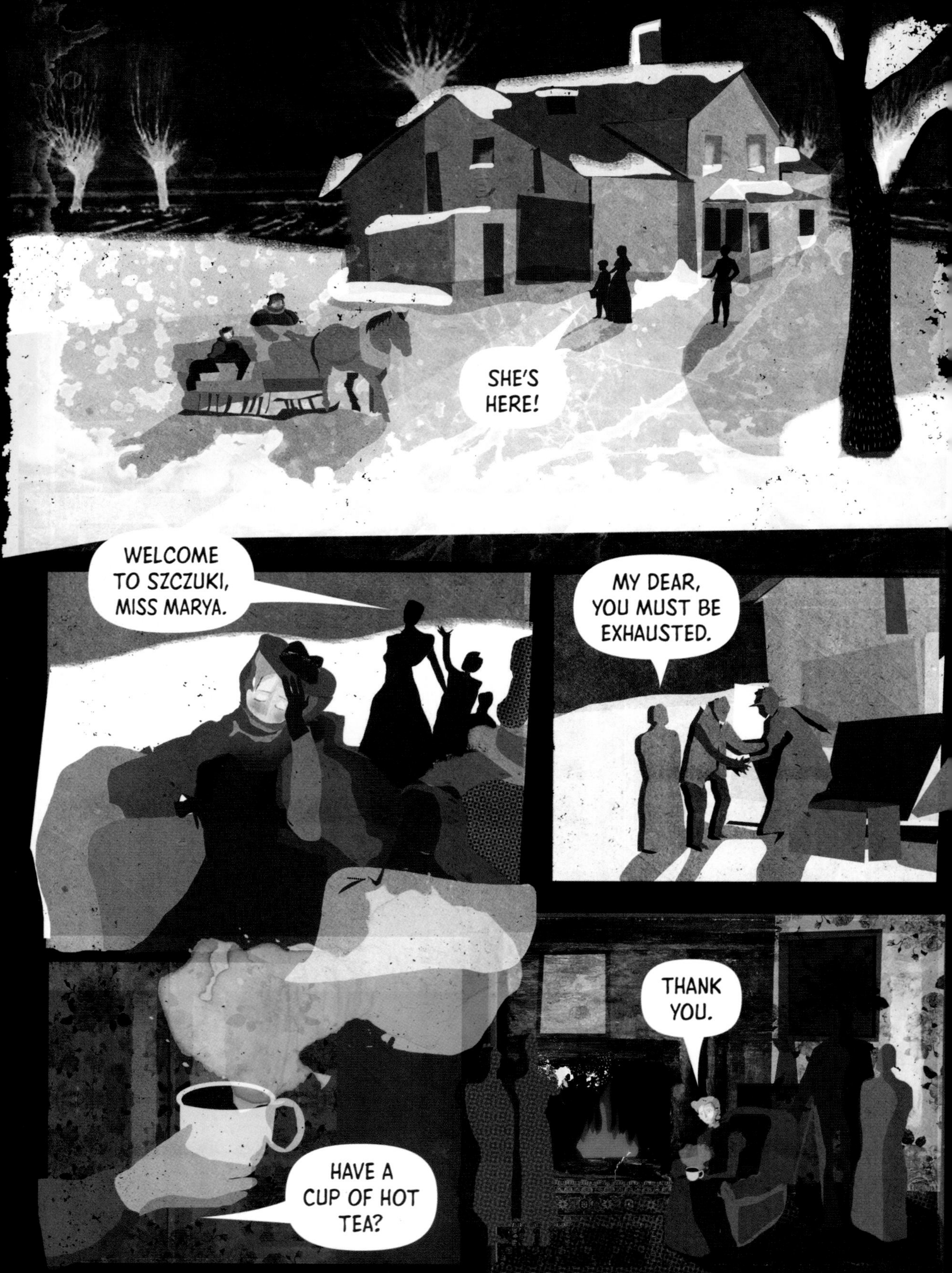
SHE'S HERE!
WELCOME TO SZCZUKI, MISS MARYA.
MY DEAR, YOU MUST BE EXHAUSTED.
HAVE A CUP OF HOT TEA?
THANK YOU.

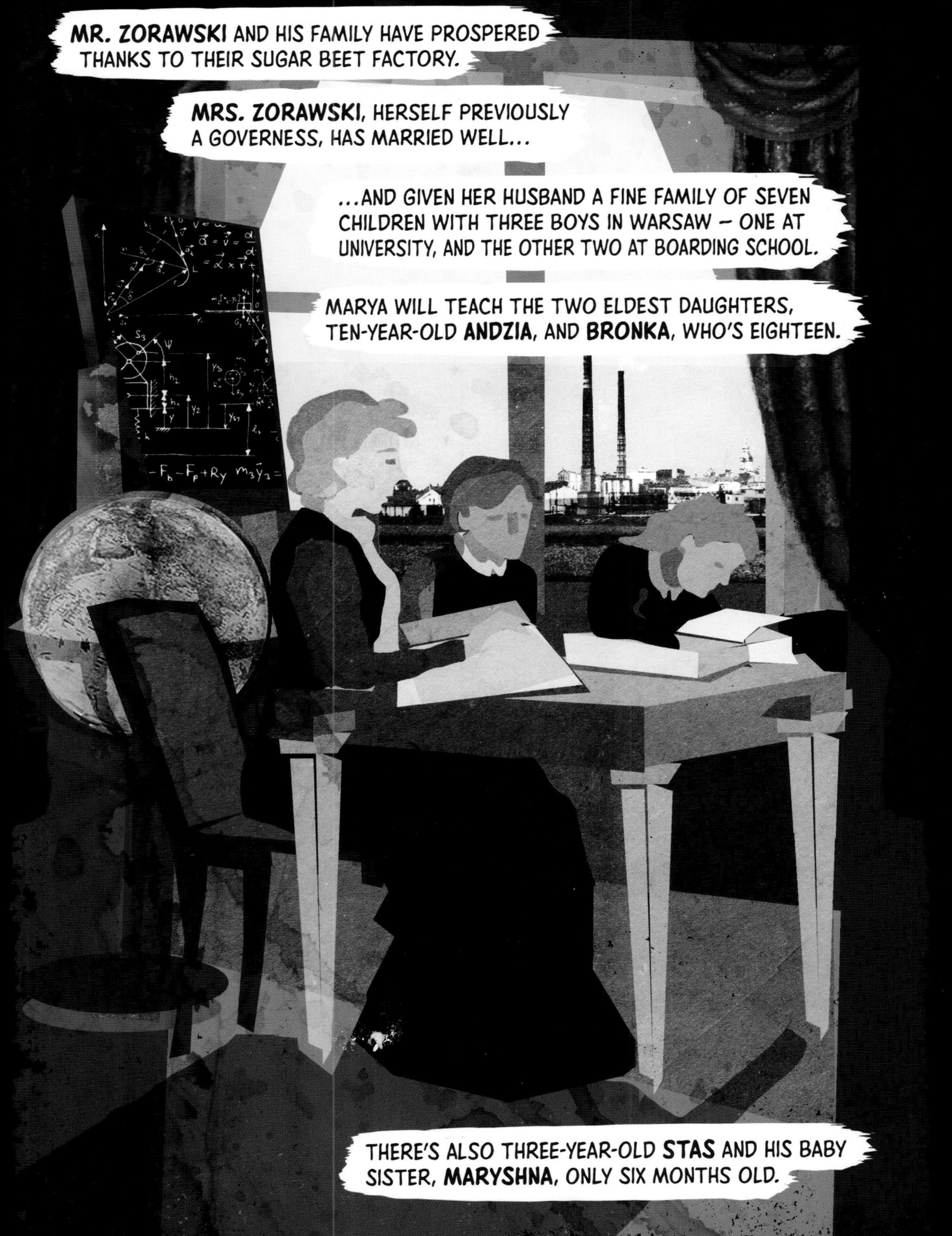
MR. ZORAWSKI AND HIS FAMILY HAVE PROSPERED THANKS TO THEIR SUGAR BEET FACTORY.
MRS. ZORAWSKI, HERSELF PREVIOUSLY A GOVERNESS, HAS MARRIED WELL...
...AND GIVEN HER HUSBAND A FINE FAMILY OF SEVEN CHILDREN WITH THREE BOYS IN WARSAW – ONE AT UNIVERSITY, AND THE OTHER TWO AT BOARDING SCHOOL.
MARYA WILL TEACH THE TWO ELDEST DAUGHTERS, TEN-YEAR-OLD ANDZIA, AND BRONKA, WHO'S EIGHTEEN.
THERE'S ALSO THREE-YEAR-OLD STAS AND HIS BABY SISTER, MARYSHNA, ONLY SIX MONTHS OLD.

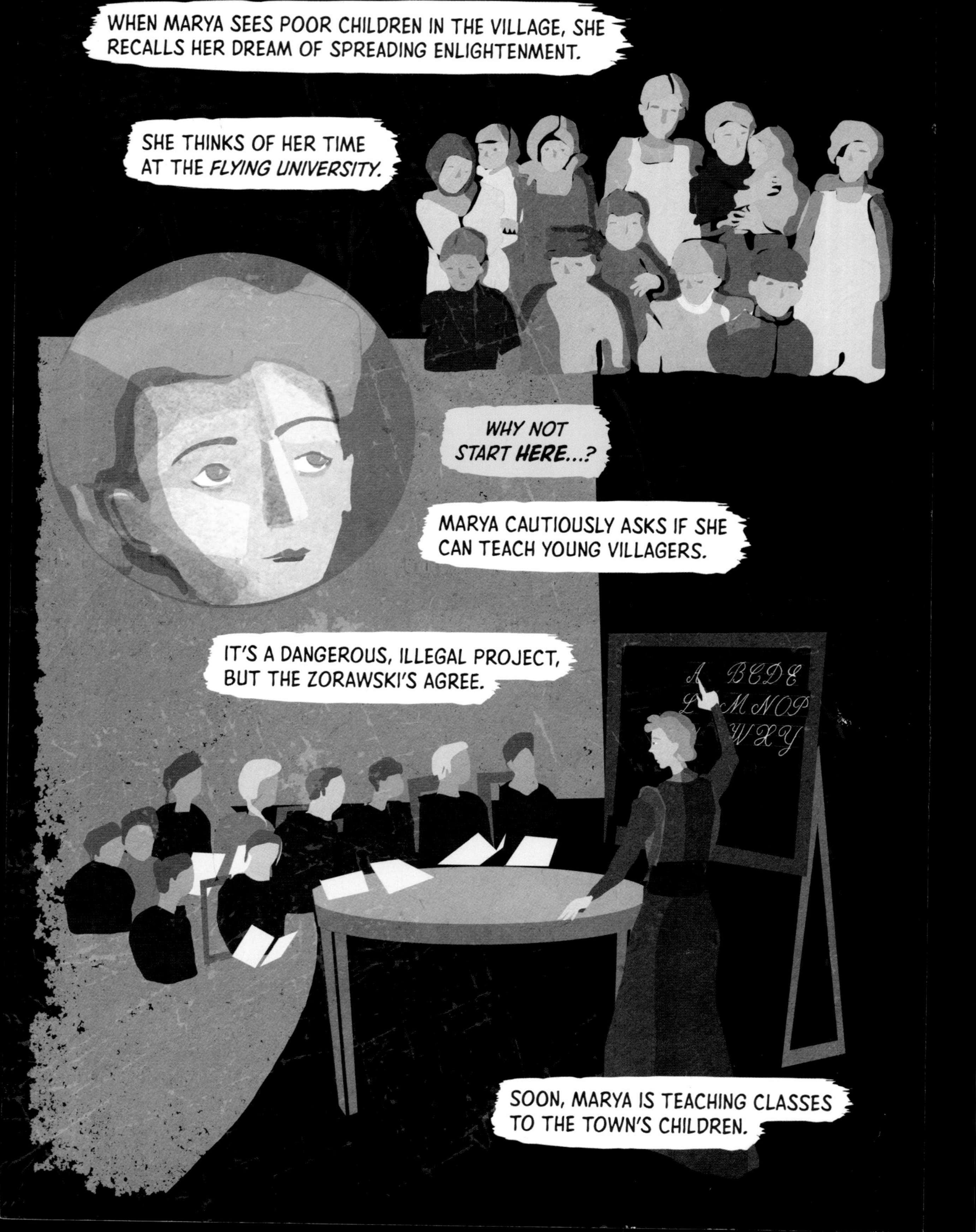
WHEN MARYA SEES POOR CHILDREN IN THE VILLAGE, SHE RECALLS HER DREAM OF SPREADING ENLIGHTENMENT.
SHE THINKS OF HER TIME AT THE *FLYING UNIVERSITY.*
*WHY NOT START **HERE**...?*
MARYA CAUTIOUSLY ASKS IF SHE CAN TEACH YOUNG VILLAGERS.
IT'S A DANGEROUS, ILLEGAL PROJECT, BUT THE ZORAWSKI'S AGREE.
SOON, MARYA IS TEACHING CLASSES TO THE TOWN'S CHILDREN.

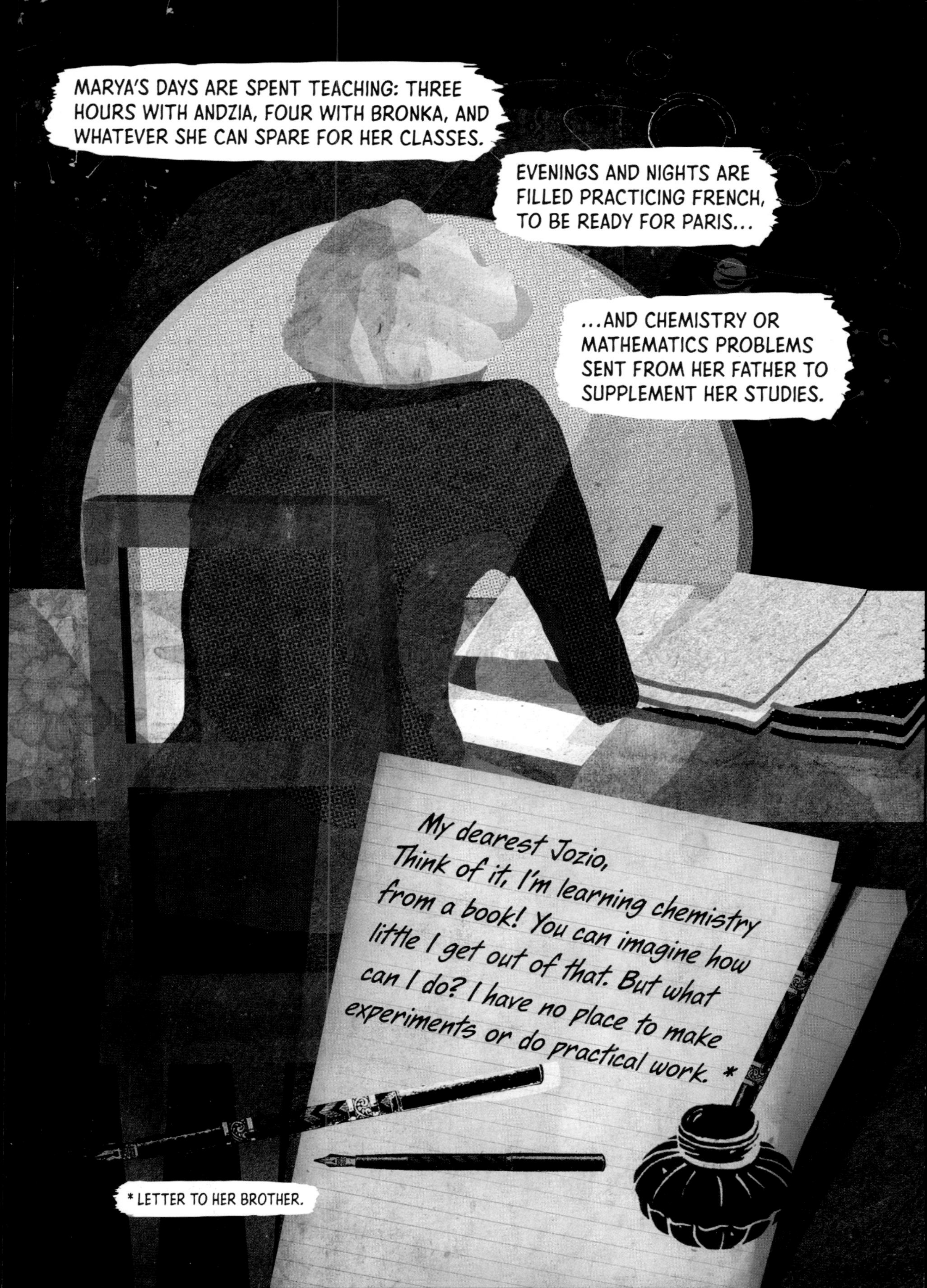
MARYA'S DAYS ARE SPENT TEACHING: THREE HOURS WITH ANDZIA, FOUR WITH BRONKA, AND WHATEVER SHE CAN SPARE FOR HER CLASSES.
EVENINGS AND NIGHTS ARE FILLED PRACTICING FRENCH, TO BE READY FOR PARIS...
...AND CHEMISTRY OR MATHEMATICS PROBLEMS SENT FROM HER FATHER TO SUPPLEMENT HER STUDIES.
My dearest Jozio, Think of it, I'm learning chemistry from a book! You can imagine how little I get out of that. But what can I do? I have no place to make experiments or do practical work. *
* LETTER TO HER BROTHER.

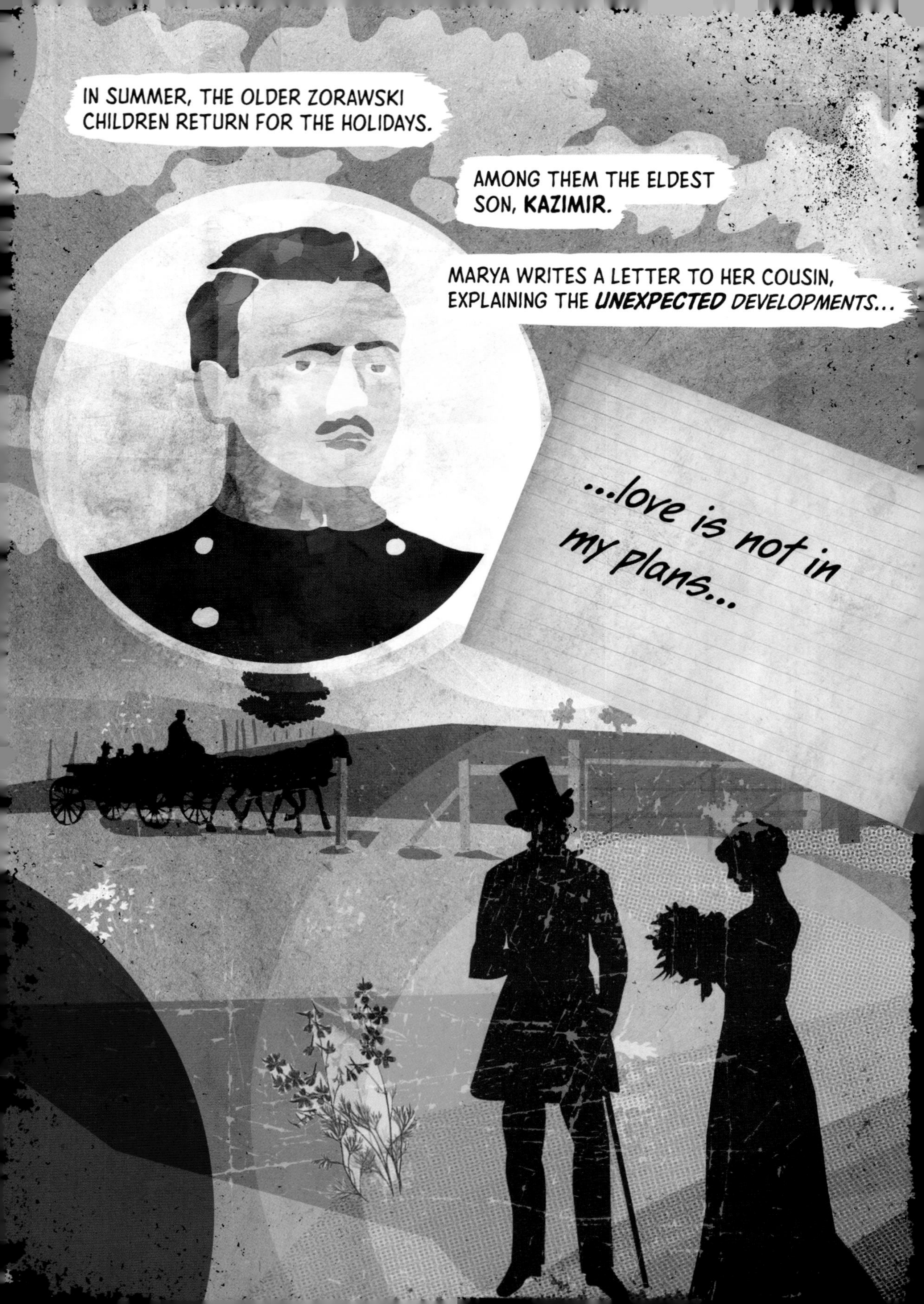
IN SUMMER, THE OLDER ZORAWSKI CHILDREN RETURN FOR THE HOLIDAYS.
AMONG THEM THE ELDEST SON, KAZIMIR.
MARYA WRITES A LETTER TO HER COUSIN, EXPLAINING THE UNEXPECTED DEVELOPMENTS...
...love is not in my plans...

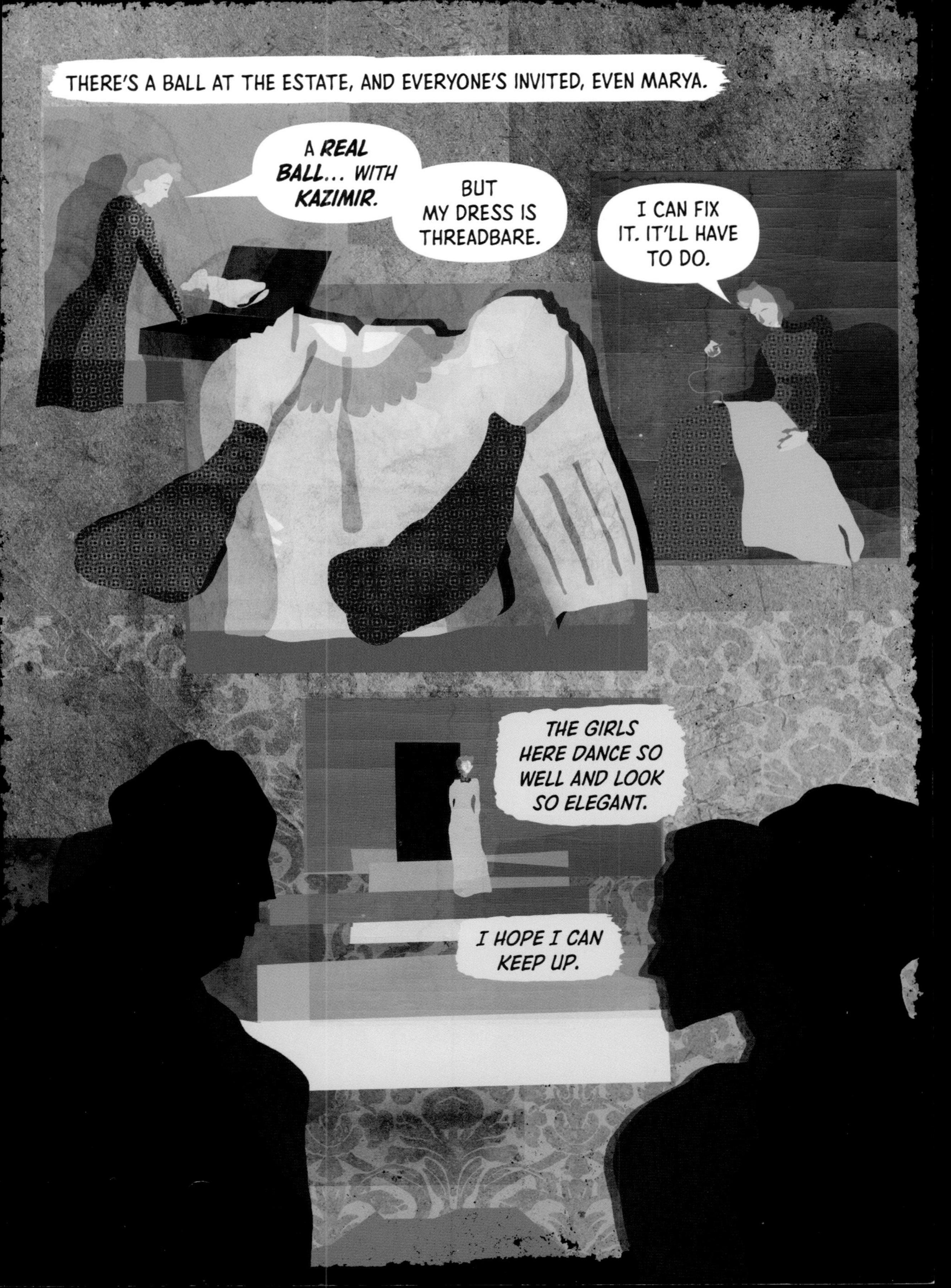
THERE'S A BALL AT THE ESTATE, AND EVERYONE'S INVITED, EVEN MARYA.
A **REAL BALL**... WITH **KAZIMIR.**
BUT MY DRESS IS THREADBARE.
I CAN FIX IT. IT'LL HAVE TO DO.
THE GIRLS HERE DANCE SO WELL AND LOOK SO ELEGANT.
I HOPE I CAN KEEP UP.

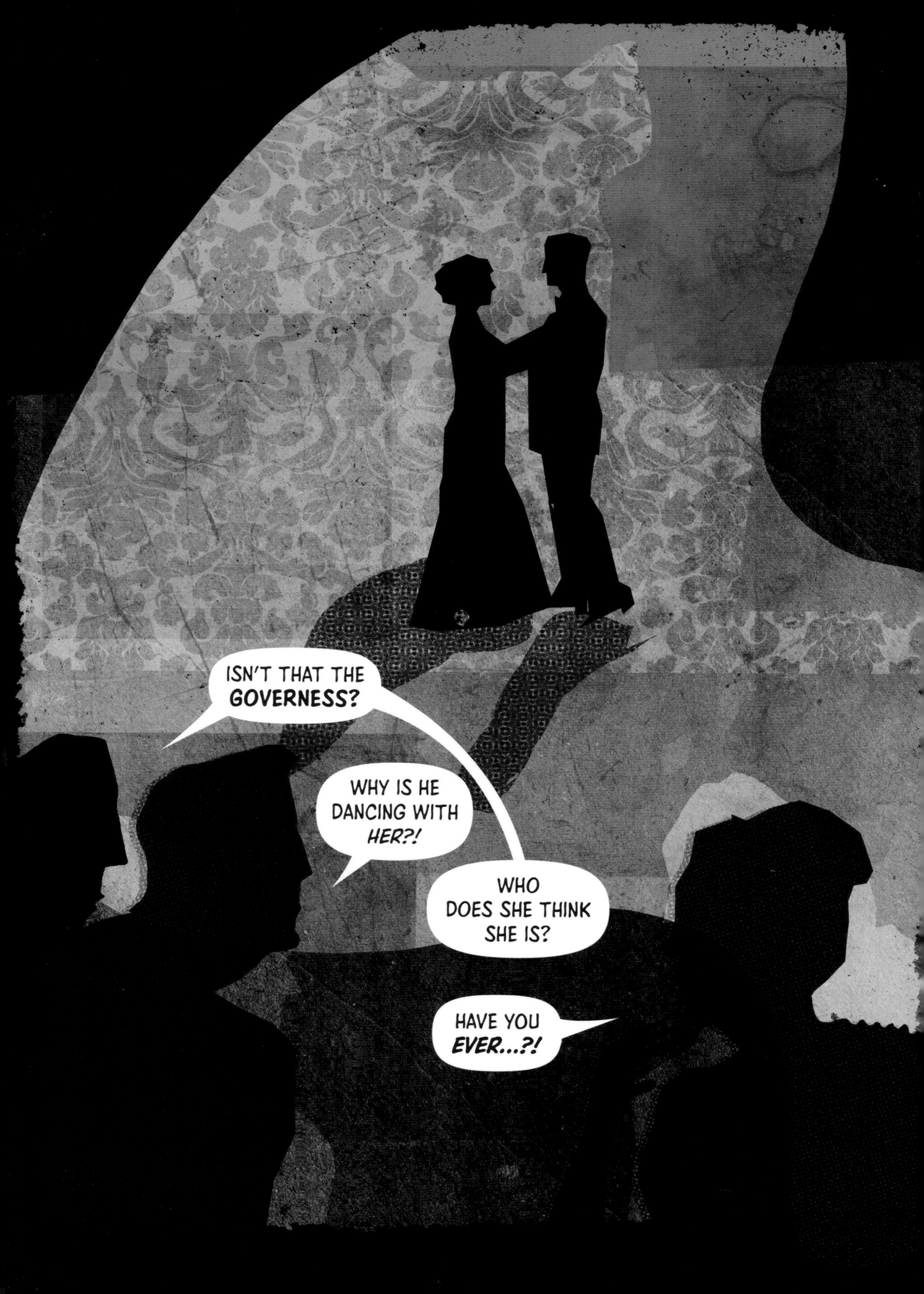
ISN'T THAT THE GOVERNESS?
WHY IS HE DANCING WITH HER?!
WHO DOES SHE THINK SHE IS?
HAVE YOU EVER...?!

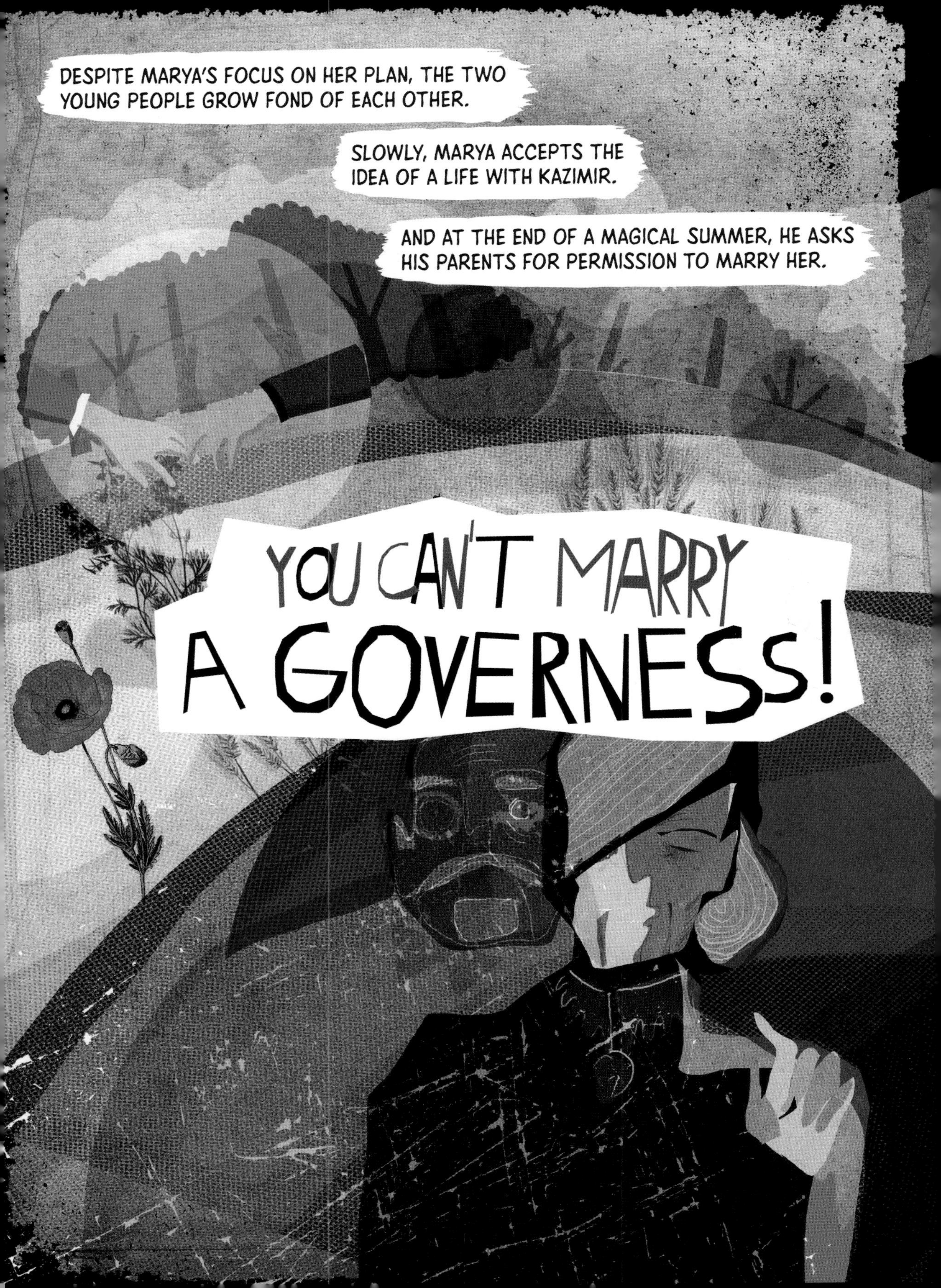
DESPITE MARYA'S FOCUS ON HER PLAN, THE TWO YOUNG PEOPLE GROW FOND OF EACH OTHER.
SLOWLY, MARYA ACCEPTS THE IDEA OF A LIFE WITH KAZIMIR.
AND AT THE END OF A MAGICAL SUMMER, HE ASKS HIS PARENTS FOR PERMISSION TO MARRY HER.
YOU CAN'T MARRY A GOVERNESS!

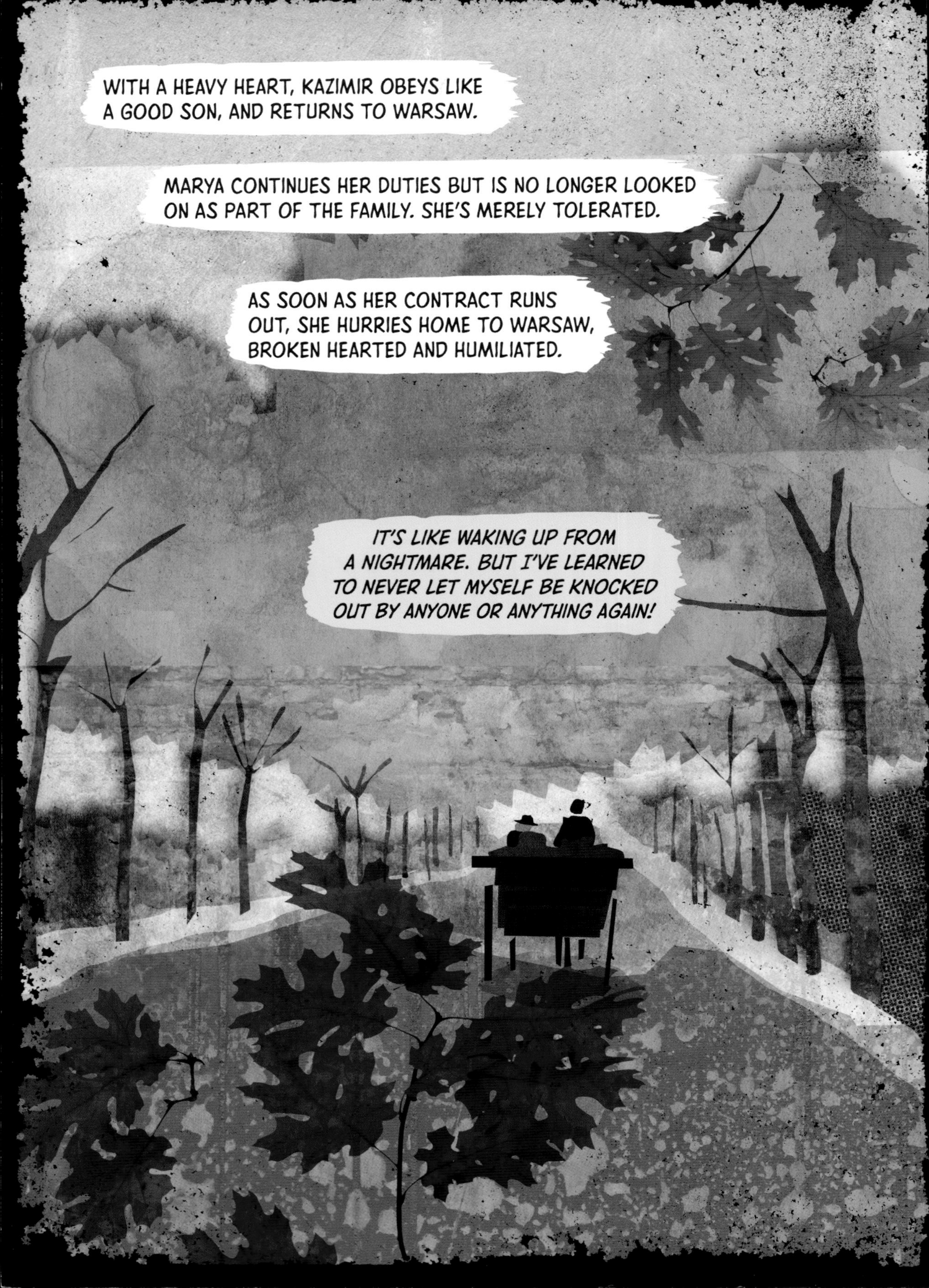
WITH A HEAVY HEART, KAZIMIR OBEYS LIKE A GOOD SON, AND RETURNS TO WARSAW.
MARYA CONTINUES HER DUTIES BUT IS NO LONGER LOOKED ON AS PART OF THE FAMILY. SHE'S MERELY TOLERATED.
AS SOON AS HER CONTRACT RUNS OUT, SHE HURRIES HOME TO WARSAW, BROKEN HEARTED AND HUMILIATED.
IT'S LIKE WAKING UP FROM A NIGHTMARE. BUT I'VE LEARNED TO NEVER LET MYSELF BE KNOCKED OUT BY ANYONE OR ANYTHING AGAIN!

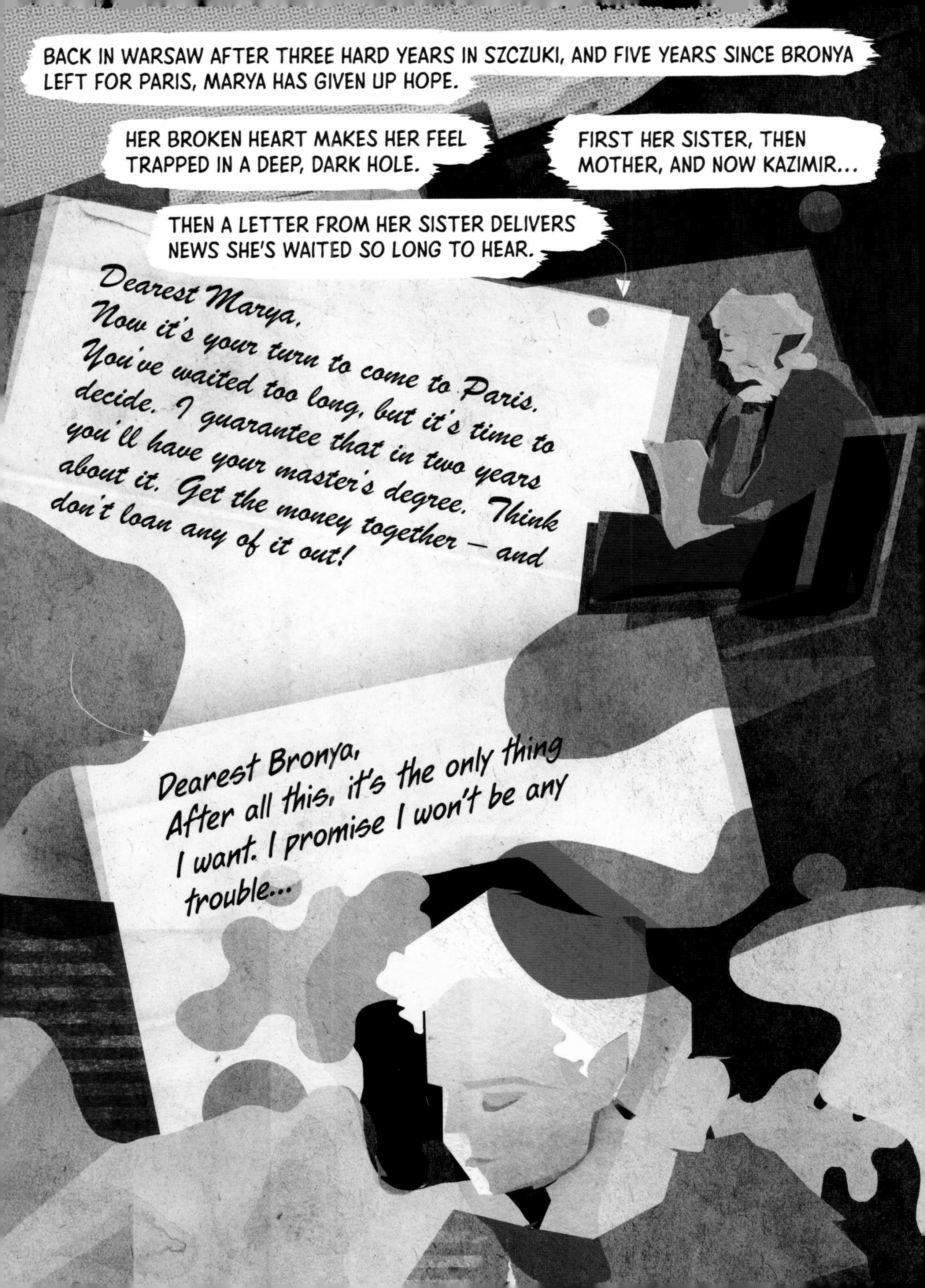
BACK IN WARSAW AFTER THREE HARD YEARS IN SZCZUKI, AND FIVE YEARS SINCE BRONYA LEFT FOR PARIS, MARYA HAS GIVEN UP HOPE.
HER BROKEN HEART MAKES HER FEEL TRAPPED IN A DEEP, DARK HOLE.
FIRST HER SISTER, THEN MOTHER, AND NOW KAZIMIR...
THEN A LETTER FROM HER SISTER DELIVERS NEWS SHE'S WAITED SO LONG TO HEAR.
Dearest Marya,
Now it's your turn to come to Paris. You've waited too long, but it's time to decide. I guarantee that in two years you'll have your master's degree. Think about it. Get the money together – and don't loan any of it out!
Dearest Bronya,
After all this, it's the only thing I want. I promise I won't be any trouble...

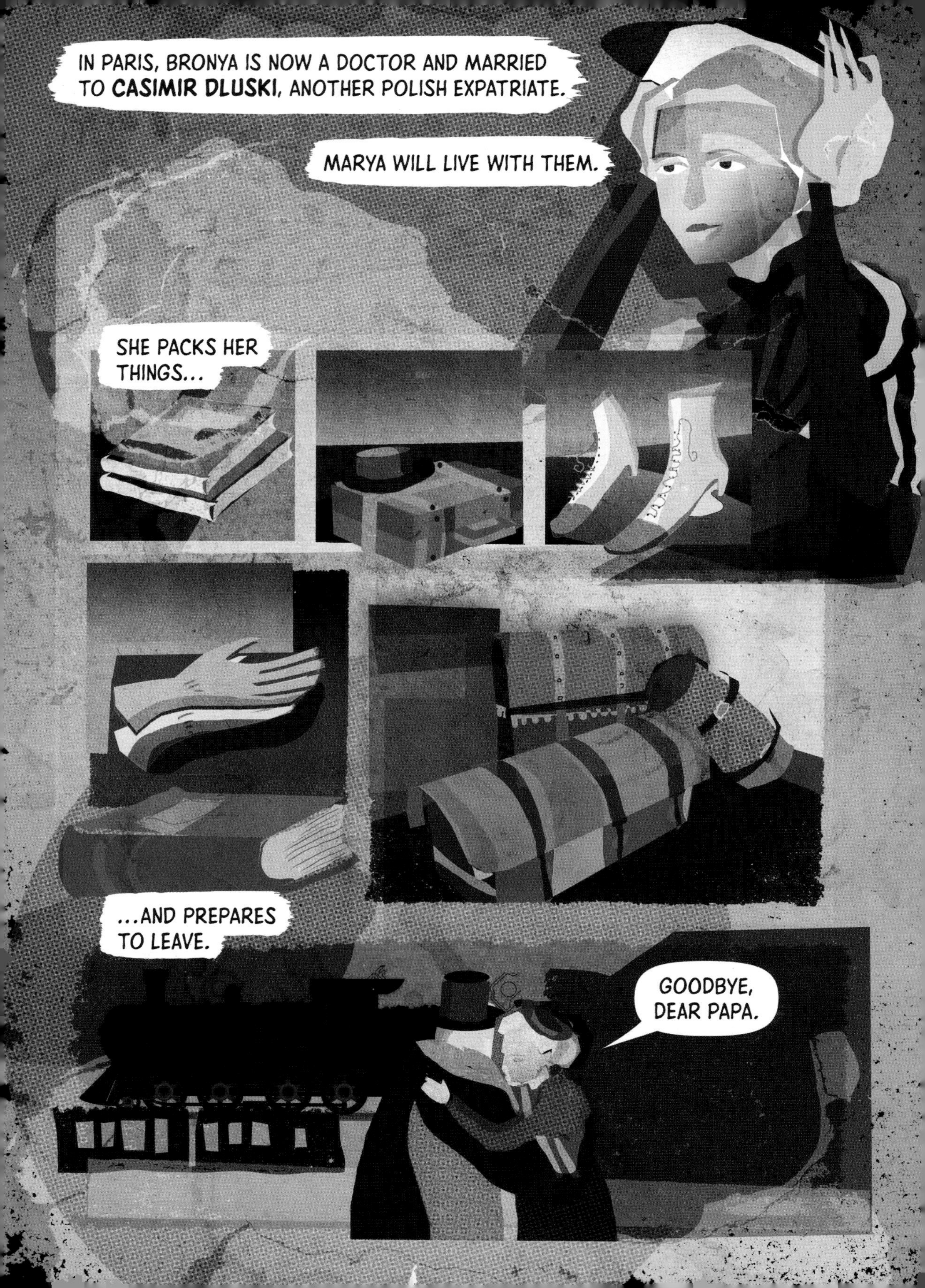
IN PARIS, BRONYA IS NOW A DOCTOR AND MARRIED TO **CASIMIR DLUSKI**, ANOTHER POLISH EXPATRIATE.
MARYA WILL LIVE WITH THEM.
SHE PACKS HER THINGS...
...AND PREPARES TO LEAVE.
GOODBYE, DEAR PAPA.

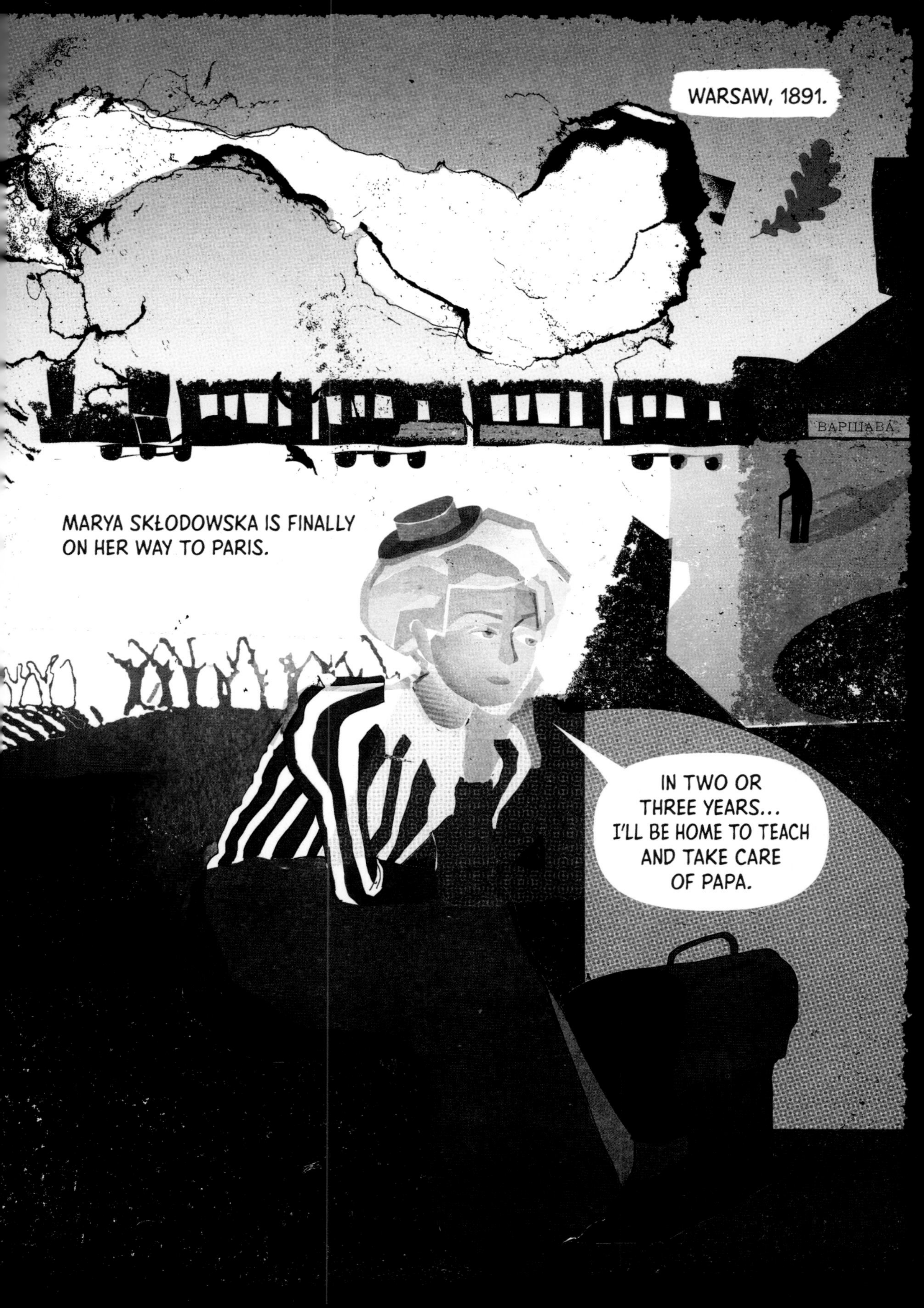
WARSAW, 1891.
ВАРШАВА
MARYA SKŁODOWSKA IS FINALLY ON HER WAY TO PARIS.
IN TWO OR THREE YEARS... I'LL BE HOME TO TEACH AND TAKE CARE OF PAPA.

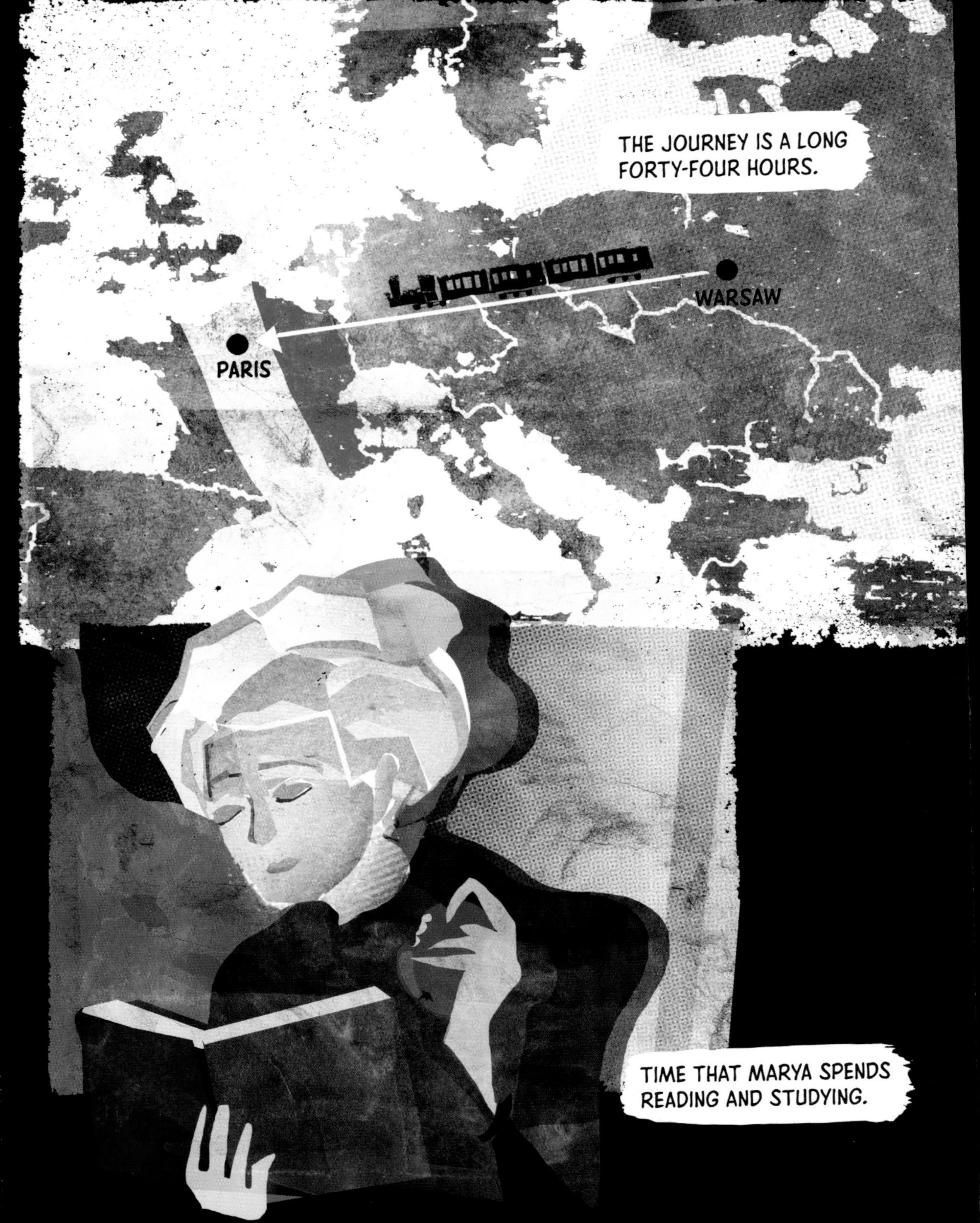
THE JOURNEY IS A LONG FORTY-FOUR HOURS.
WARSAW
PARIS
TIME THAT MARYA SPENDS READING AND STUDYING.

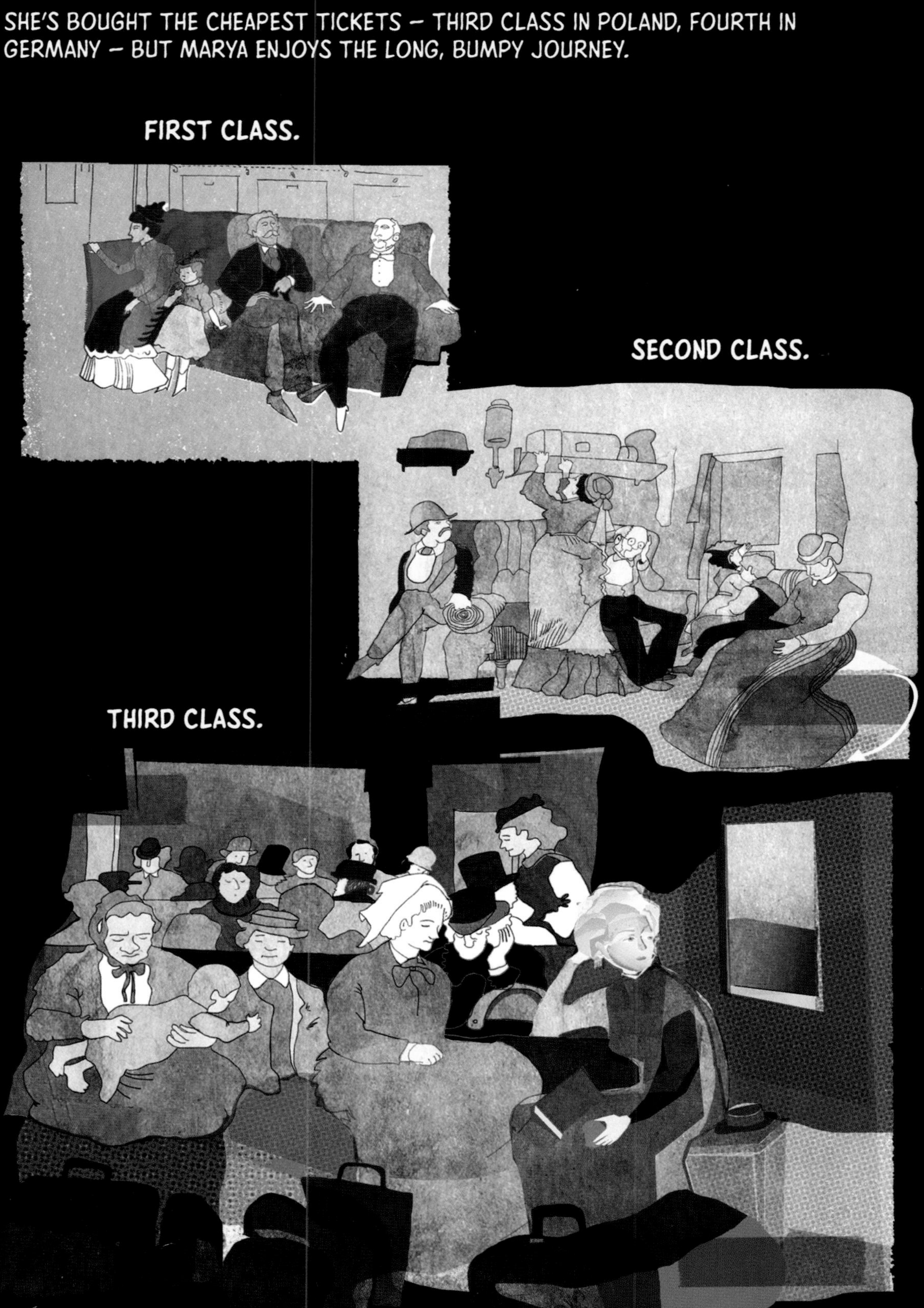
SHE'S BOUGHT THE CHEAPEST TICKETS – THIRD CLASS IN POLAND, FOURTH IN GERMANY – BUT MARYA ENJOYS THE LONG, BUMPY JOURNEY.
FIRST CLASS.
SECOND CLASS.
THIRD CLASS.

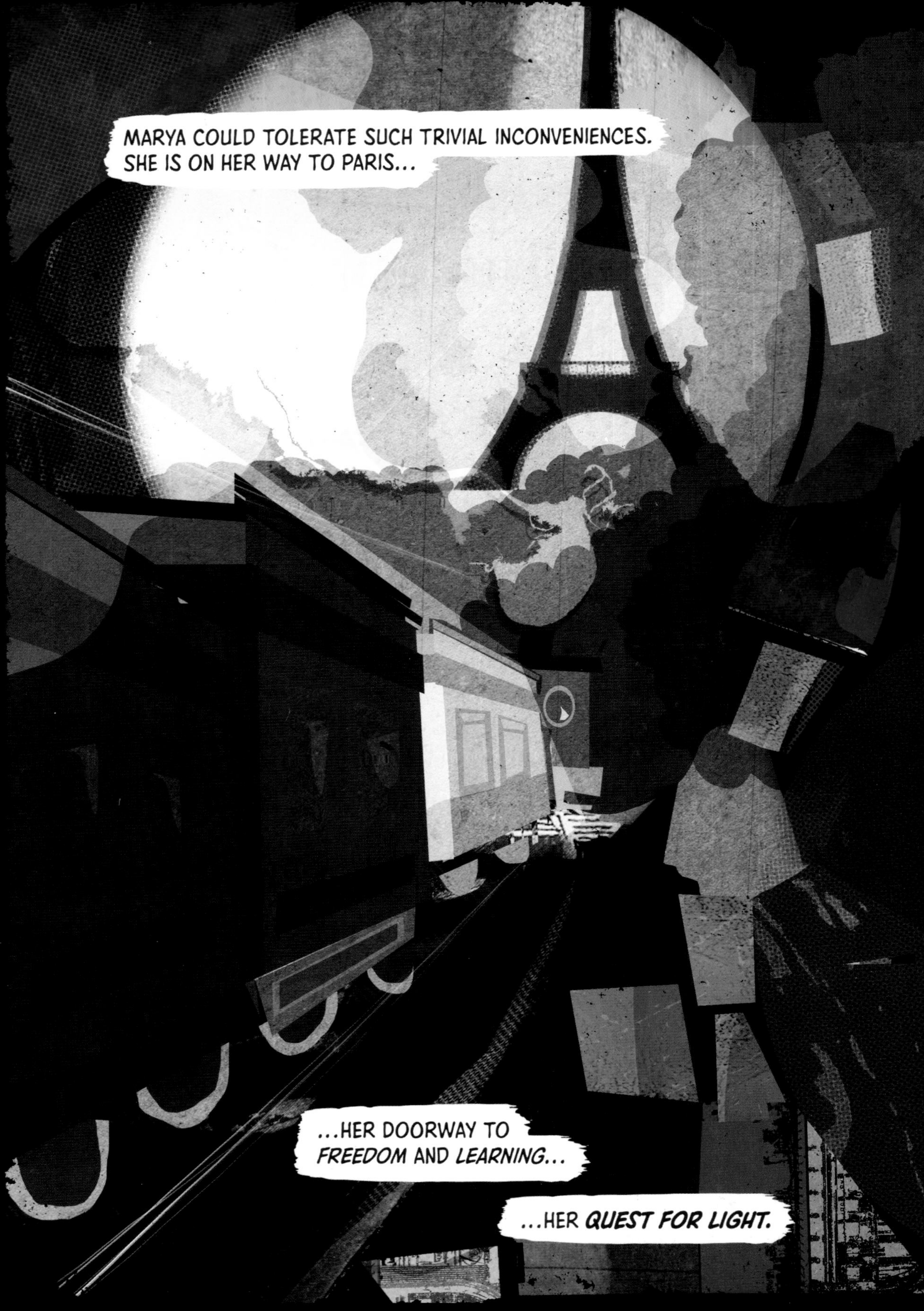
MARYA COULD TOLERATE SUCH TRIVIAL INCONVENIENCES. SHE IS ON HER WAY TO PARIS...
...HER DOORWAY TO *FREEDOM* AND *LEARNING*...
...HER ***QUEST FOR LIGHT.***

Chapter 3

1891-1895

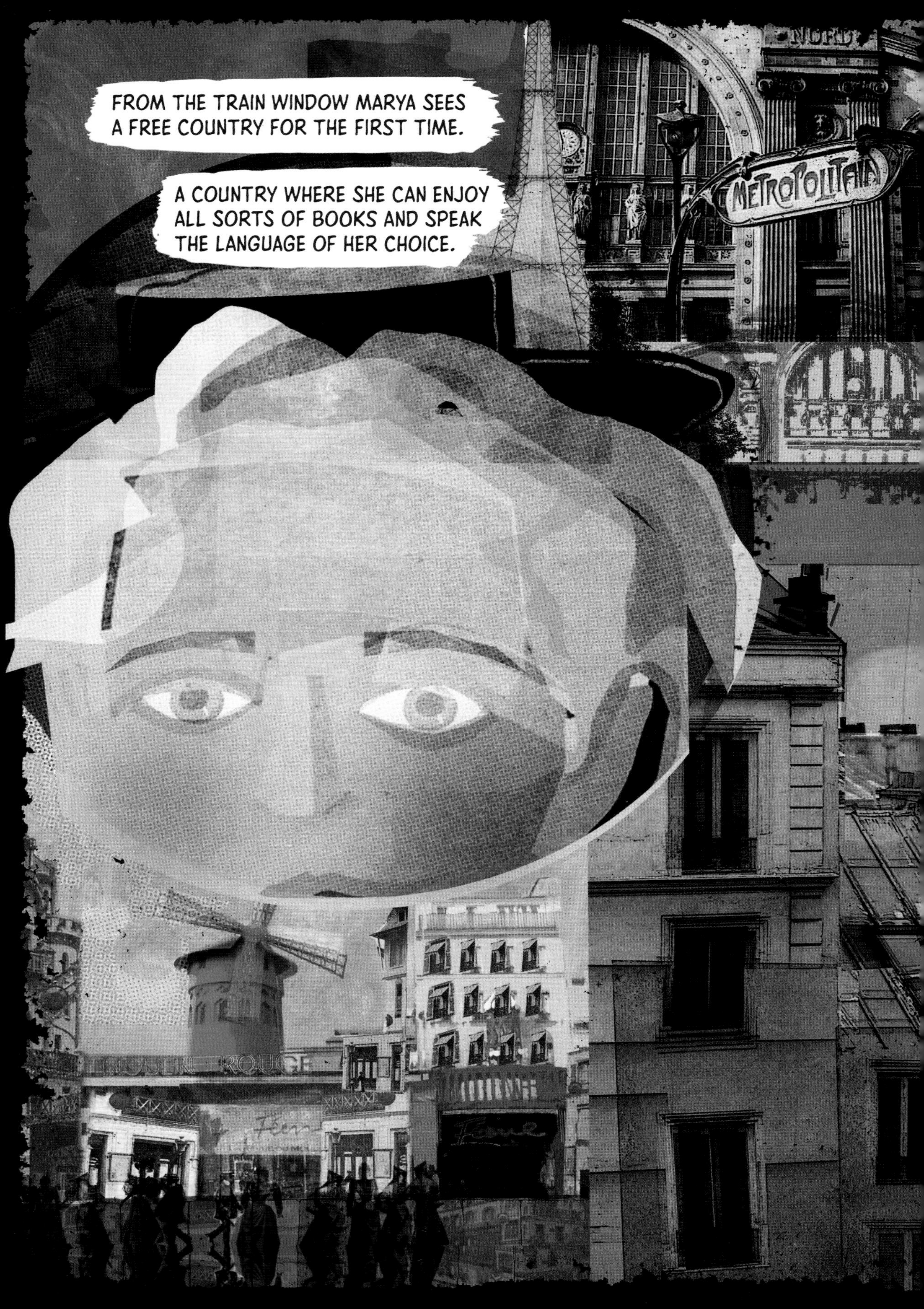
FROM THE TRAIN WINDOW MARYA SEES A FREE COUNTRY FOR THE FIRST TIME.
A COUNTRY WHERE SHE CAN ENJOY ALL SORTS OF BOOKS AND SPEAK THE LANGUAGE OF HER CHOICE.
NORD
METROPOLITAIN
ROUGE

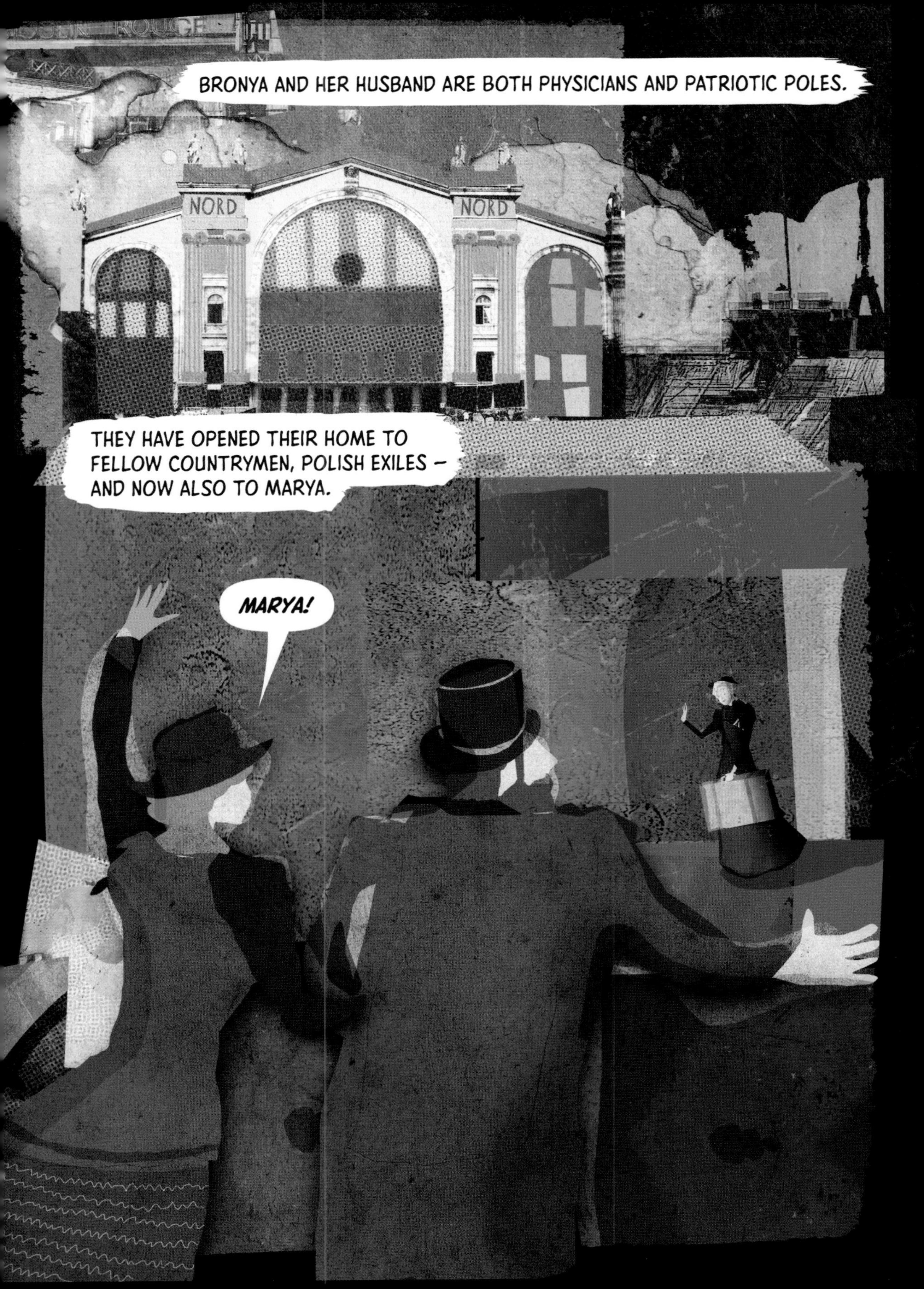
BRONYA AND HER HUSBAND ARE BOTH PHYSICIANS AND PATRIOTIC POLES.
NORD
NORD
THEY HAVE OPENED THEIR HOME TO FELLOW COUNTRYMEN, POLISH EXILES – AND NOW ALSO TO MARYA.
MARYA!

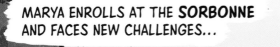

MARYA ENROLLS AT THE **SORBONNE** AND FACES NEW CHALLENGES...

...SUCH AS IMPROVING HER FRENCH...

...AND FILLING IN GAPS — CHEMISTRY AND PHYSICS — FROM HER SECRETIVE HOME STUDIES IN POLAND.

French Republic
Faculty of Sciences, First Quarter
Courses will begin
at the Sorbonne on November 3, 1891

5ᵉ Arrᵗ

PLACE
DE LA
SORBONNE

I STUDIED SO HARD, BUT MY PREPARATION IN POLAND WAS NOT ENOUGH. THE FRENCH STUDENTS ARE FAR MORE ADVANCED, ESPECIALLY IN MATHEMATICS.

IT'S A NEW LIFE IN A NEW COUNTRY. WHEN MARYA ENROLLS AT THE SORBONNE, SHE'S NOW *MARIE*. THE QUIET GIRL WITH THE IMPOSSIBLE LAST NAME: **MARIE SKŁODOWSKA**.

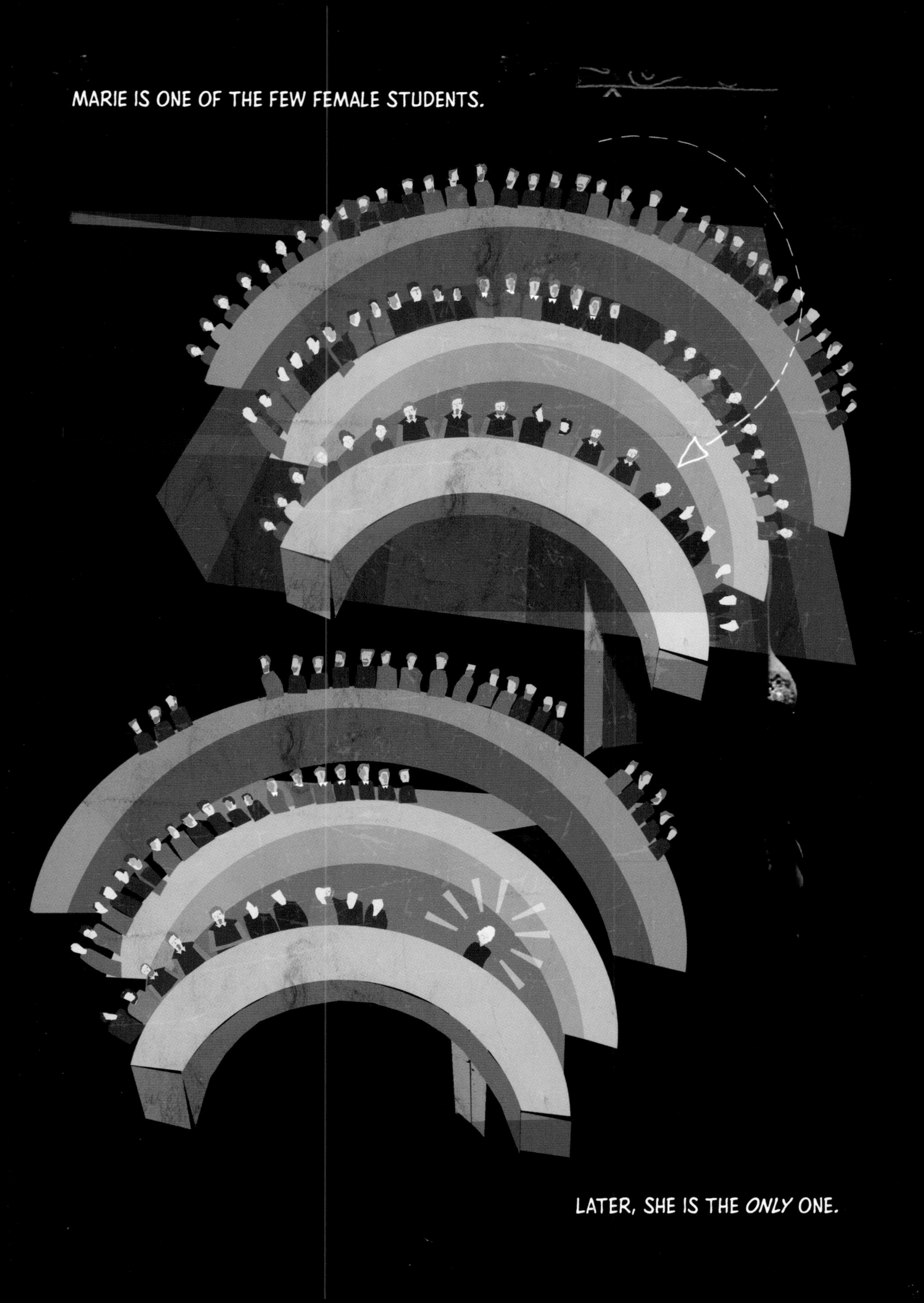
MARIE IS ONE OF THE FEW FEMALE STUDENTS.
LATER, SHE IS THE *ONLY* ONE.

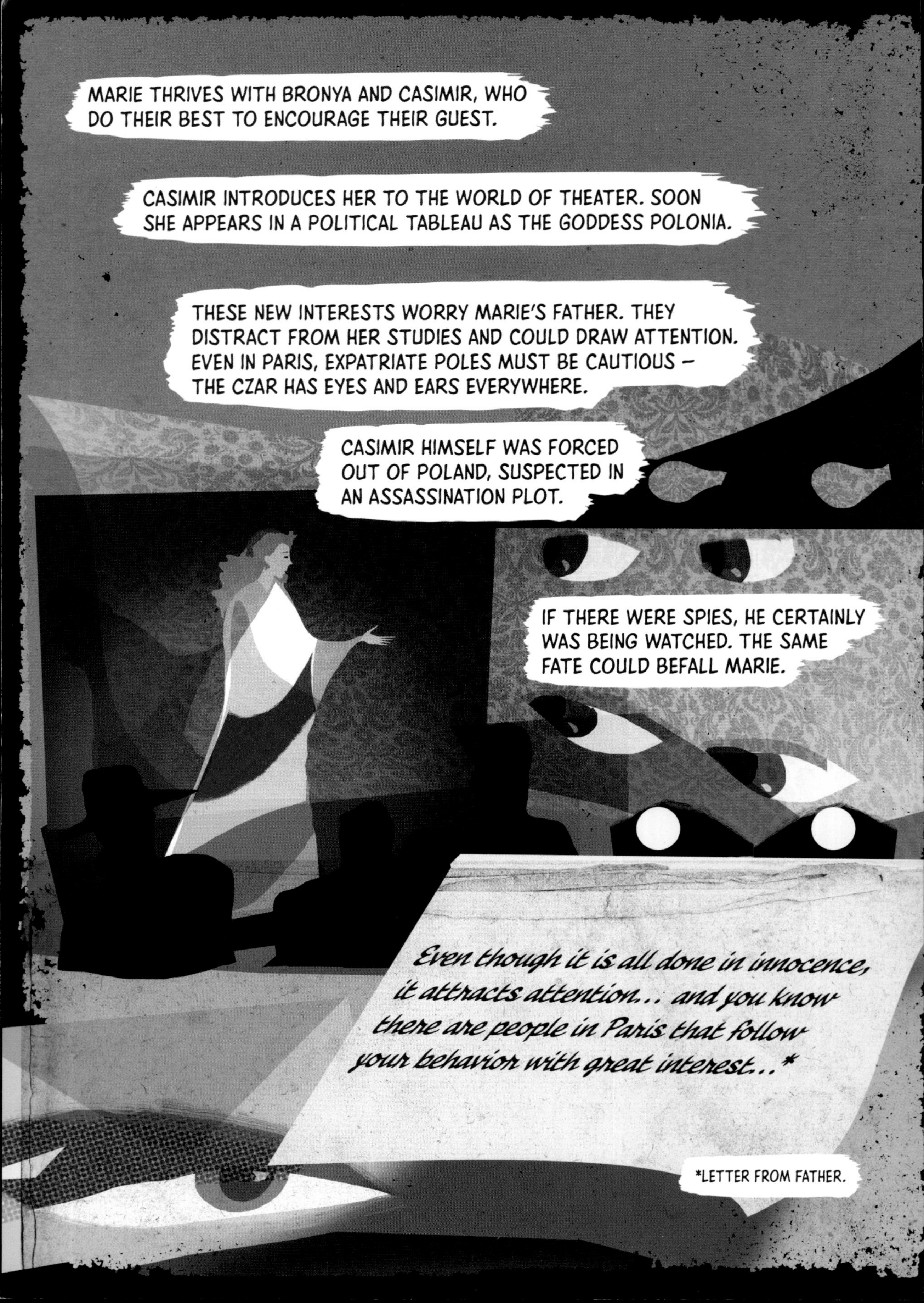
MARIE THRIVES WITH BRONYA AND CASIMIR, WHO DO THEIR BEST TO ENCOURAGE THEIR GUEST.
CASIMIR INTRODUCES HER TO THE WORLD OF THEATER. SOON SHE APPEARS IN A POLITICAL TABLEAU AS THE GODDESS POLONIA.
THESE NEW INTERESTS WORRY MARIE'S FATHER. THEY DISTRACT FROM HER STUDIES AND COULD DRAW ATTENTION. EVEN IN PARIS, EXPATRIATE POLES MUST BE CAUTIOUS – THE CZAR HAS EYES AND EARS EVERYWHERE.
CASIMIR HIMSELF WAS FORCED OUT OF POLAND, SUSPECTED IN AN ASSASSINATION PLOT.
IF THERE WERE SPIES, HE CERTAINLY WAS BEING WATCHED. THE SAME FATE COULD BEFALL MARIE.
Even though it is all done in innocence, it attracts attention... and you know there are people in Paris that follow your behavior with great interest...*
*LETTER FROM FATHER.

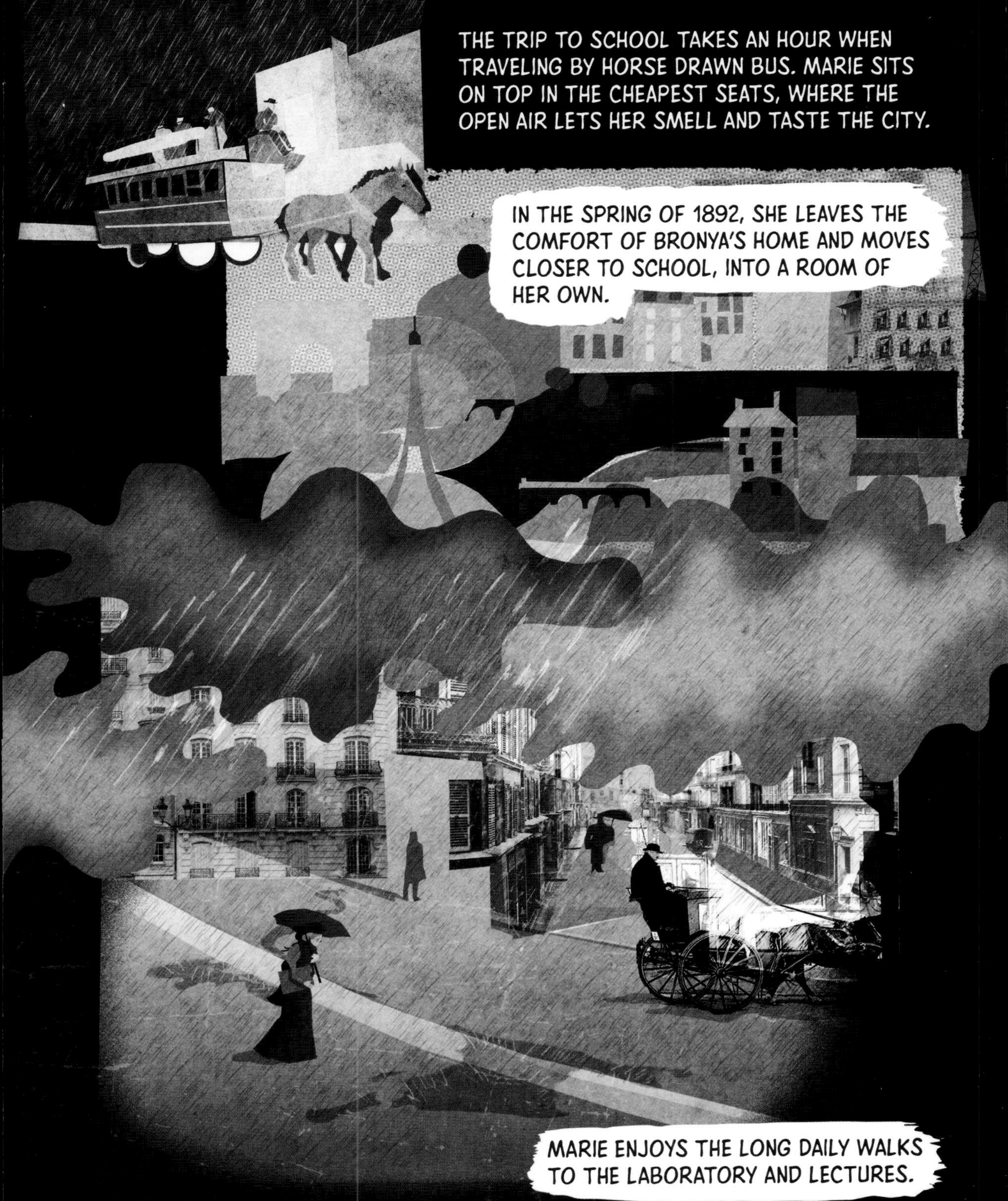
THE TRIP TO SCHOOL TAKES AN HOUR WHEN TRAVELING BY HORSE DRAWN BUS. MARIE SITS ON TOP IN THE CHEAPEST SEATS, WHERE THE OPEN AIR LETS HER SMELL AND TASTE THE CITY.
IN THE SPRING OF 1892, SHE LEAVES THE COMFORT OF BRONYA'S HOME AND MOVES CLOSER TO SCHOOL, INTO A ROOM OF HER OWN.
MARIE ENJOYS THE LONG DAILY WALKS TO THE LABORATORY AND LECTURES.

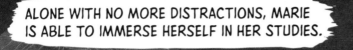

ALONE WITH NO MORE DISTRACTIONS, MARIE IS ABLE TO IMMERSE HERSELF IN HER STUDIES.

Life is not easy for any of us. But what of it?... We must hold on to our belief that we are fated for something and this something must be achieved. *

*FROM A LETTER TO HER BROTHER.

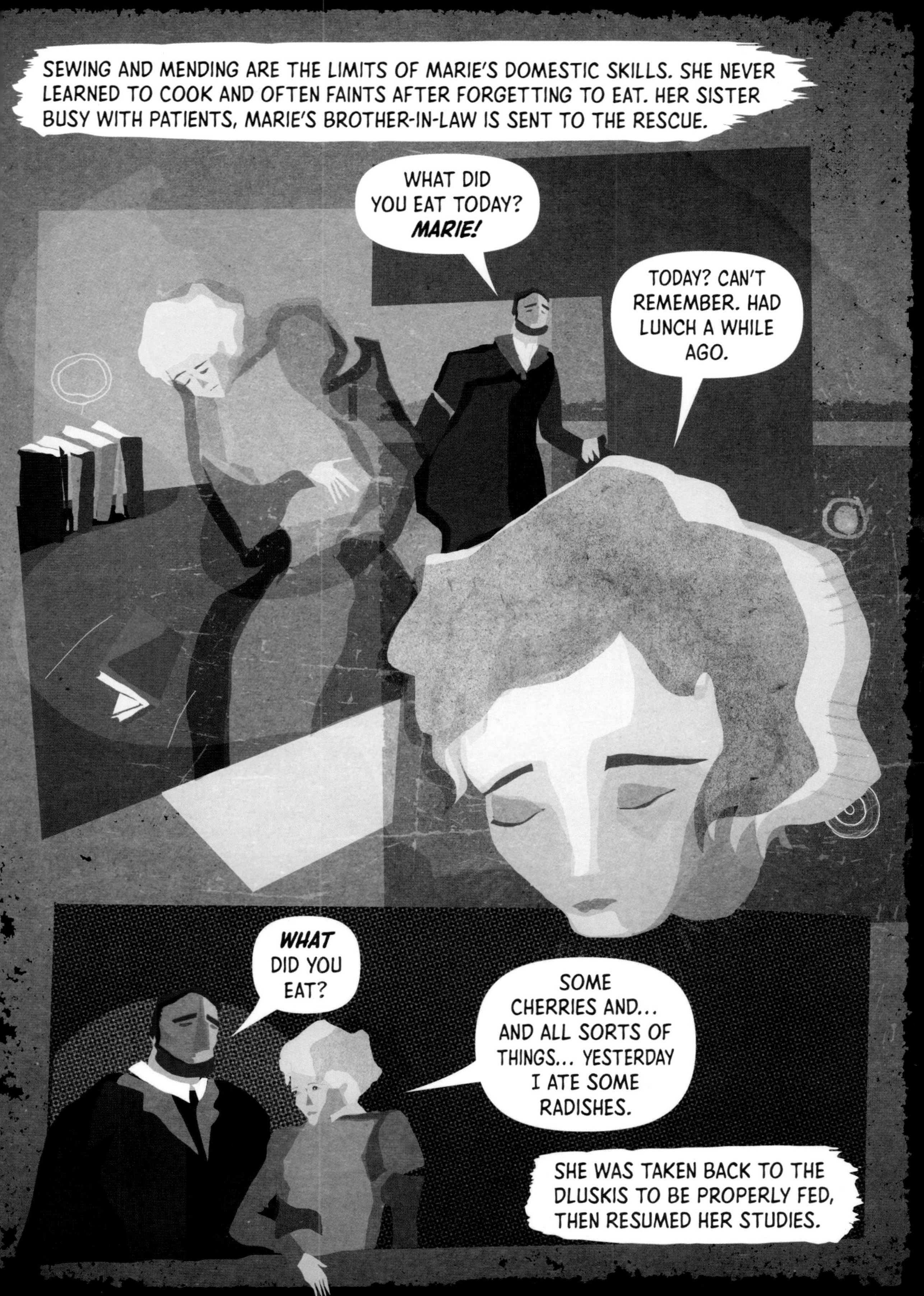
SEWING AND MENDING ARE THE LIMITS OF MARIE'S DOMESTIC SKILLS. SHE NEVER LEARNED TO COOK AND OFTEN FAINTS AFTER FORGETTING TO EAT. HER SISTER BUSY WITH PATIENTS, MARIE'S BROTHER-IN-LAW IS SENT TO THE RESCUE.
WHAT DID YOU EAT TODAY? MARIE!
TODAY? CAN'T REMEMBER. HAD LUNCH A WHILE AGO.
WHAT DID YOU EAT?
SOME CHERRIES AND... AND ALL SORTS OF THINGS... YESTERDAY I ATE SOME RADISHES.
SHE WAS TAKEN BACK TO THE DLUSKIS TO BE PROPERLY FED, THEN RESUMED HER STUDIES.

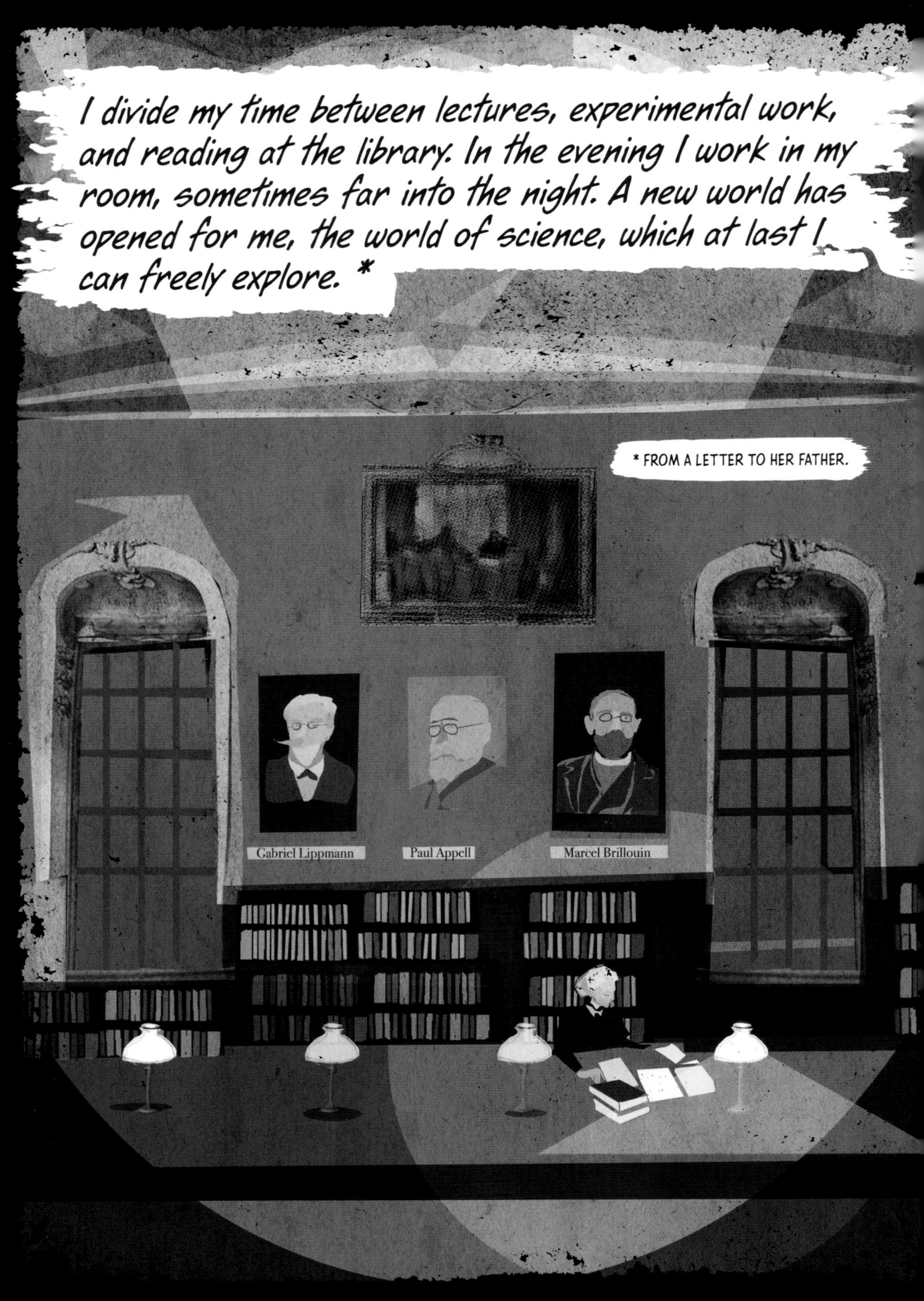
I divide my time between lectures, experimental work, and reading at the library. In the evening I work in my room, sometimes far into the night. A new world has opened for me, the world of science, which at last I can freely explore. *
* FROM A LETTER TO HER FATHER.
Gabriel Lippmann
Paul Appell
Marcel Brillouin

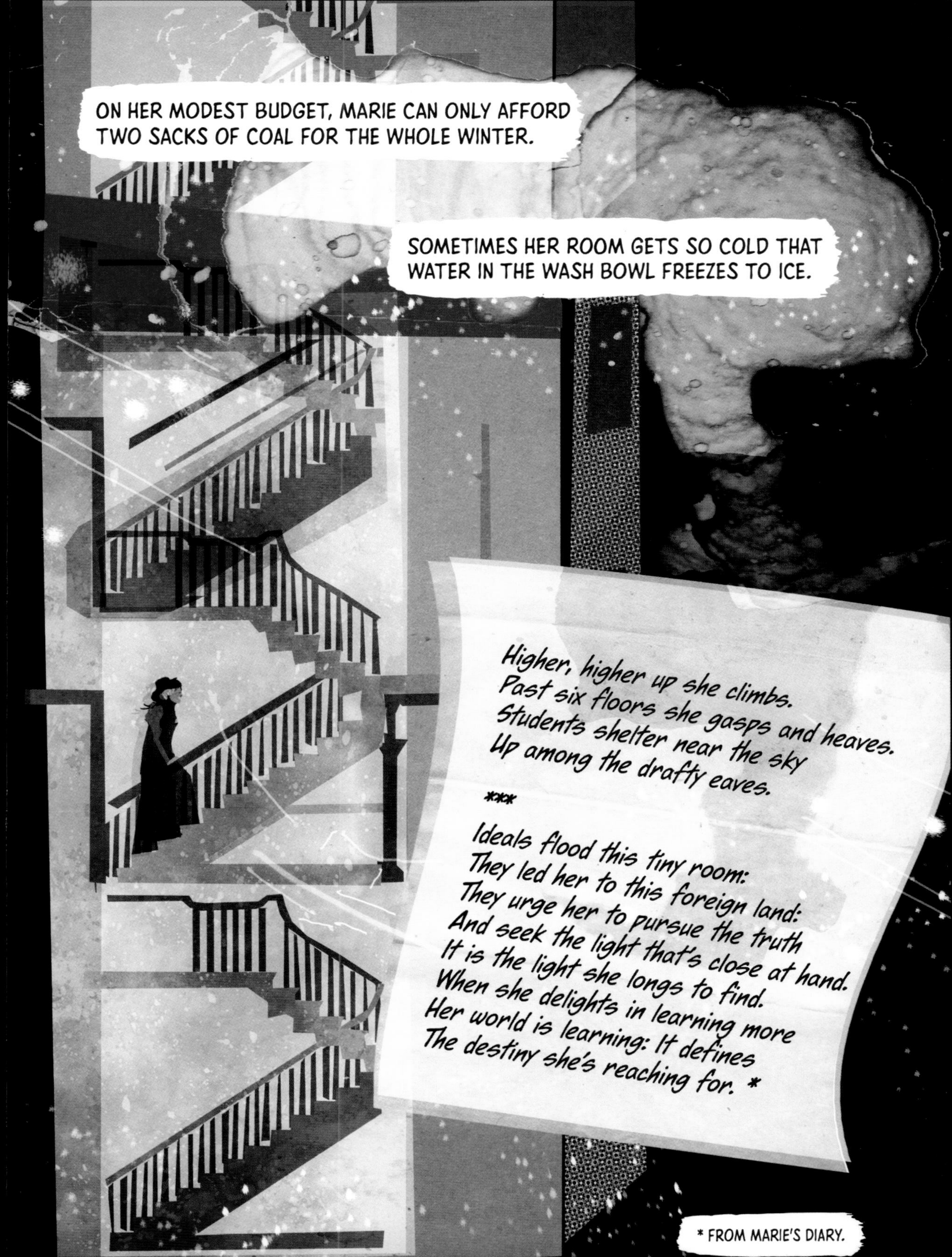
ON HER MODEST BUDGET, MARIE CAN ONLY AFFORD TWO SACKS OF COAL FOR THE WHOLE WINTER.
SOMETIMES HER ROOM GETS SO COLD THAT WATER IN THE WASH BOWL FREEZES TO ICE.
Higher, higher up she climbs.
Past six floors she gasps and heaves.
Students shelter near the sky
Up among the drafty eaves.
***
Ideals flood this tiny room:
They led her to this foreign land:
They urge her to pursue the truth
And seek the light that's close at hand.
It is the light she longs to find.
When she delights in learning more
Her world is learning: It defines
The destiny she's reaching for. *
* FROM MARIE'S DIARY.

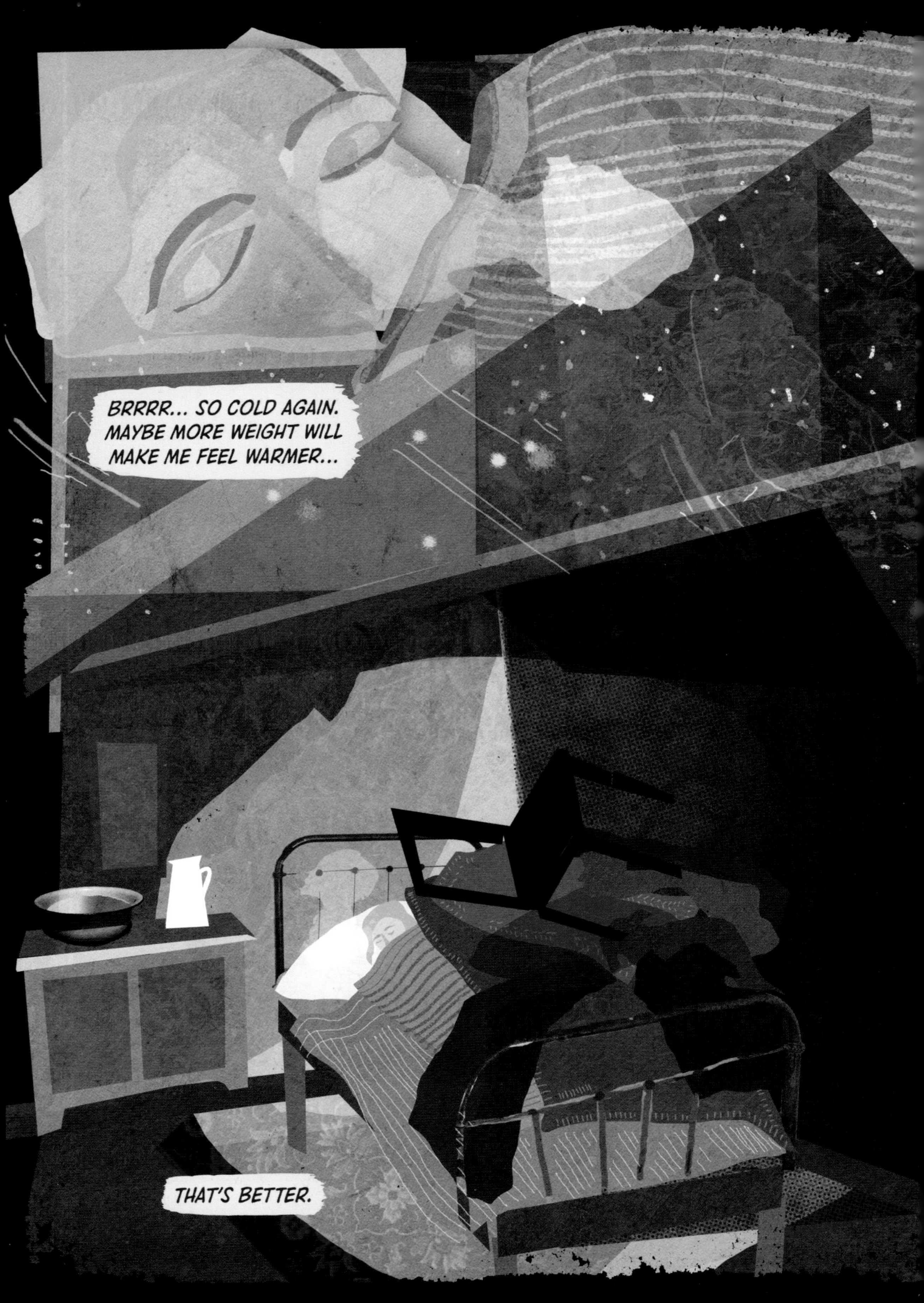
BRRRR... SO COLD AGAIN. MAYBE MORE WEIGHT WILL MAKE ME FEEL WARMER...
THAT'S BETTER.

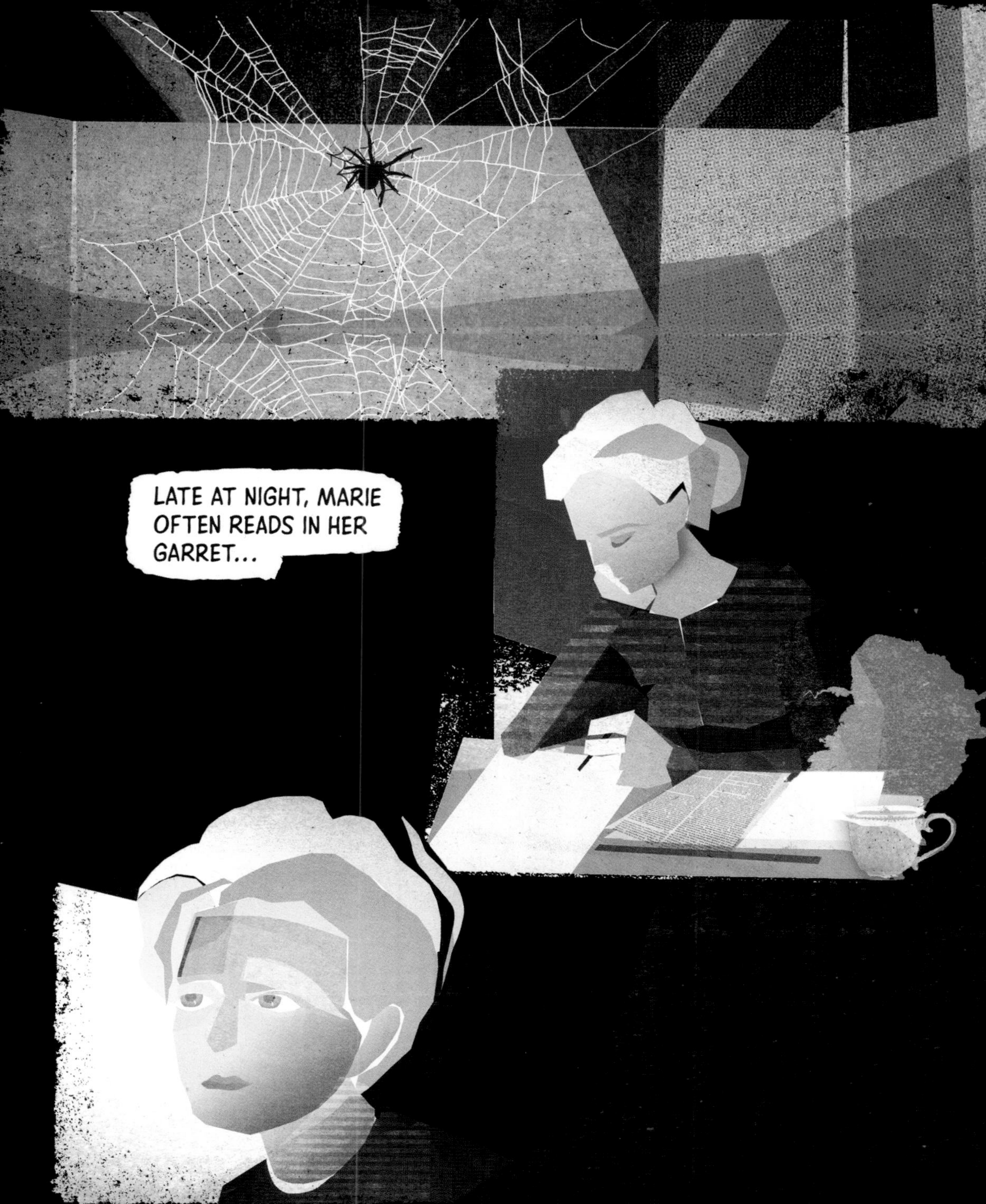
LATE AT NIGHT, MARIE OFTEN READS IN HER GARRET...

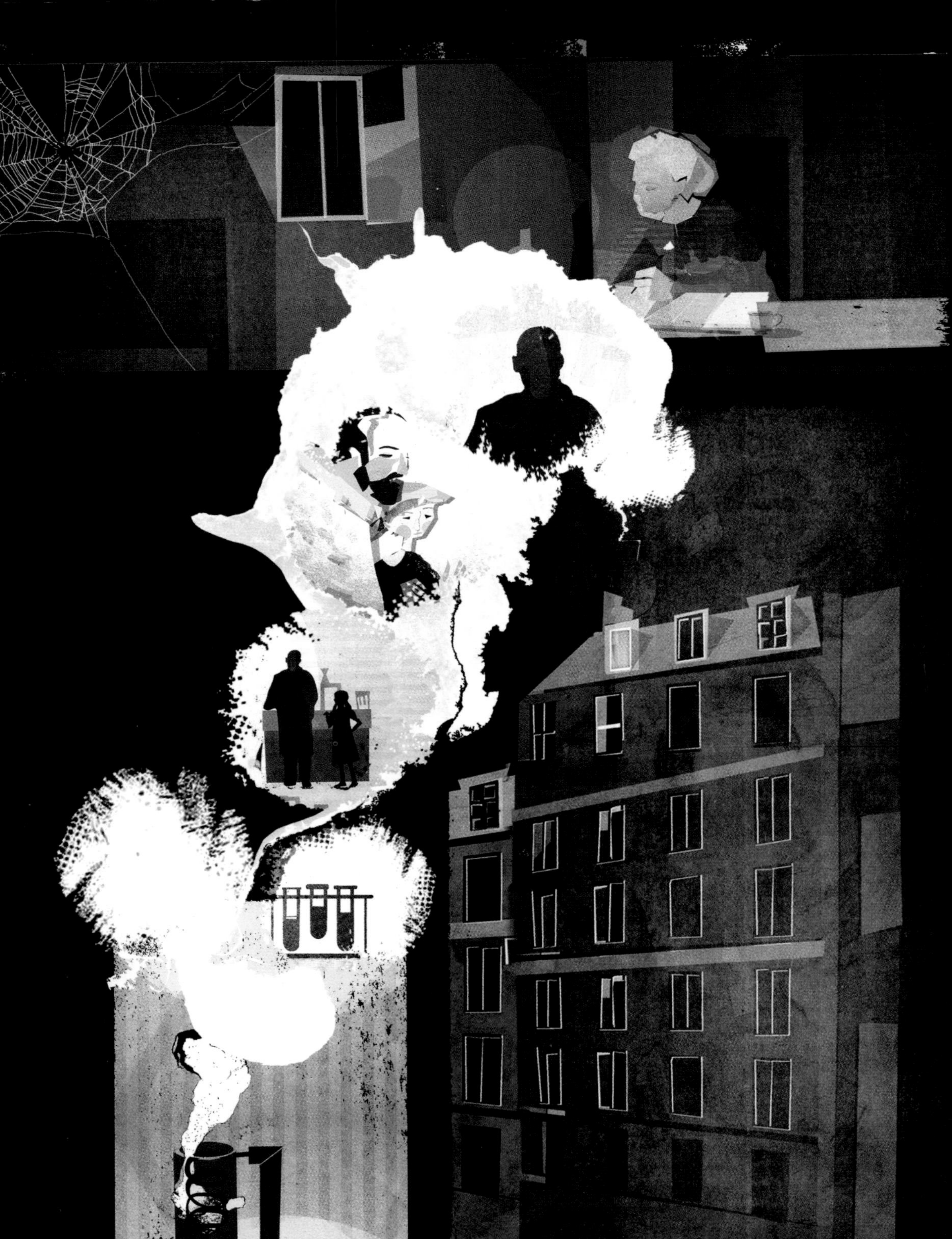

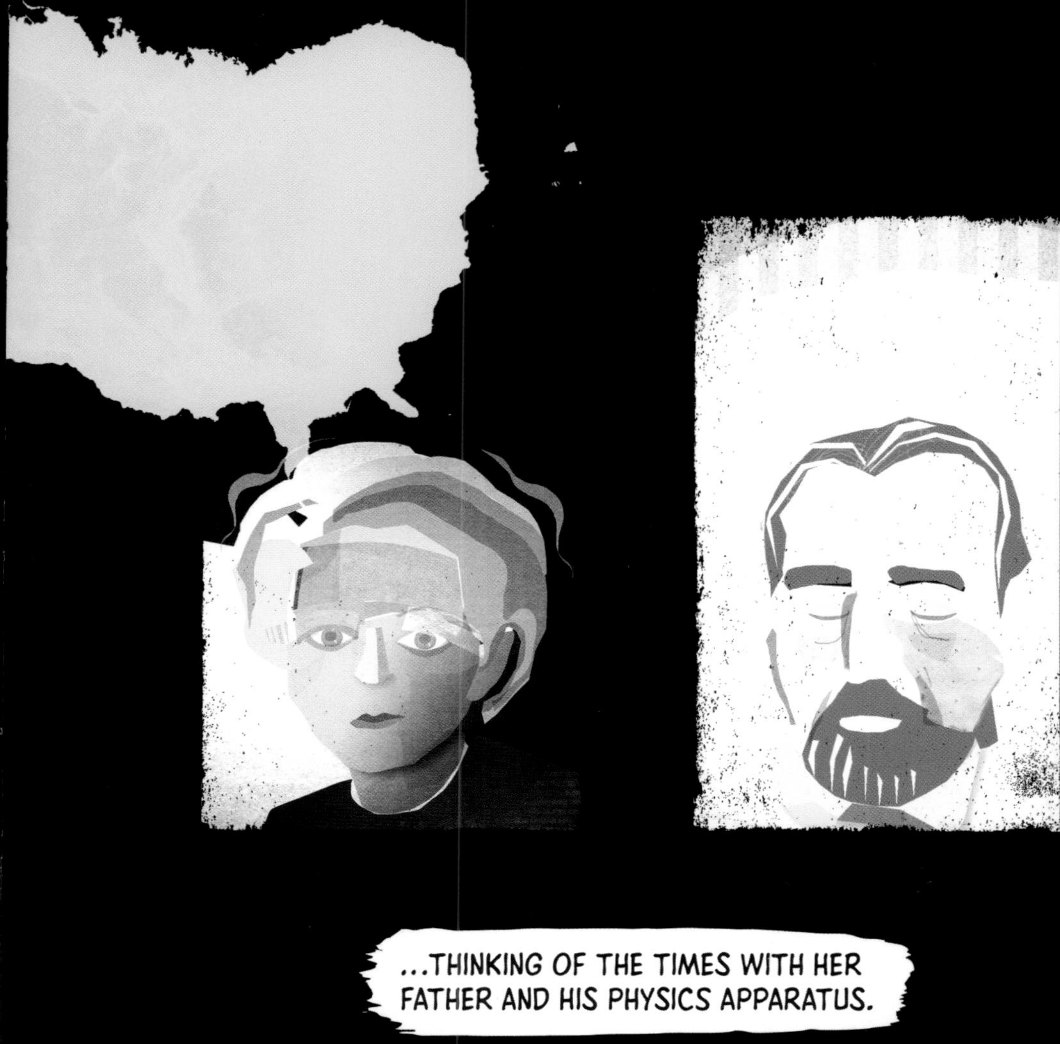
...THINKING OF THE TIMES WITH HER FATHER AND HIS PHYSICS APPARATUS.

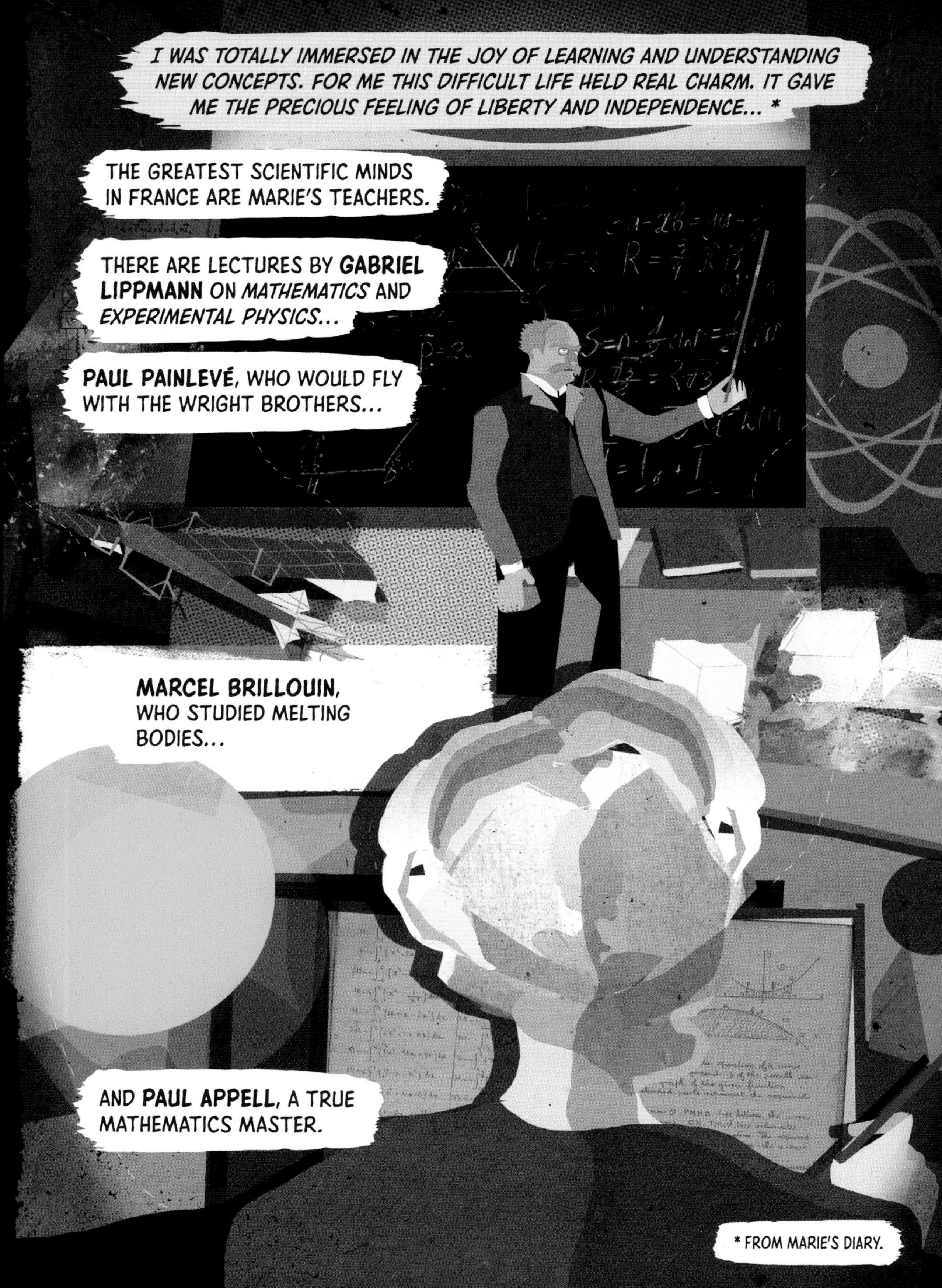
I WAS TOTALLY IMMERSED IN THE JOY OF LEARNING AND UNDERSTANDING NEW CONCEPTS. FOR ME THIS DIFFICULT LIFE HELD REAL CHARM. IT GAVE ME THE PRECIOUS FEELING OF LIBERTY AND INDEPENDENCE... *
THE GREATEST SCIENTIFIC MINDS IN FRANCE ARE MARIE'S TEACHERS.
THERE ARE LECTURES BY **GABRIEL LIPPMANN** ON *MATHEMATICS* AND *EXPERIMENTAL PHYSICS*...
PAUL PAINLEVÉ, WHO WOULD FLY WITH THE WRIGHT BROTHERS...
MARCEL BRILLOUIN, WHO STUDIED MELTING BODIES...
AND **PAUL APPELL**, A TRUE MATHEMATICS MASTER.
* FROM MARIE'S DIARY.

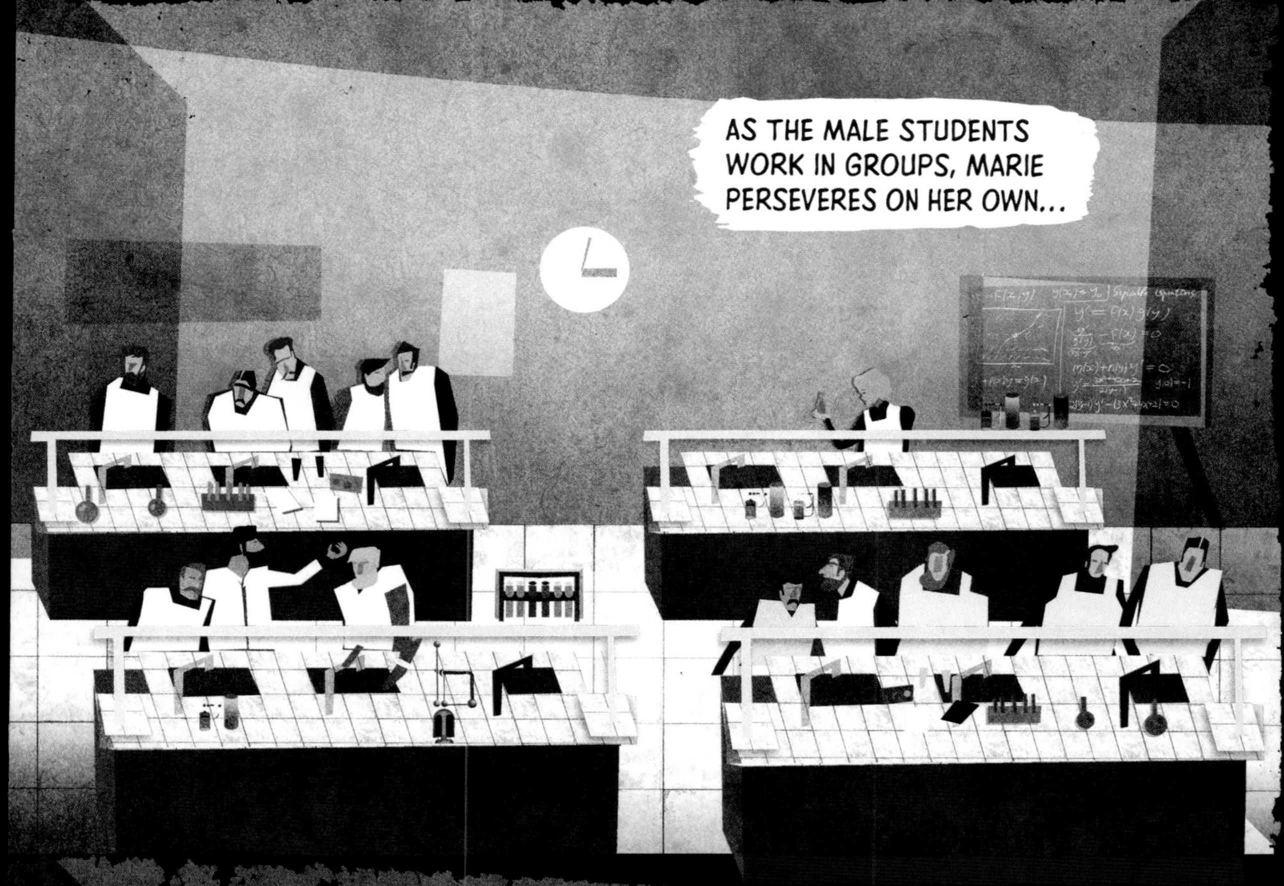
AS THE MALE STUDENTS WORK IN GROUPS, MARIE PERSEVERES ON HER OWN...

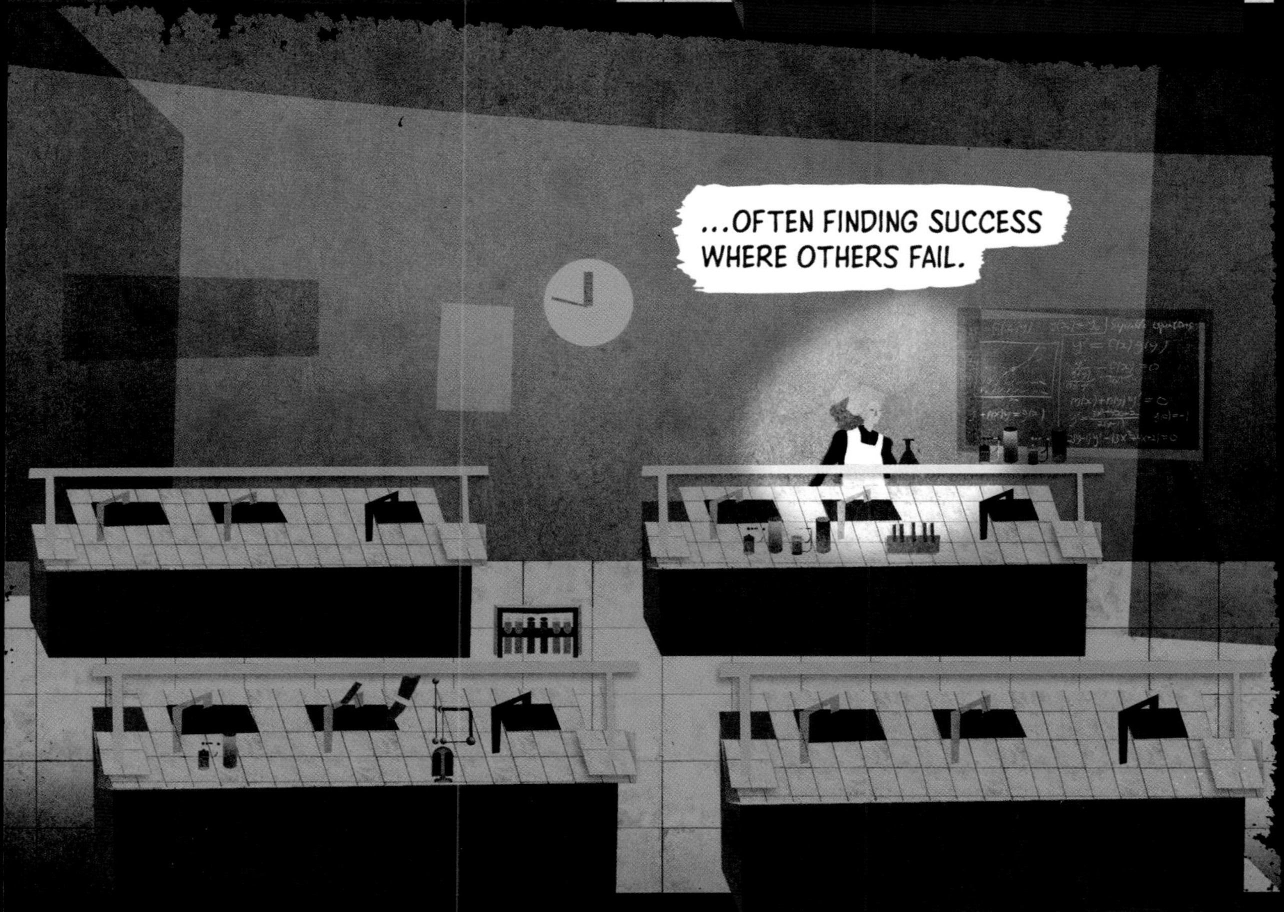
...OFTEN FINDING SUCCESS WHERE OTHERS FAIL.

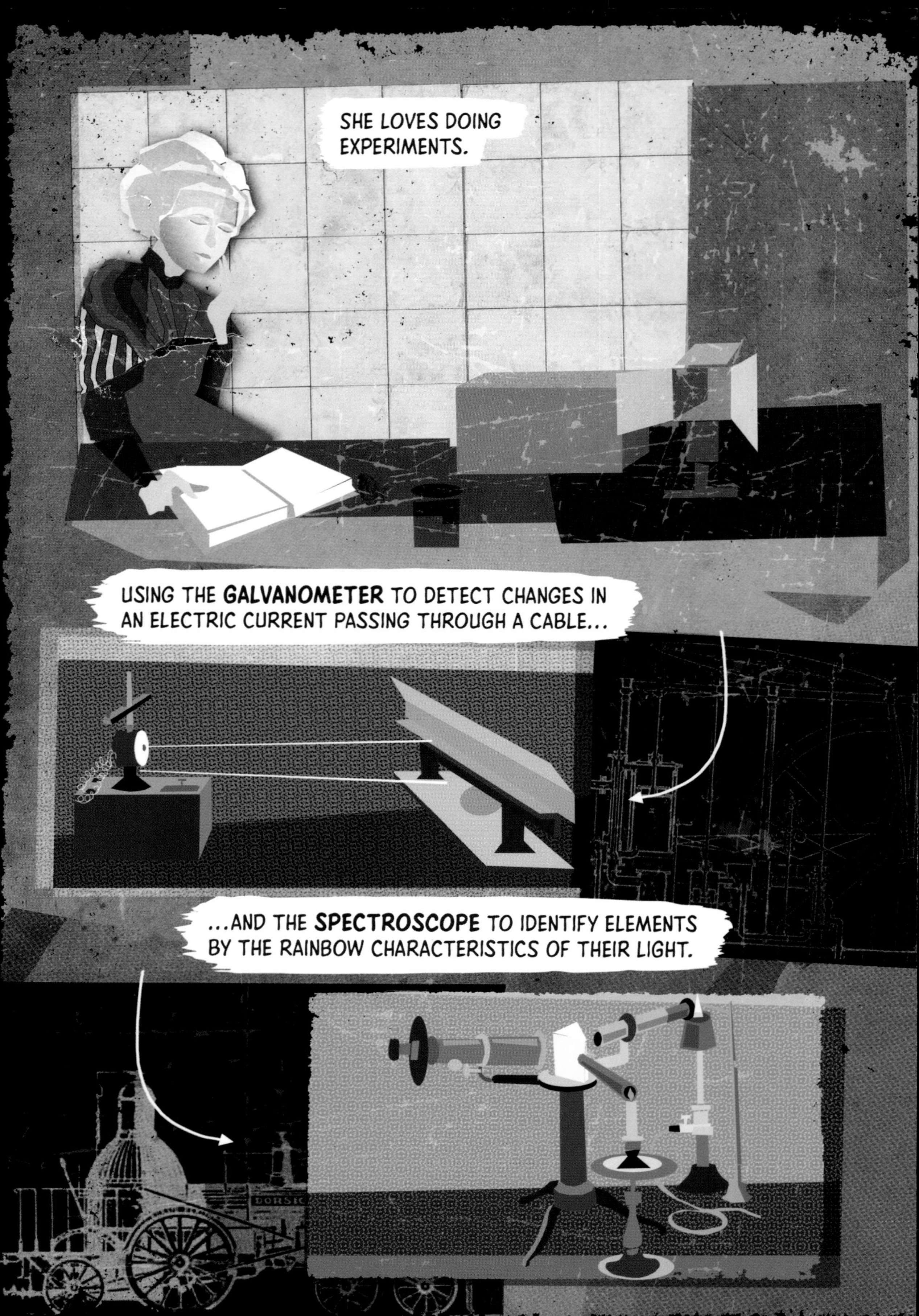
SHE LOVES DOING EXPERIMENTS.
USING THE GALVANOMETER TO DETECT CHANGES IN AN ELECTRIC CURRENT PASSING THROUGH A CABLE...
...AND THE SPECTROSCOPE TO IDENTIFY ELEMENTS BY THE RAINBOW CHARACTERISTICS OF THEIR LIGHT.

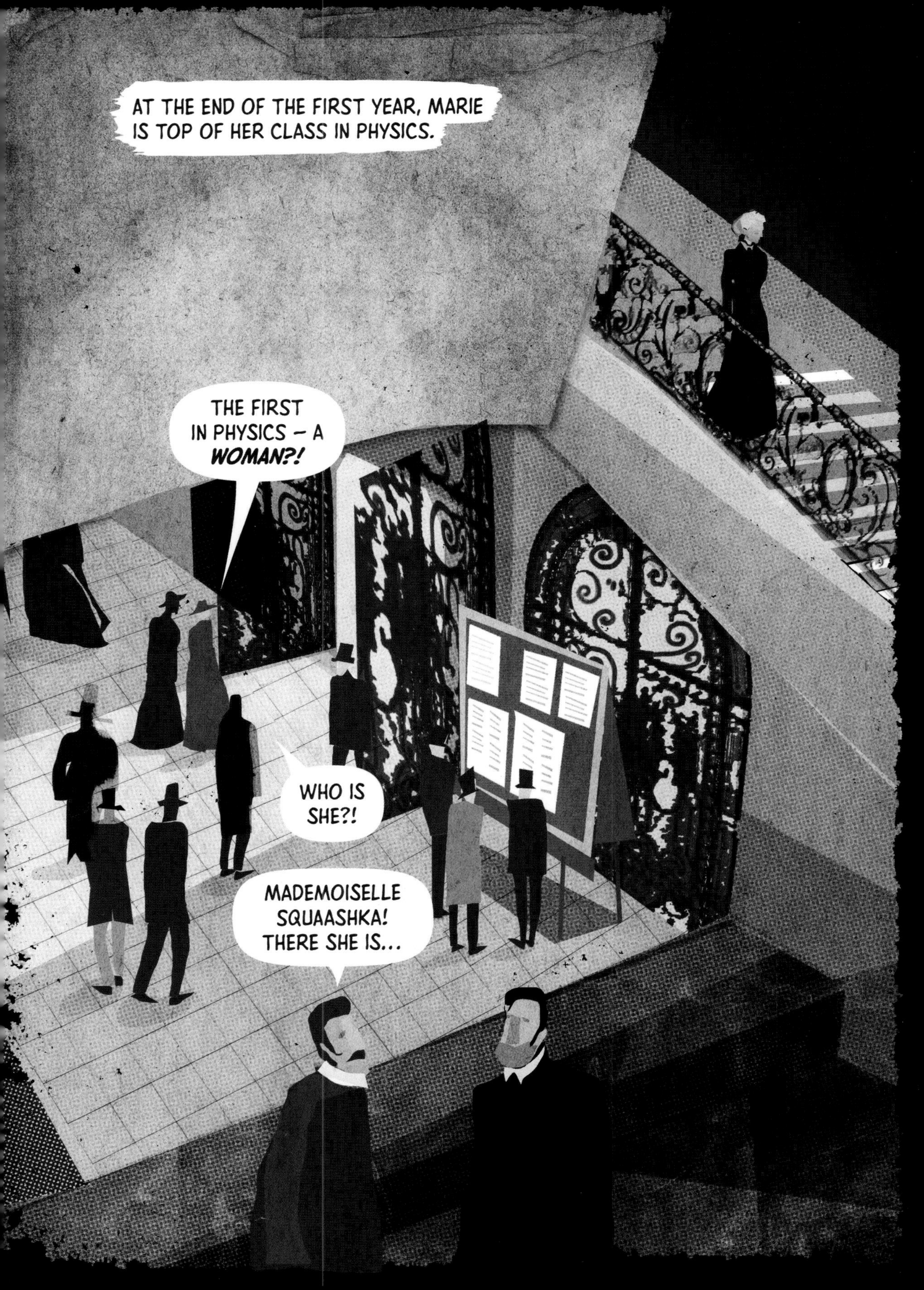
AT THE END OF THE FIRST YEAR, MARIE IS TOP OF HER CLASS IN PHYSICS.
THE FIRST IN PHYSICS – A ***WOMAN?!***
WHO IS SHE?!
MADEMOISELLE SQUAASHKA! THERE SHE IS...

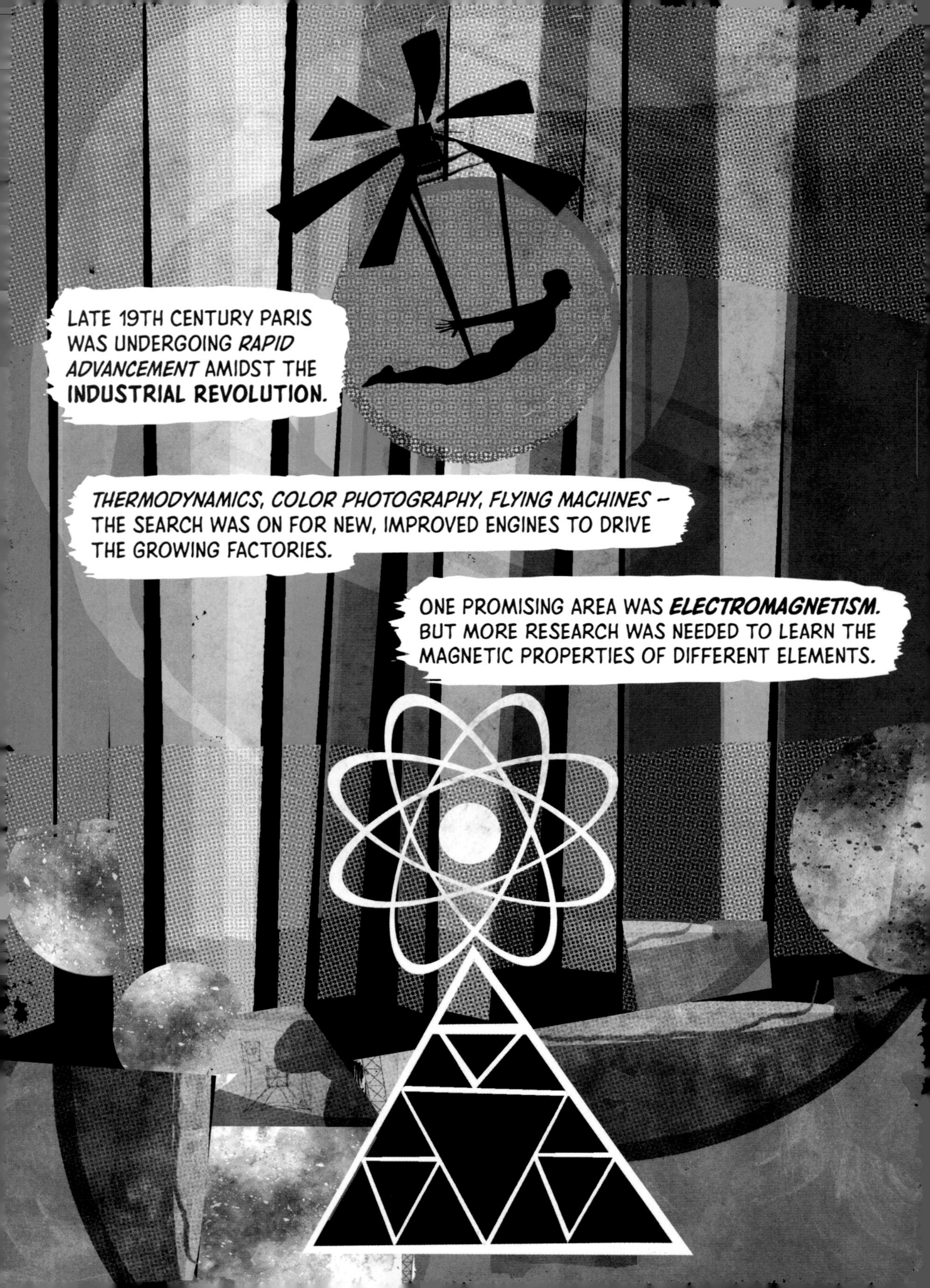
LATE 19TH CENTURY PARIS WAS UNDERGOING *RAPID ADVANCEMENT* AMIDST THE **INDUSTRIAL REVOLUTION.**
THERMODYNAMICS, COLOR PHOTOGRAPHY, FLYING MACHINES – THE SEARCH WAS ON FOR NEW, IMPROVED ENGINES TO DRIVE THE GROWING FACTORIES.
ONE PROMISING AREA WAS ***ELECTROMAGNETISM.*** BUT MORE RESEARCH WAS NEEDED TO LEARN THE MAGNETIC PROPERTIES OF DIFFERENT ELEMENTS.

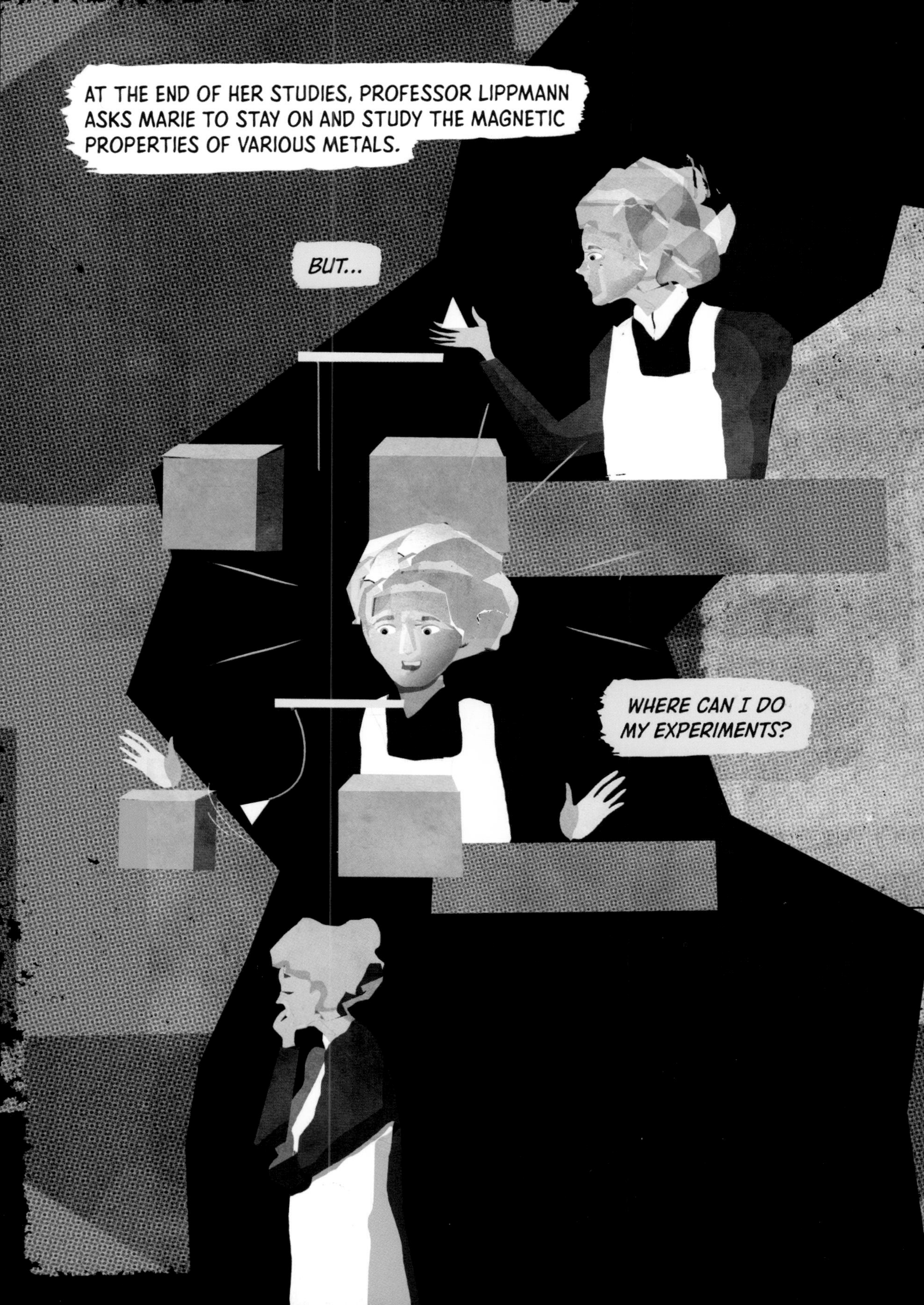
AT THE END OF HER STUDIES, PROFESSOR LIPPMANN ASKS MARIE TO STAY ON AND STUDY THE MAGNETIC PROPERTIES OF VARIOUS METALS.
BUT...
WHERE CAN I DO MY EXPERIMENTS?

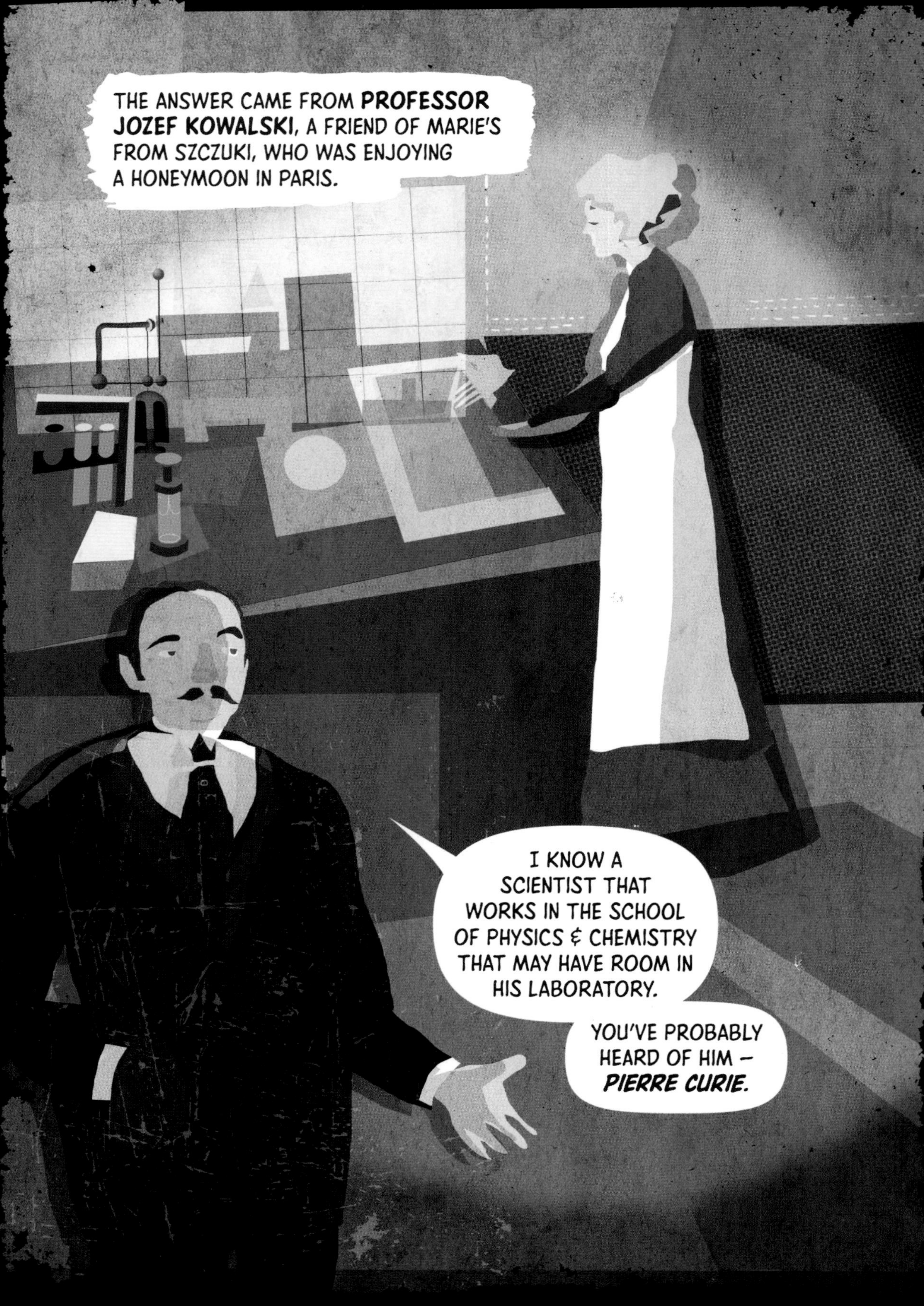
THE ANSWER CAME FROM PROFESSOR JOZEF KOWALSKI, A FRIEND OF MARIE'S FROM SZCZUKI, WHO WAS ENJOYING A HONEYMOON IN PARIS.
I KNOW A SCIENTIST THAT WORKS IN THE SCHOOL OF PHYSICS & CHEMISTRY THAT MAY HAVE ROOM IN HIS LABORATORY.
YOU'VE PROBABLY HEARD OF HIM – PIERRE CURIE.

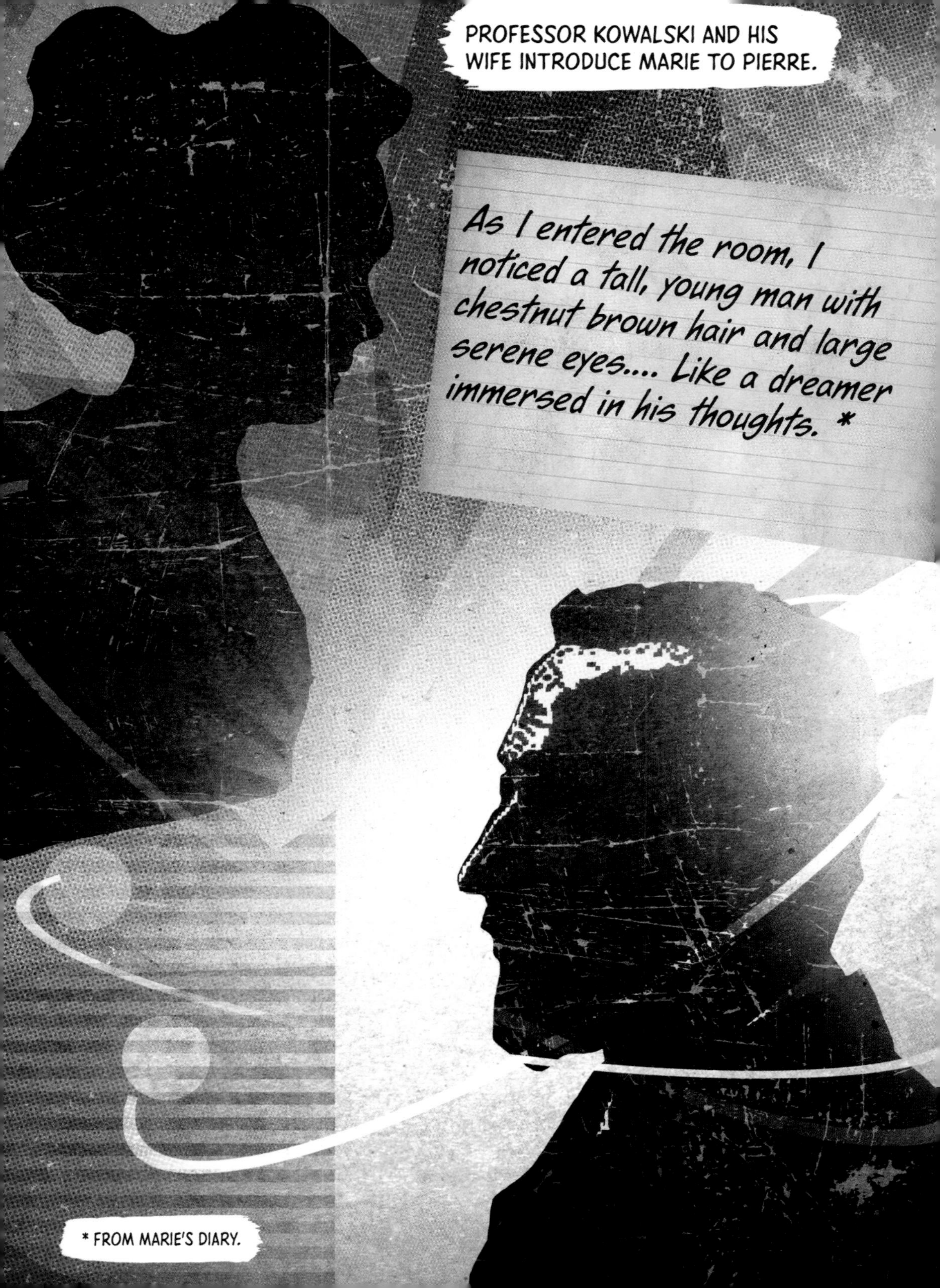
PROFESSOR KOWALSKI AND HIS WIFE INTRODUCE MARIE TO PIERRE.
As I entered the room, I noticed a tall, young man with chestnut brown hair and large serene eyes.... Like a dreamer immersed in his thoughts. *
* FROM MARIE'S DIARY.

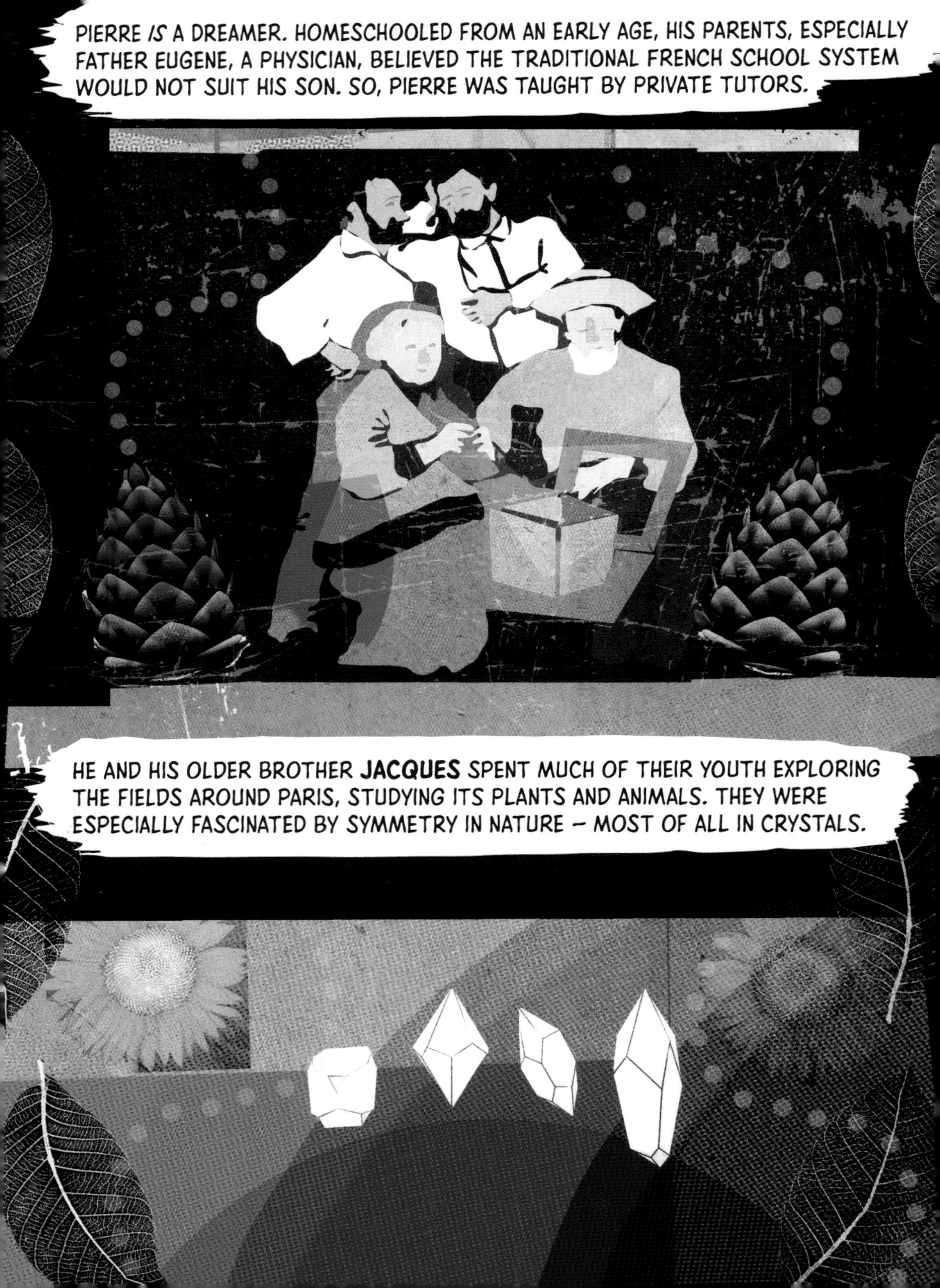
PIERRE *IS* A DREAMER. HOMESCHOOLED FROM AN EARLY AGE, HIS PARENTS, ESPECIALLY FATHER EUGENE, A PHYSICIAN, BELIEVED THE TRADITIONAL FRENCH SCHOOL SYSTEM WOULD NOT SUIT HIS SON. SO, PIERRE WAS TAUGHT BY PRIVATE TUTORS.
HE AND HIS OLDER BROTHER **JACQUES** SPENT MUCH OF THEIR YOUTH EXPLORING THE FIELDS AROUND PARIS, STUDYING ITS PLANTS AND ANIMALS. THEY WERE ESPECIALLY FASCINATED BY SYMMETRY IN NATURE – MOST OF ALL IN CRYSTALS.

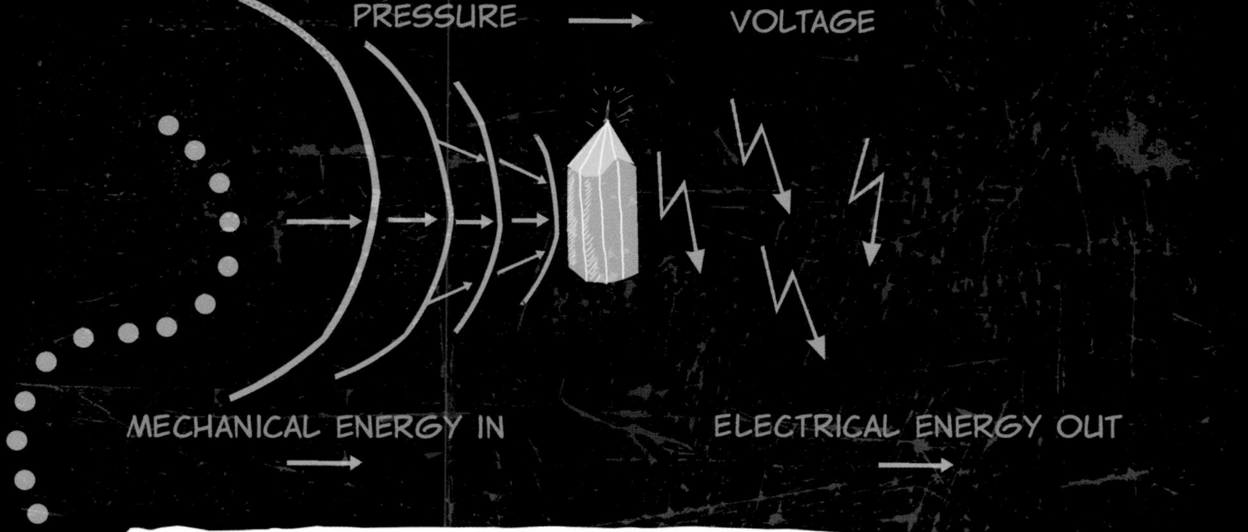
PRESSURE
VOLTAGE
MECHANICAL ENERGY IN
ELECTRICAL ENERGY OUT

BY THE AGE OF 35, PIERRE WAS A SCIENTIST OF RENOWN. HE AND JACQUES HAD DISCOVERED **PIEZOELECTRICITY** (*PIEZO* FROM THE GREEK, MEANING TO PRESS OR SQUEEZE), WHICH IS THE ELECTRICAL CURRENT CREATED WHEN A CRYSTAL IS PUT UNDER PRESSURE.

THIS DISCOVERY LED TO THE DEVELOPMENT OF NEW TECHNOLOGIES, SUCH AS SONAR, AND CAN IN THE FUTURE BE A SOURCE OF ALTERNATIVE ENERGY, AS IN **WIND STALKS**, HOLLOW FIBERGLASS POLES CONTAINING CRYSTALS THAT CREATE ENERGY AS THEY SWAY IN THE WIND.

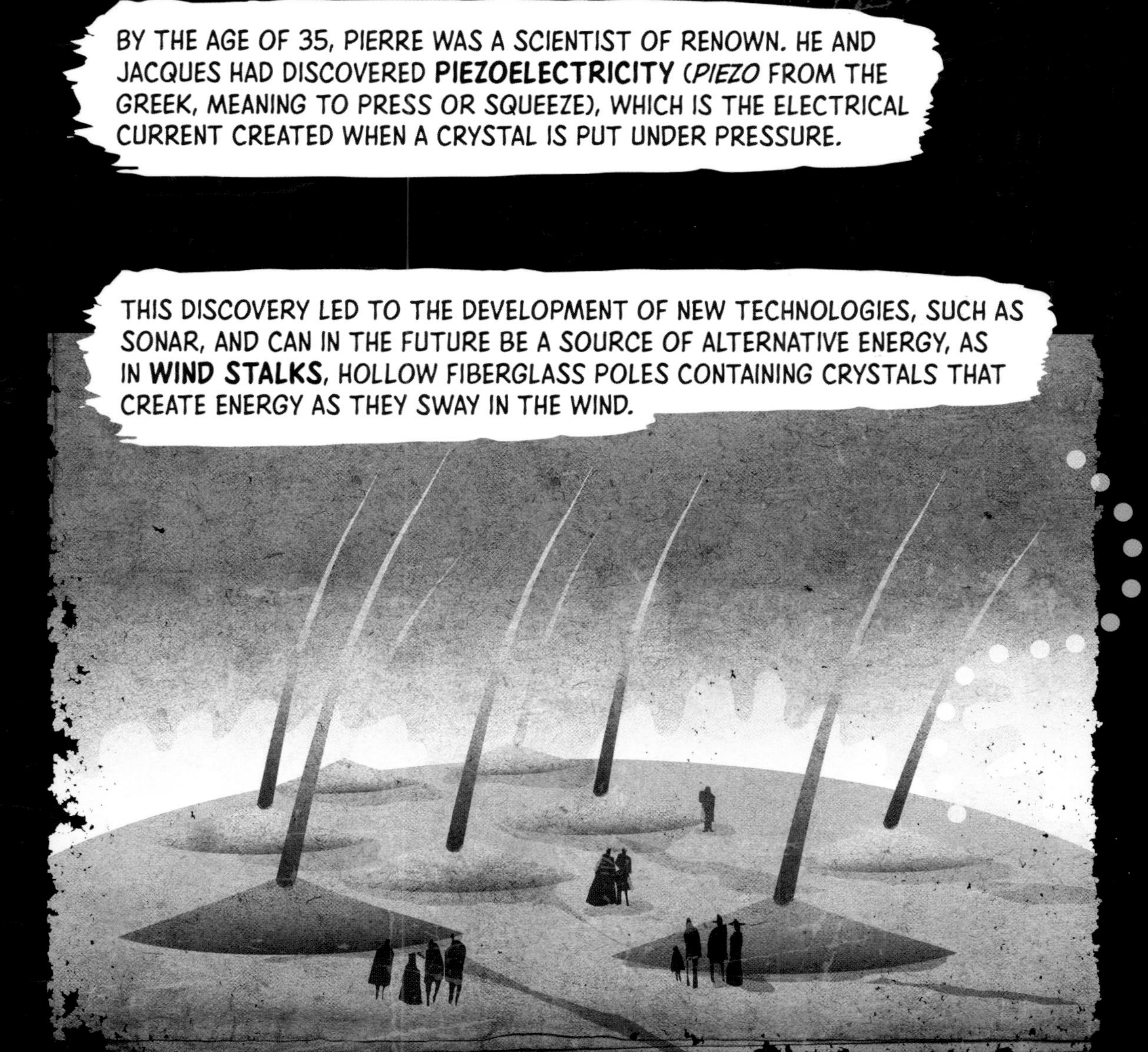

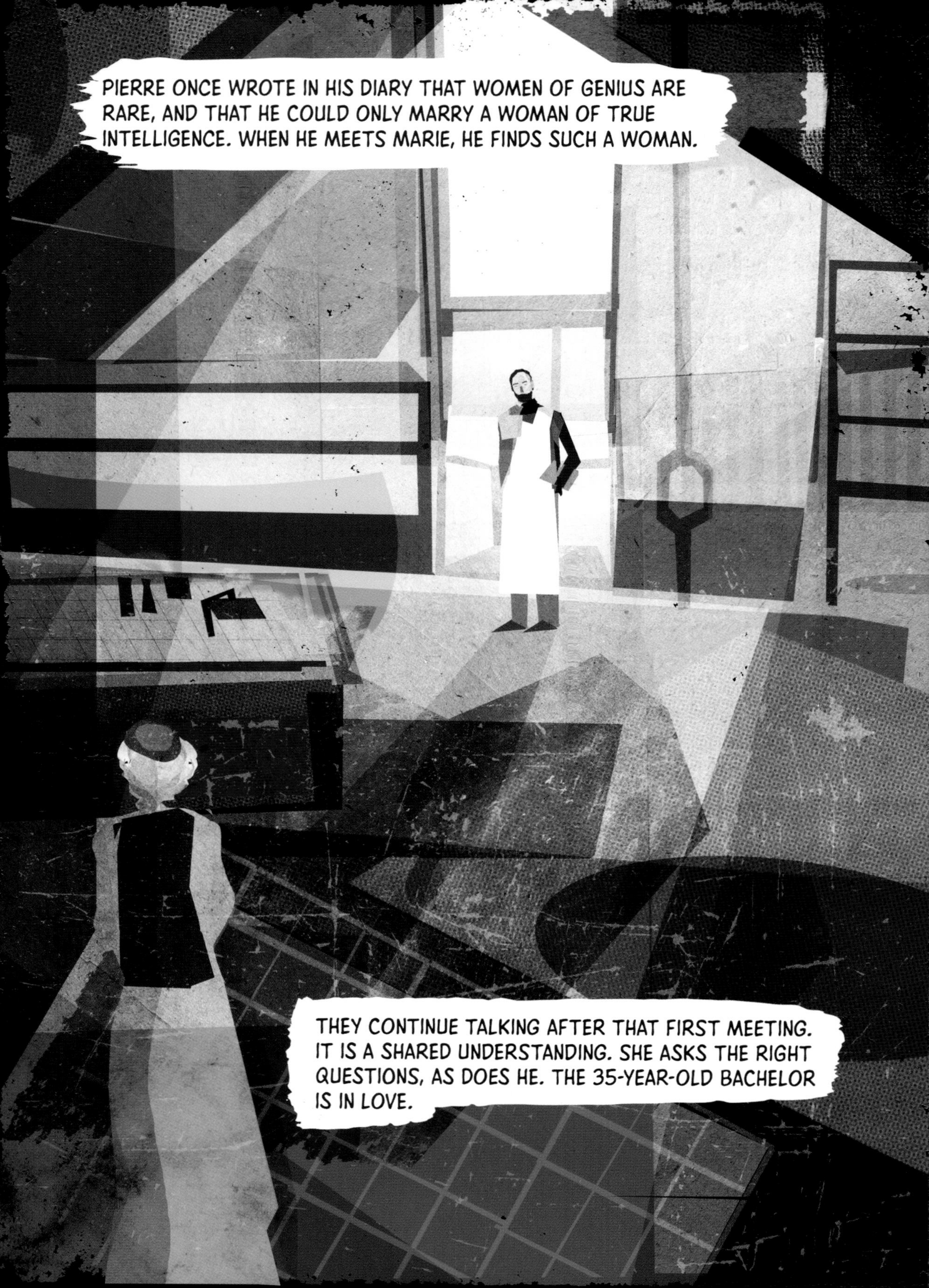
PIERRE ONCE WROTE IN HIS DIARY THAT WOMEN OF GENIUS ARE RARE, AND THAT HE COULD ONLY MARRY A WOMAN OF TRUE INTELLIGENCE. WHEN HE MEETS MARIE, HE FINDS SUCH A WOMAN.
THEY CONTINUE TALKING AFTER THAT FIRST MEETING. IT IS A SHARED UNDERSTANDING. SHE ASKS THE RIGHT QUESTIONS, AS DOES HE. THE 35-YEAR-OLD BACHELOR IS IN LOVE.

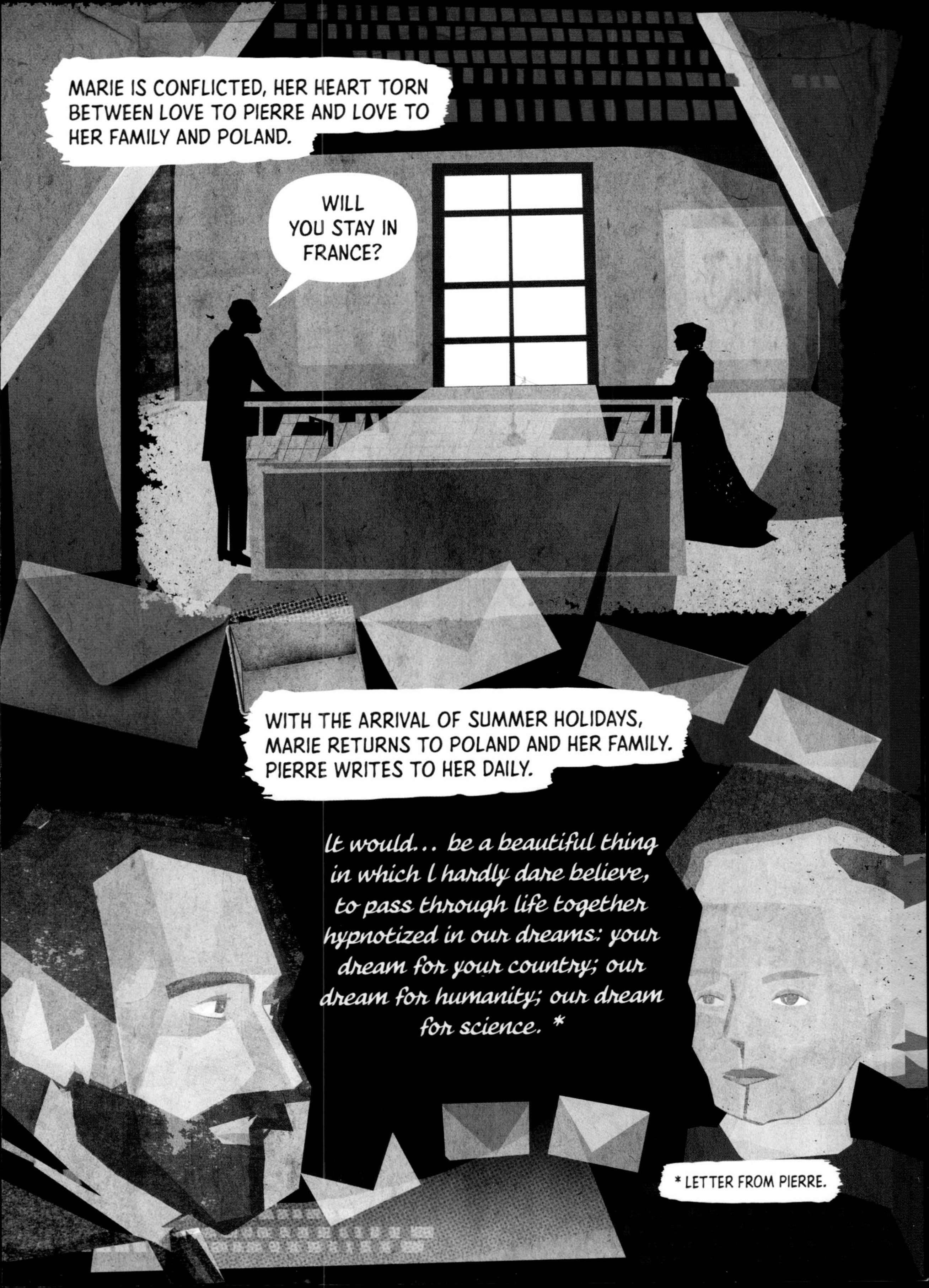
MARIE IS CONFLICTED, HER HEART TORN BETWEEN LOVE TO PIERRE AND LOVE TO HER FAMILY AND POLAND.
WILL YOU STAY IN FRANCE?
WITH THE ARRIVAL OF SUMMER HOLIDAYS, MARIE RETURNS TO POLAND AND HER FAMILY. PIERRE WRITES TO HER DAILY.
It would... be a beautiful thing in which I hardly dare believe, to pass through life together hypnotized in our dreams: your dream for your country; our dream for humanity; our dream for science. *
* LETTER FROM PIERRE.

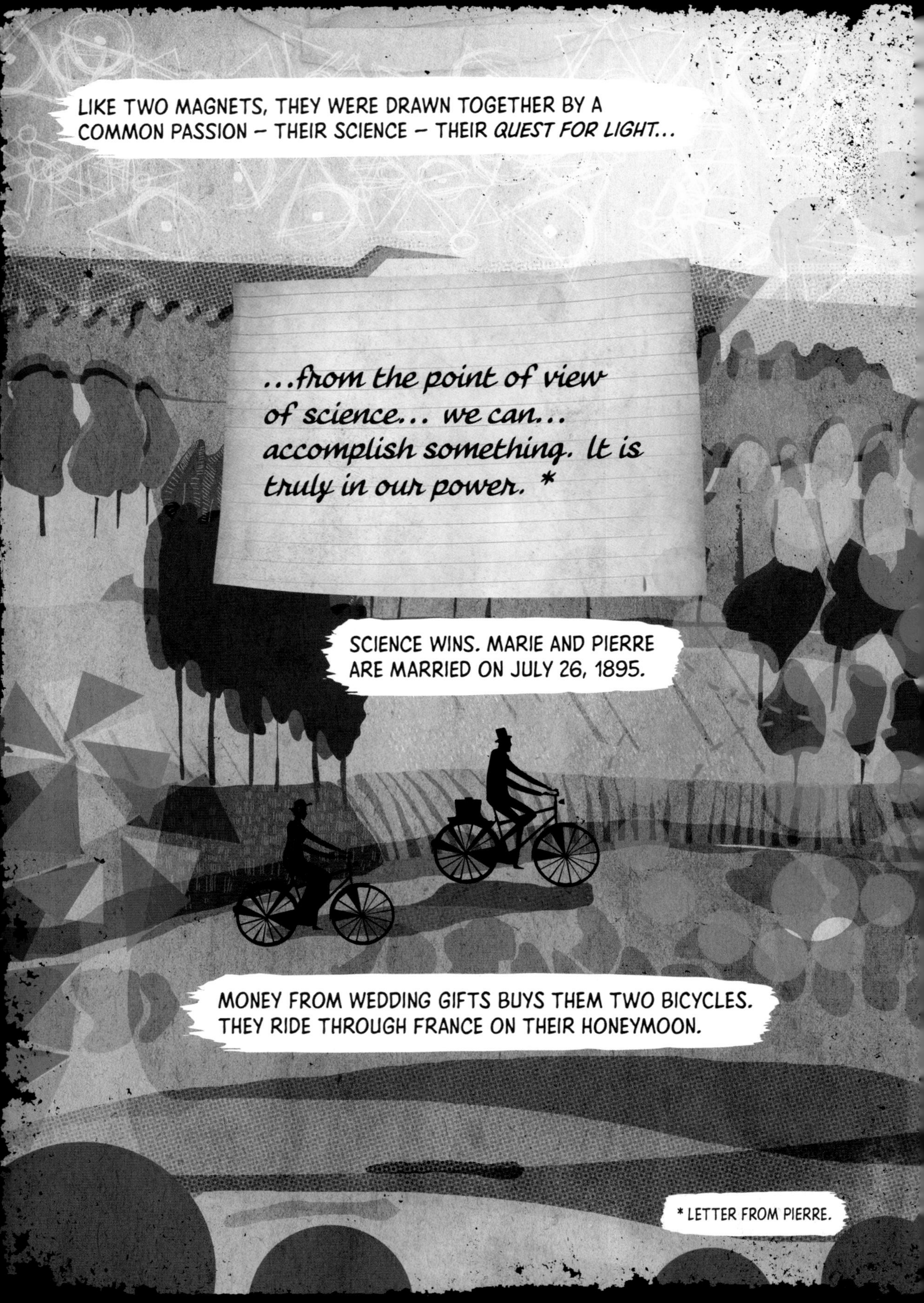
LIKE TWO MAGNETS, THEY WERE DRAWN TOGETHER BY A COMMON PASSION – THEIR SCIENCE – THEIR *QUEST FOR LIGHT*...
...from the point of view of science... we can... accomplish something. It is truly in our power. *
SCIENCE WINS. MARIE AND PIERRE ARE MARRIED ON JULY 26, 1895.
MONEY FROM WEDDING GIFTS BUYS THEM TWO BICYCLES. THEY RIDE THROUGH FRANCE ON THEIR HONEYMOON.
* LETTER FROM PIERRE.

Chapter 4

Ra

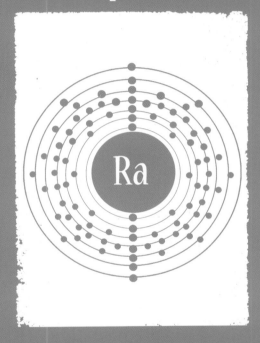

1895-1903

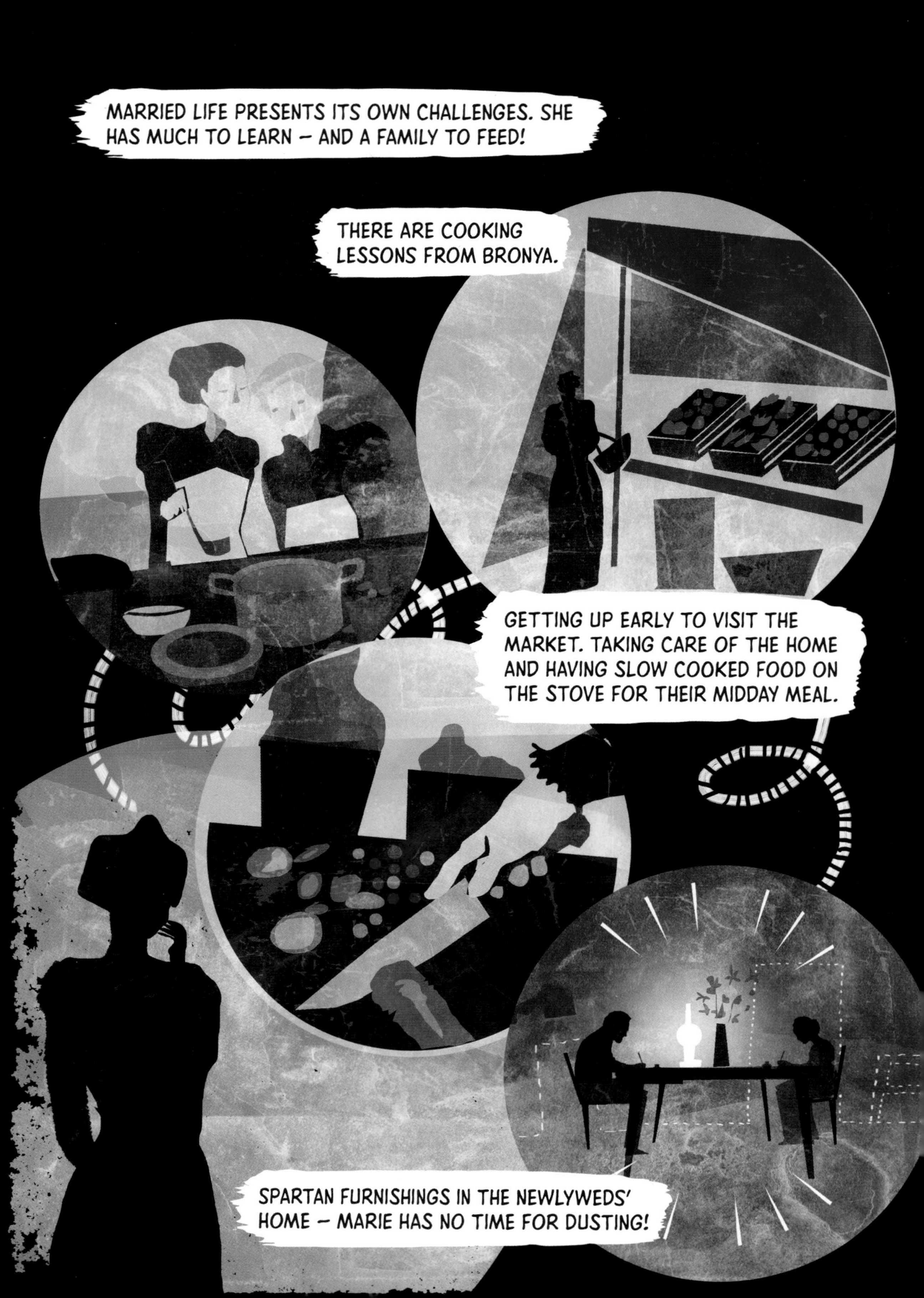
MARRIED LIFE PRESENTS ITS OWN CHALLENGES. SHE HAS MUCH TO LEARN – AND A FAMILY TO FEED!
THERE ARE COOKING LESSONS FROM BRONYA.
GETTING UP EARLY TO VISIT THE MARKET. TAKING CARE OF THE HOME AND HAVING SLOW COOKED FOOD ON THE STOVE FOR THEIR MIDDAY MEAL.
SPARTAN FURNISHINGS IN THE NEWLYWEDS' HOME – MARIE HAS NO TIME FOR DUSTING!

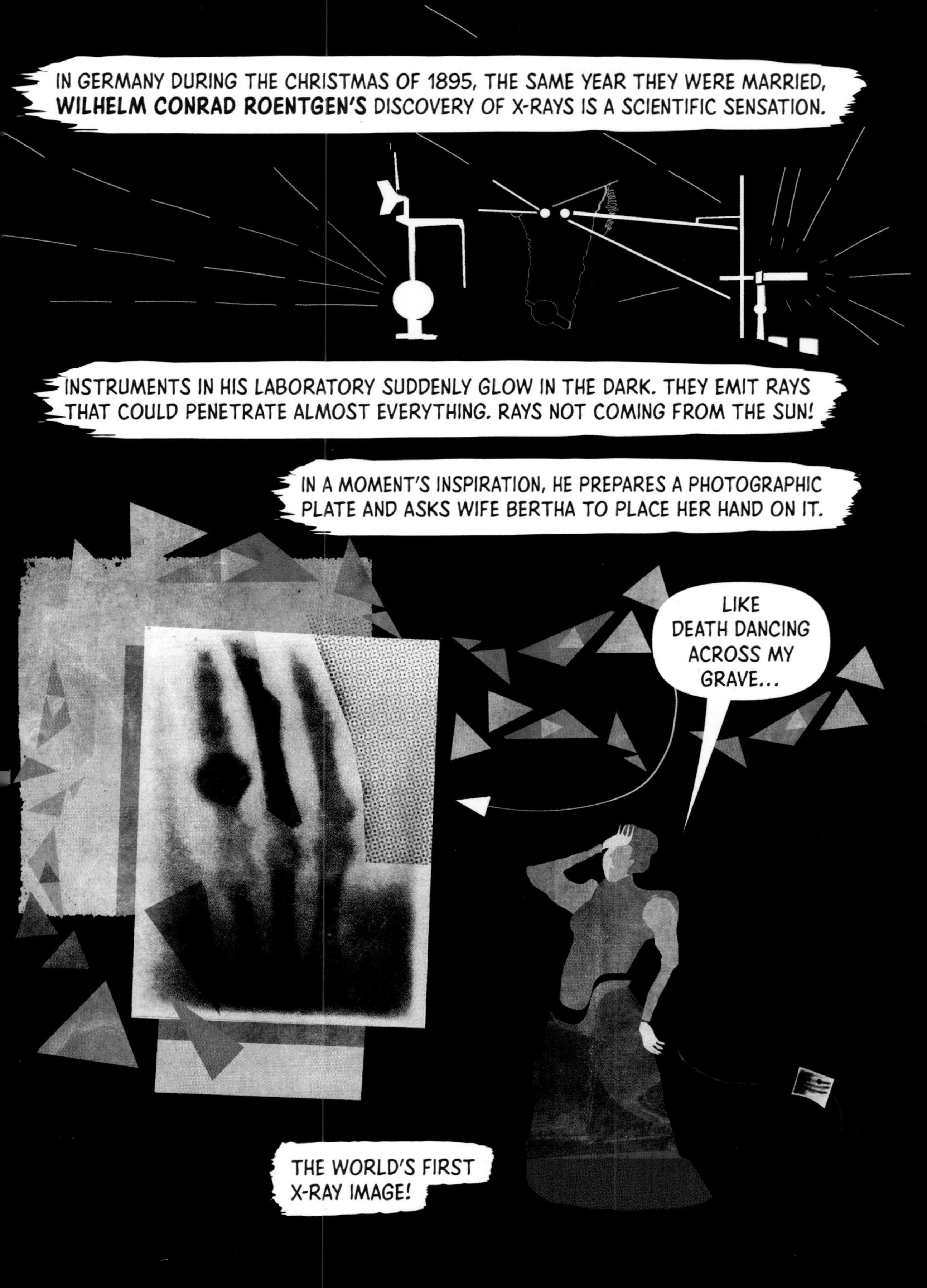
IN GERMANY DURING THE CHRISTMAS OF 1895, THE SAME YEAR THEY WERE MARRIED, **WILHELM CONRAD ROENTGEN'S** DISCOVERY OF X-RAYS IS A SCIENTIFIC SENSATION.
INSTRUMENTS IN HIS LABORATORY SUDDENLY GLOW IN THE DARK. THEY EMIT RAYS THAT COULD PENETRATE ALMOST EVERYTHING. RAYS NOT COMING FROM THE SUN!
IN A MOMENT'S INSPIRATION, HE PREPARES A PHOTOGRAPHIC PLATE AND ASKS WIFE BERTHA TO PLACE HER HAND ON IT.
LIKE DEATH DANCING ACROSS MY GRAVE...
THE WORLD'S FIRST X-RAY IMAGE!

IN JANUARY 1896, AN AUSTRIAN JOURNALIST GETS WIND OF THE ROENTGEN'S DISCOVERY. THE RESULTING ARTICLE IS A SENSATION – AND NOT JUST FOR SCIENCE. PEOPLE ARE FASCINATED AND FRIGHTENED – LOOKING AT PICTURES OF THEIR BONES WAS LIKE LOOKING INTO THE EYES OF DEATH.

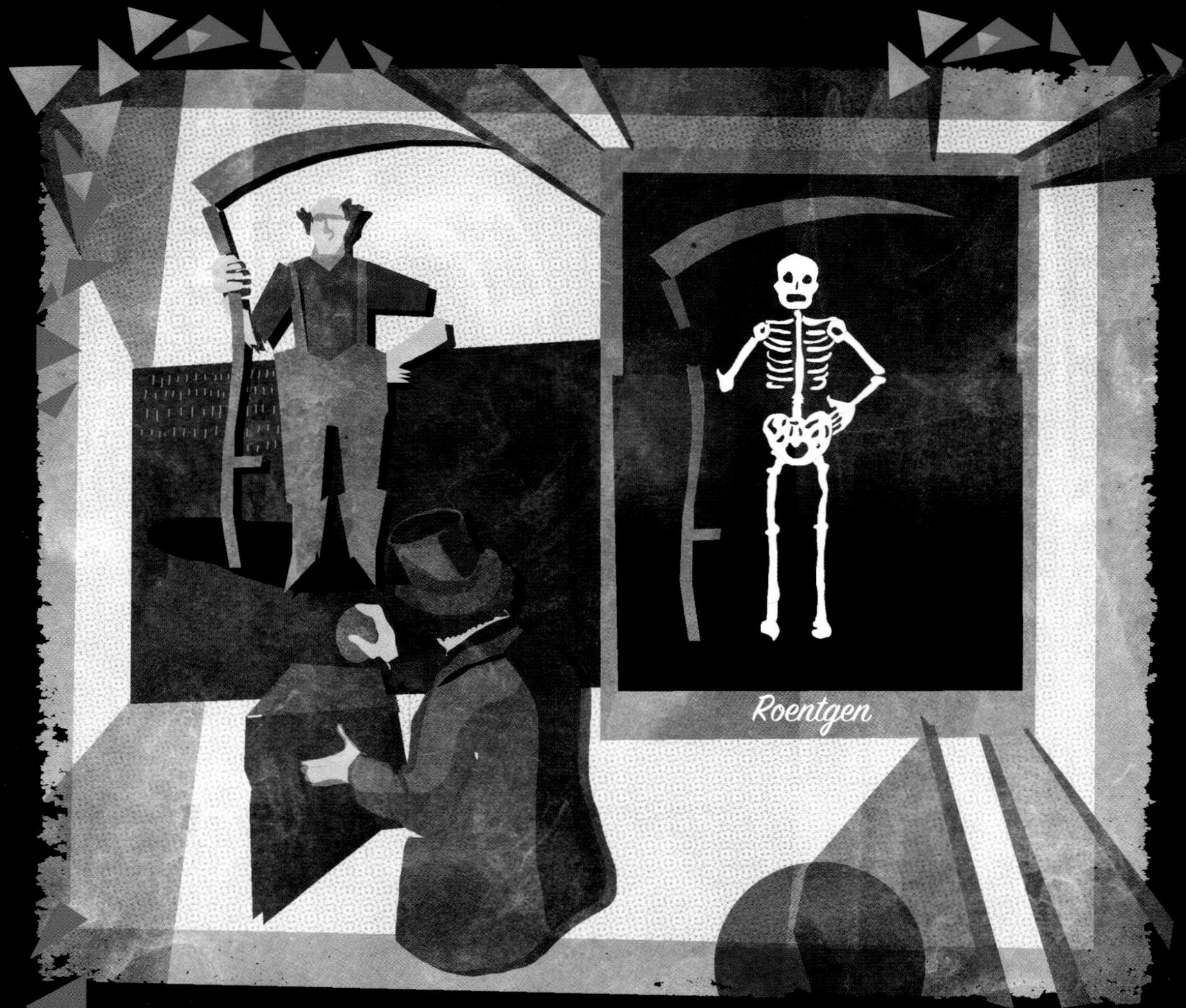
Roentgen

MAGNETISM, ELECTROMAGNETISM, AND NOW **X-RAYS!** SCIENTISTS EVERYWHERE TURN OVER ROCKS AND STONES TO FIND THE EXPLANATION FOR THIS MYSTERY. CAN THERE BE OTHER RAYS INVISIBLE TO THE HUMAN EYE – AND WHAT ARE THEY?

THE SEARCH IS ON...

X-RAYS ARE THE TALK OF THE SCIENTIFIC COMMUNITY. **HENRI BECQUEREL**, A FRENCH SCIENTIST FROM A PROMINENT SCIENTIFIC FAMILY, RECALLS SOMETHING HE'D READ IN ONE OF HIS FATHER'S BOOKS...

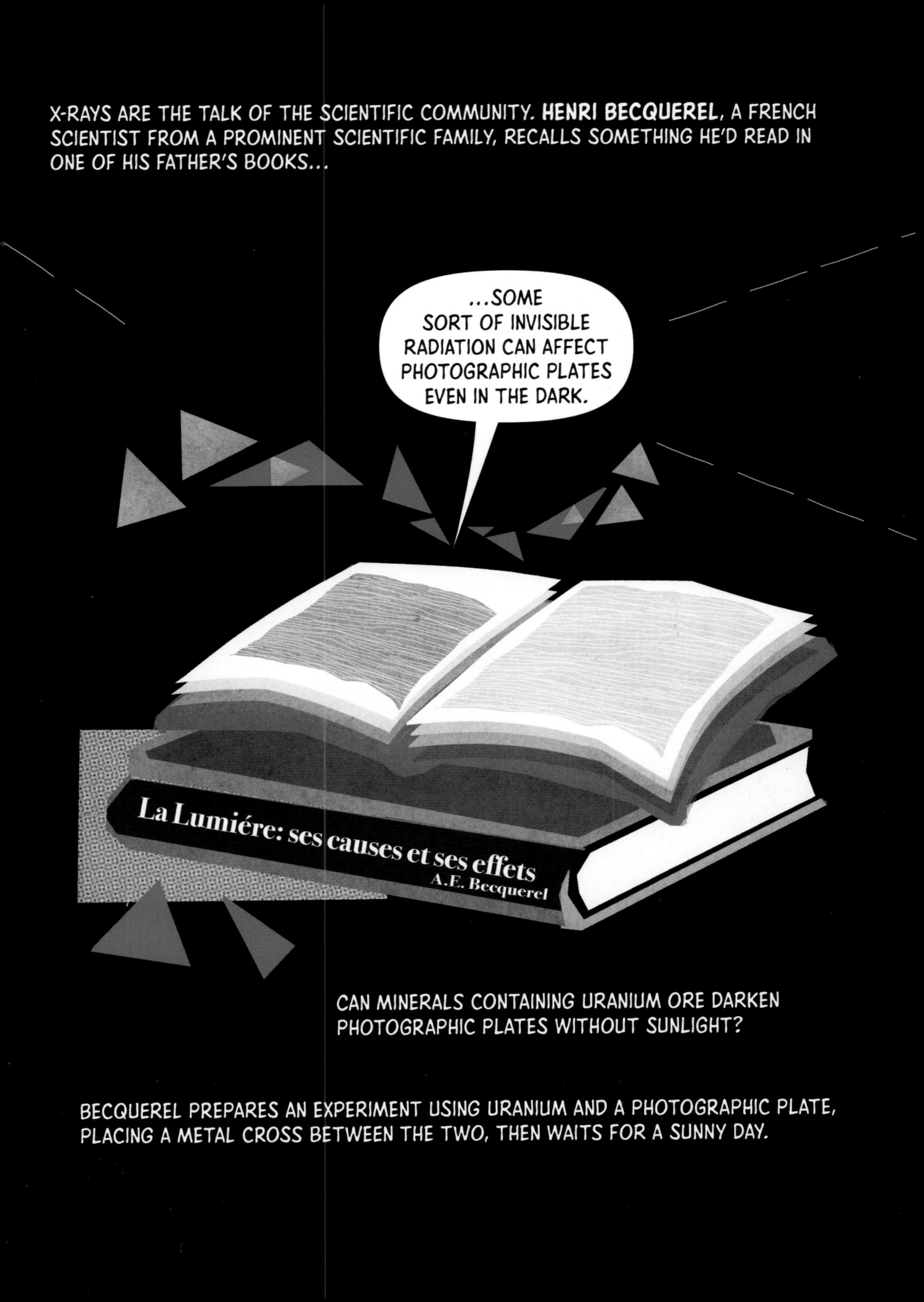
...SOME SORT OF INVISIBLE RADIATION CAN AFFECT PHOTOGRAPHIC PLATES EVEN IN THE DARK.
La Lumiére: ses causes et ses effets
A.E. Becquerel

CAN MINERALS CONTAINING URANIUM ORE DARKEN PHOTOGRAPHIC PLATES WITHOUT SUNLIGHT?

BECQUEREL PREPARES AN EXPERIMENT USING URANIUM AND A PHOTOGRAPHIC PLATE, PLACING A METAL CROSS BETWEEN THE TWO, THEN WAITS FOR A SUNNY DAY.

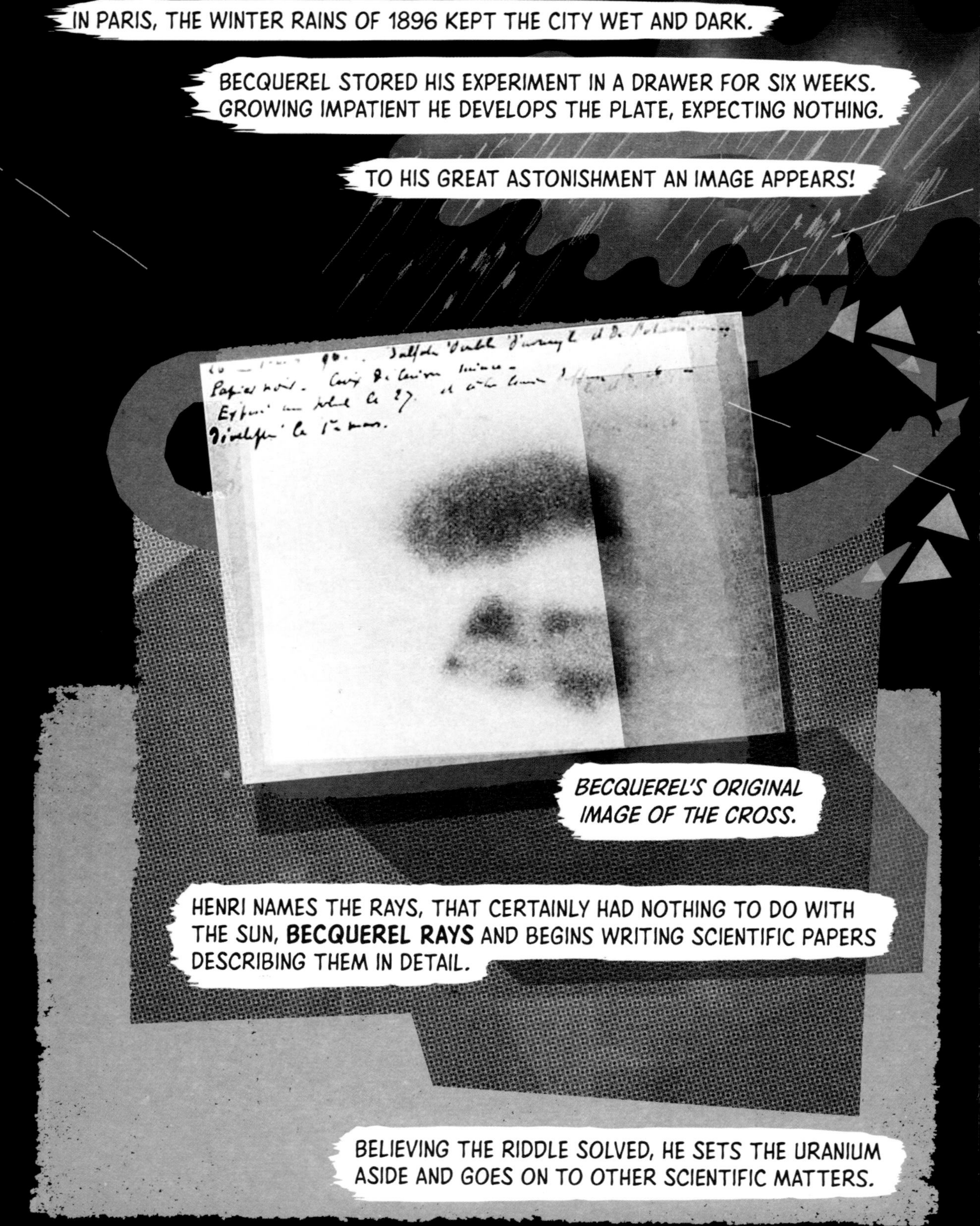
IN PARIS, THE WINTER RAINS OF 1896 KEPT THE CITY WET AND DARK.
BECQUEREL STORED HIS EXPERIMENT IN A DRAWER FOR SIX WEEKS. GROWING IMPATIENT HE DEVELOPS THE PLATE, EXPECTING NOTHING.
TO HIS GREAT ASTONISHMENT AN IMAGE APPEARS!
BECQUEREL'S ORIGINAL IMAGE OF THE CROSS.
HENRI NAMES THE RAYS, THAT CERTAINLY HAD NOTHING TO DO WITH THE SUN, BECQUEREL RAYS AND BEGINS WRITING SCIENTIFIC PAPERS DESCRIBING THEM IN DETAIL.
BELIEVING THE RIDDLE SOLVED, HE SETS THE URANIUM ASIDE AND GOES ON TO OTHER SCIENTIFIC MATTERS.

IN 1897, MARIE AND PIERRE HAVE THEIR FIRST DAUGHTER, **IRENE.**
THE NEW MOTHER IS CONSIDERING TOPICS FOR HER DOCTORAL THESIS.
AS IF THE URANIUM IN BECQUEREL'S DESK ITSELF CALLS OUT TO HER...
...MARIE DECIDES TO RESEARCH IF OTHER METALS GIVE OFF *BECQUEREL RAYS.*

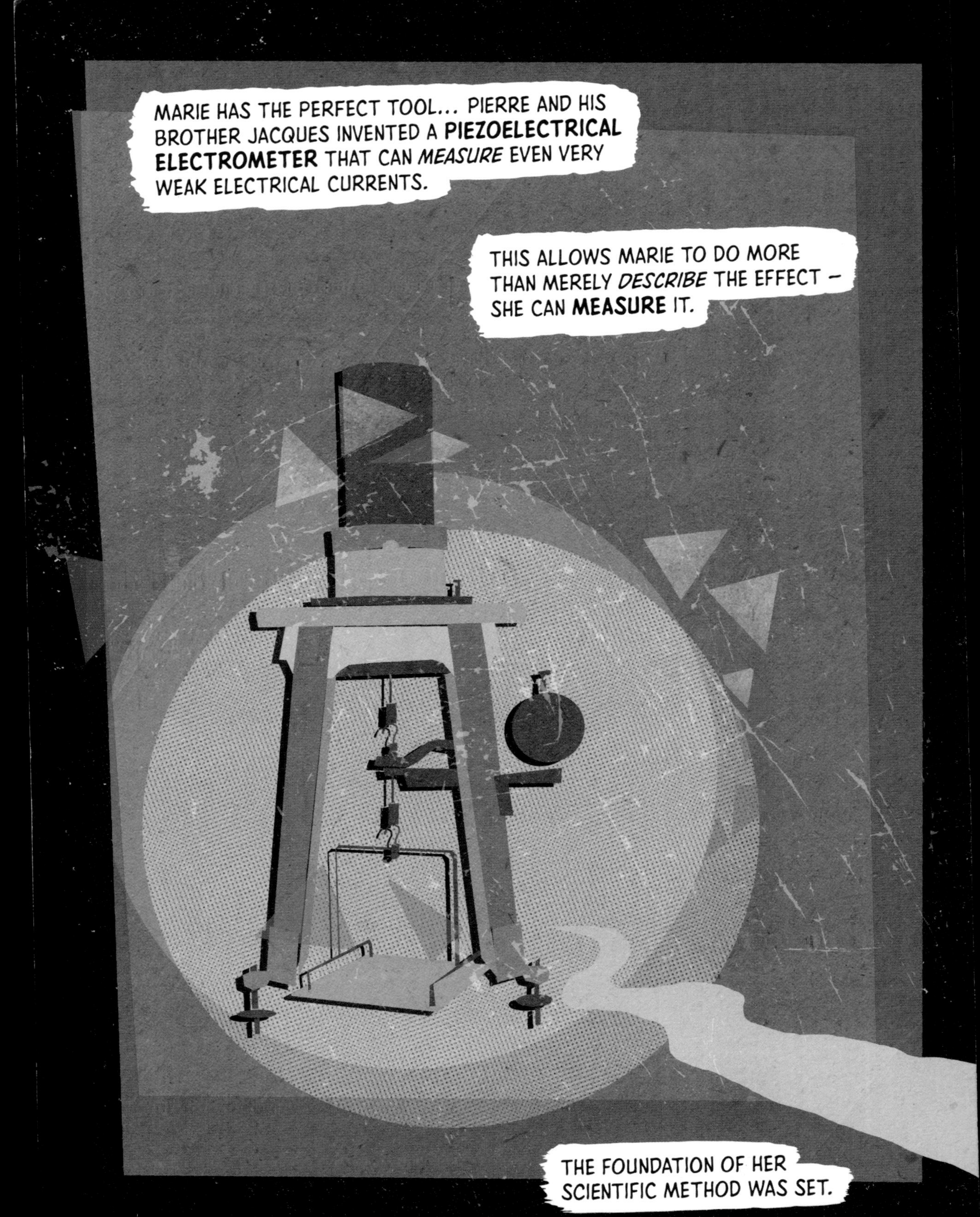
MARIE HAS THE PERFECT TOOL... PIERRE AND HIS BROTHER JACQUES INVENTED A **PIEZOELECTRICAL ELECTROMETER** THAT CAN *MEASURE* EVEN VERY WEAK ELECTRICAL CURRENTS.
THIS ALLOWS MARIE TO DO MORE THAN MERELY *DESCRIBE* THE EFFECT – SHE CAN **MEASURE** IT.
THE FOUNDATION OF HER SCIENTIFIC METHOD WAS SET.

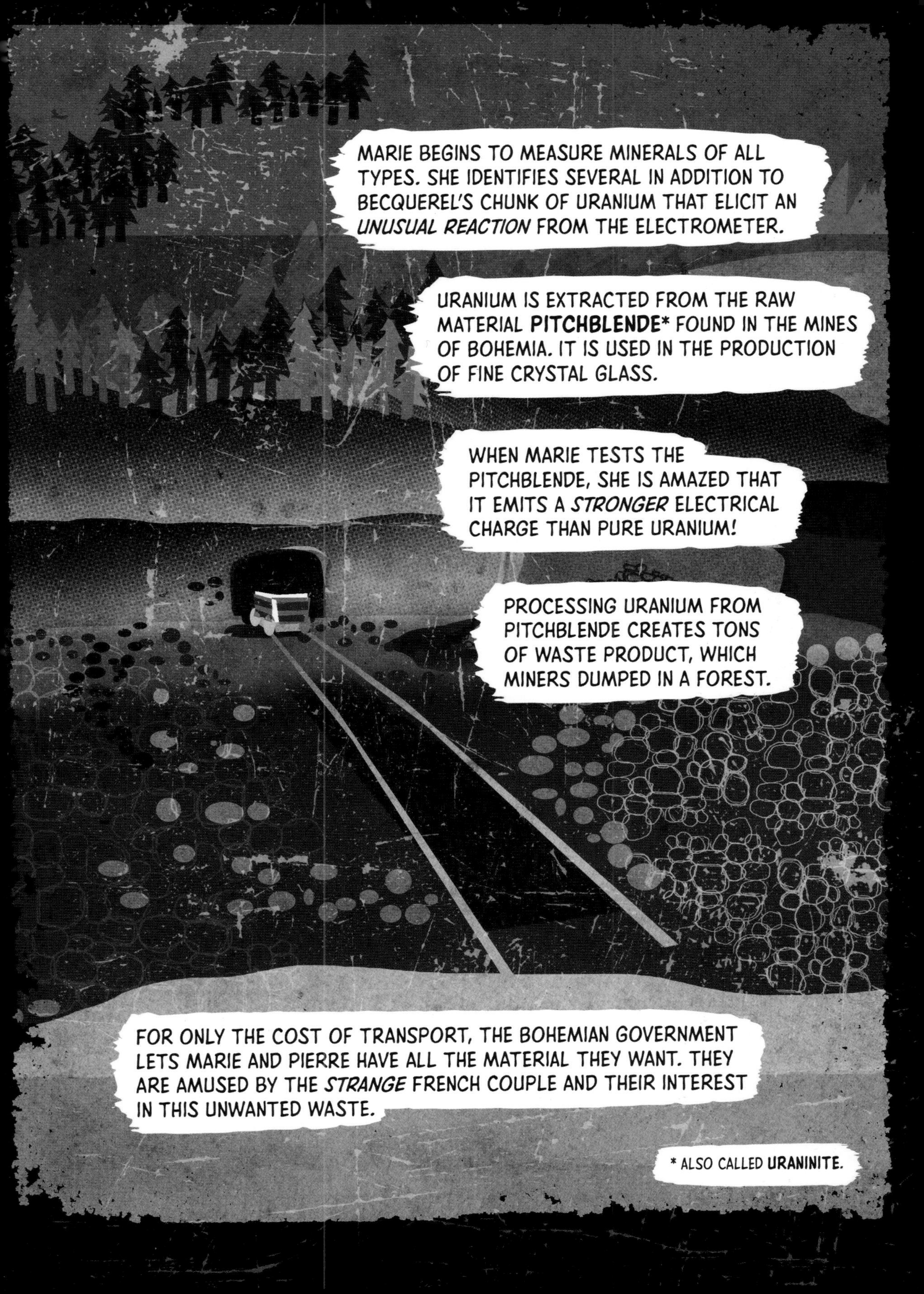
MARIE BEGINS TO MEASURE MINERALS OF ALL TYPES. SHE IDENTIFIES SEVERAL IN ADDITION TO BECQUEREL'S CHUNK OF URANIUM THAT ELICIT AN *UNUSUAL REACTION* FROM THE ELECTROMETER.
URANIUM IS EXTRACTED FROM THE RAW MATERIAL **PITCHBLENDE*** FOUND IN THE MINES OF BOHEMIA. IT IS USED IN THE PRODUCTION OF FINE CRYSTAL GLASS.
WHEN MARIE TESTS THE PITCHBLENDE, SHE IS AMAZED THAT IT EMITS A *STRONGER* ELECTRICAL CHARGE THAN PURE URANIUM!
PROCESSING URANIUM FROM PITCHBLENDE CREATES TONS OF WASTE PRODUCT, WHICH MINERS DUMPED IN A FOREST.
FOR ONLY THE COST OF TRANSPORT, THE BOHEMIAN GOVERNMENT LETS MARIE AND PIERRE HAVE ALL THE MATERIAL THEY WANT. THEY ARE AMUSED BY THE *STRANGE* FRENCH COUPLE AND THEIR INTEREST IN THIS UNWANTED WASTE.
* ALSO CALLED **URANINITE**.

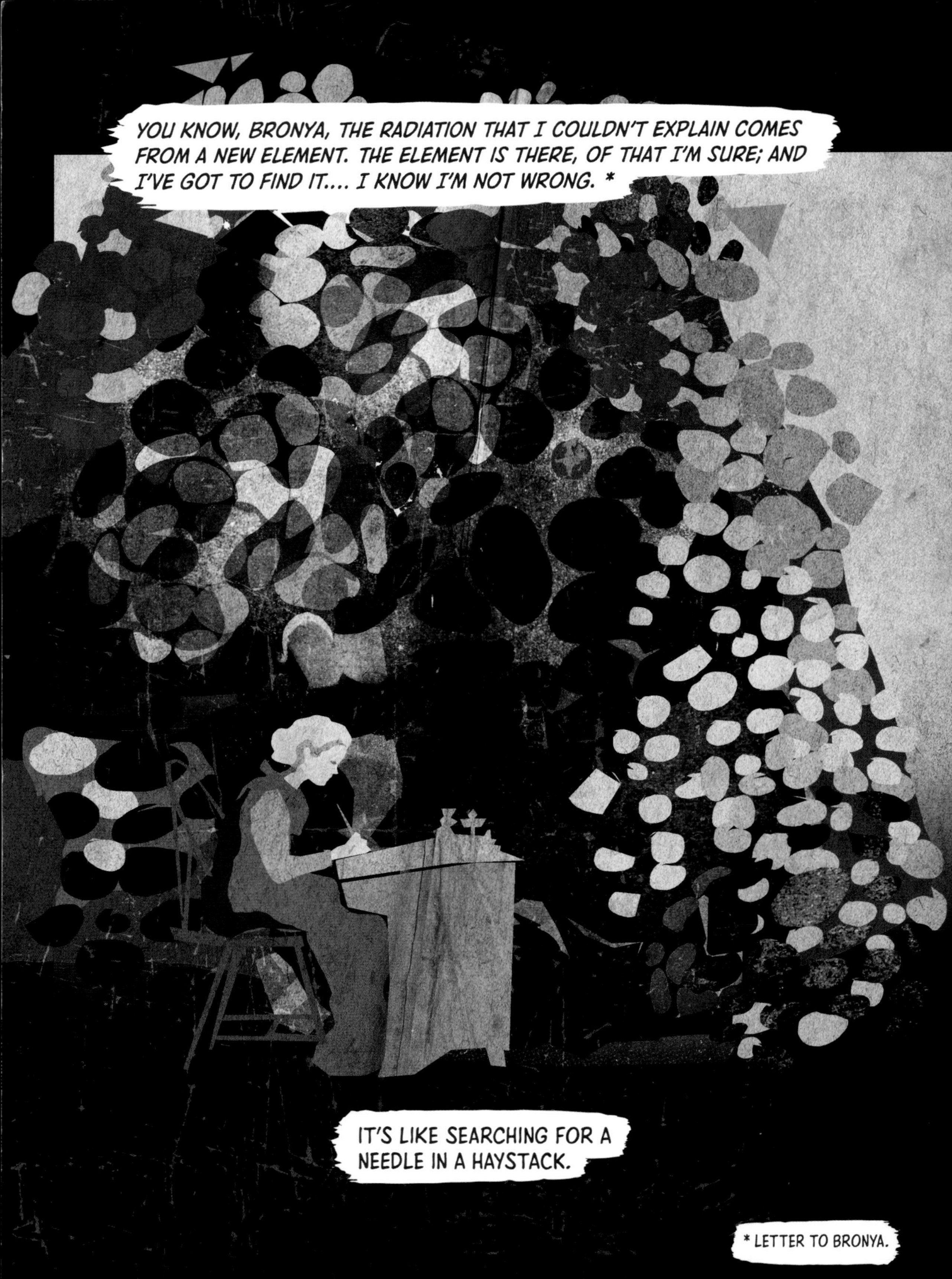
YOU KNOW, BRONYA, THE RADIATION THAT I COULDN'T EXPLAIN COMES FROM A NEW ELEMENT. THE ELEMENT IS THERE, OF THAT I'M SURE; AND I'VE GOT TO FIND IT.... I KNOW I'M NOT WRONG. *
IT'S LIKE SEARCHING FOR A NEEDLE IN A HAYSTACK.
* LETTER TO BRONYA.

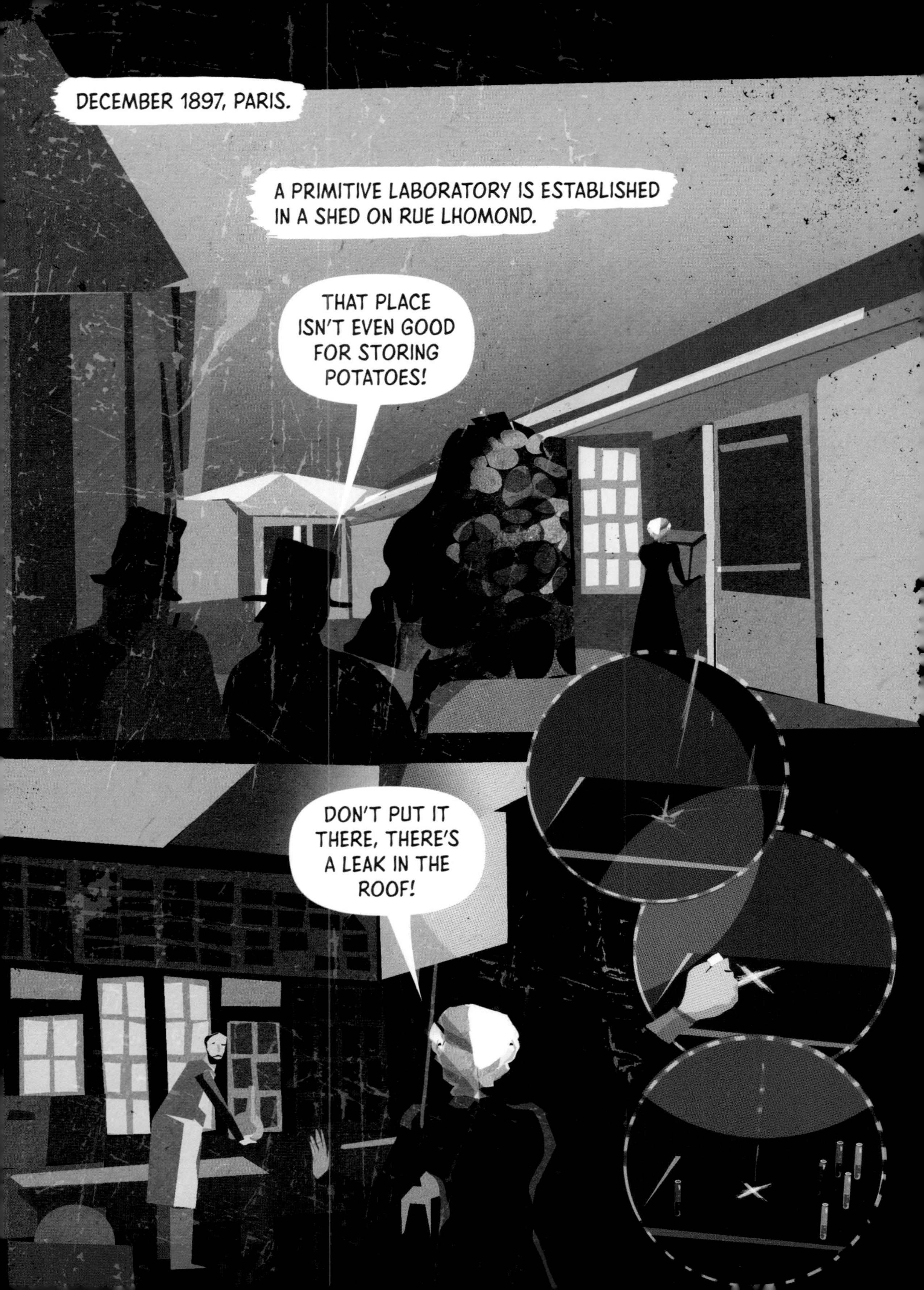
DECEMBER 1897, PARIS.
A PRIMITIVE LABORATORY IS ESTABLISHED IN A SHED ON RUE LHOMOND.
THAT PLACE ISN'T EVEN GOOD FOR STORING POTATOES!
DON'T PUT IT THERE, THERE'S A LEAK IN THE ROOF!

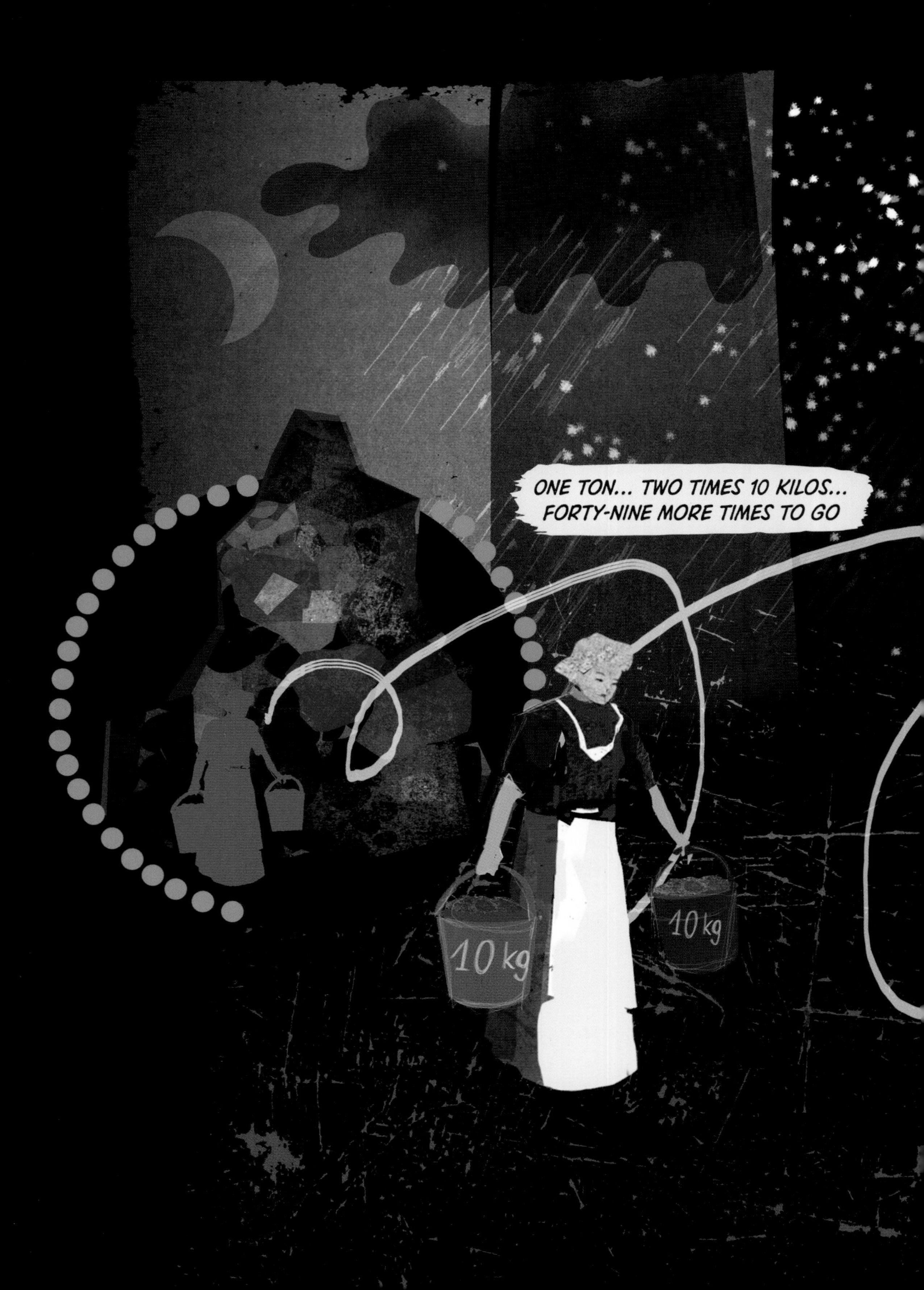
ONE TON... TWO TIMES 10 KILOS... FORTY-NINE MORE TIMES TO GO
10 kg
10 kg

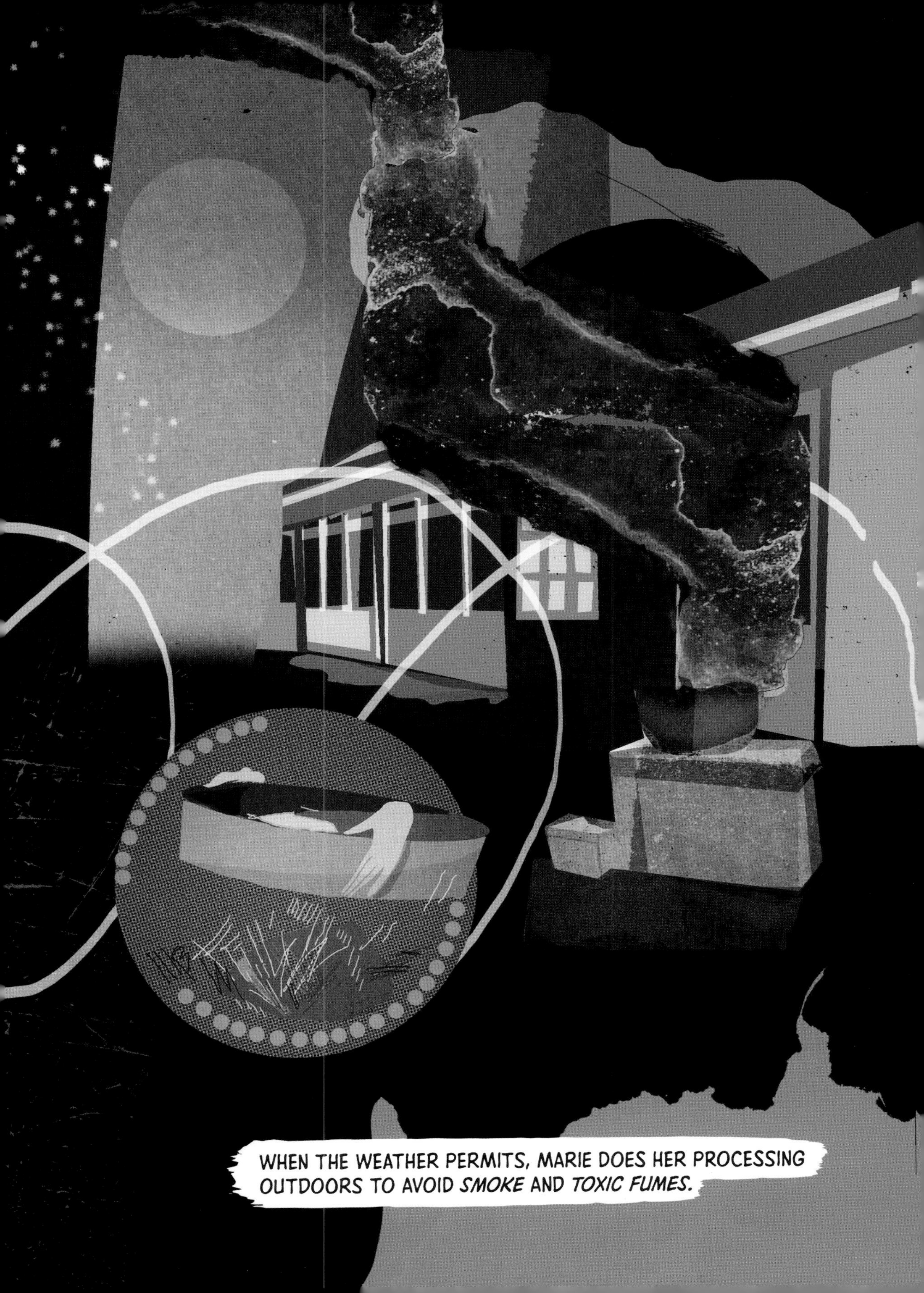
WHEN THE WEATHER PERMITS, MARIE DOES HER PROCESSING OUTDOORS TO AVOID *SMOKE* AND *TOXIC FUMES.*

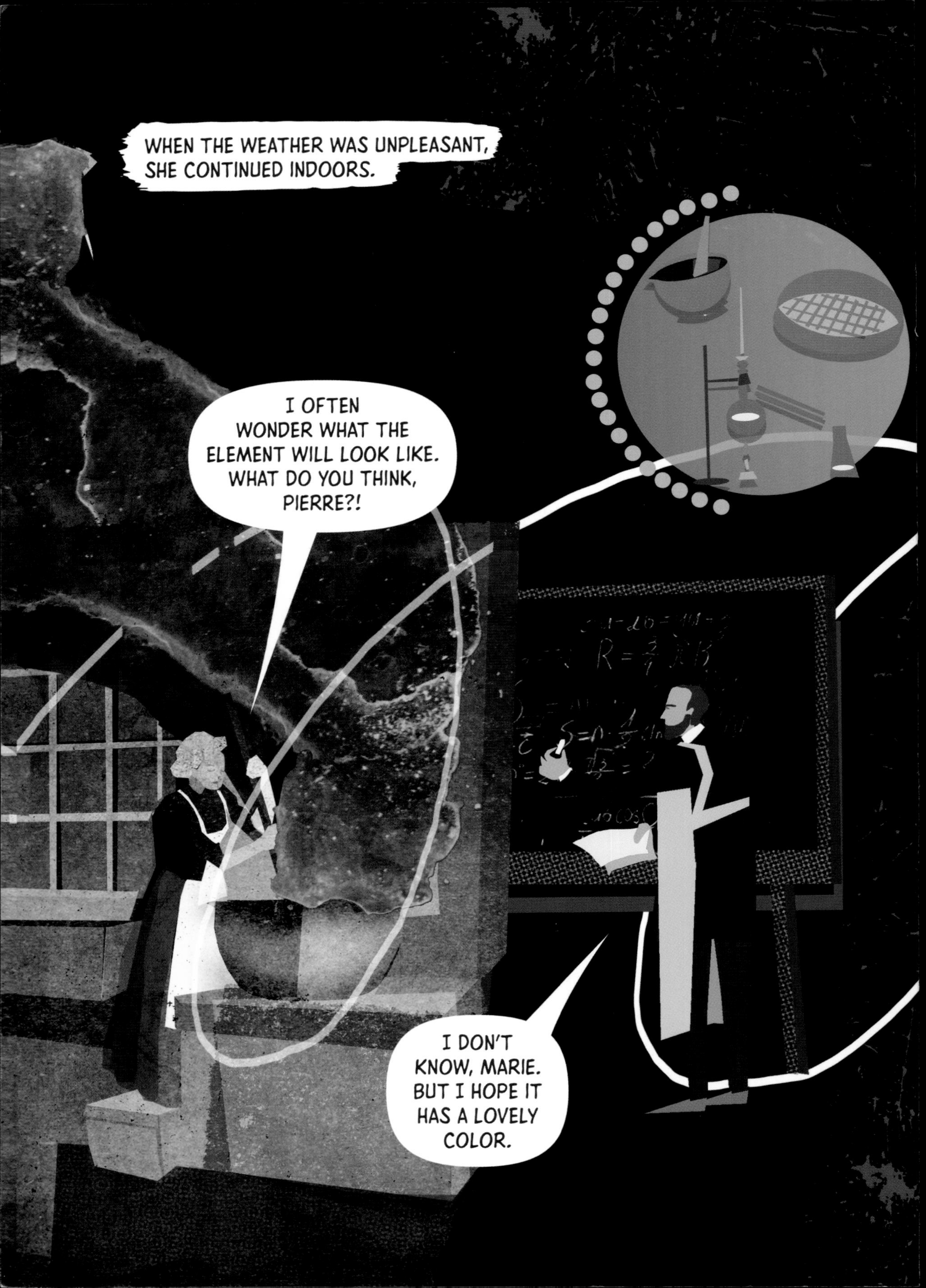
WHEN THE WEATHER WAS UNPLEASANT, SHE CONTINUED INDOORS.
I OFTEN WONDER WHAT THE ELEMENT WILL LOOK LIKE. WHAT DO YOU THINK, PIERRE?!
I DON'T KNOW, MARIE. BUT I HOPE IT HAS A LOVELY COLOR.

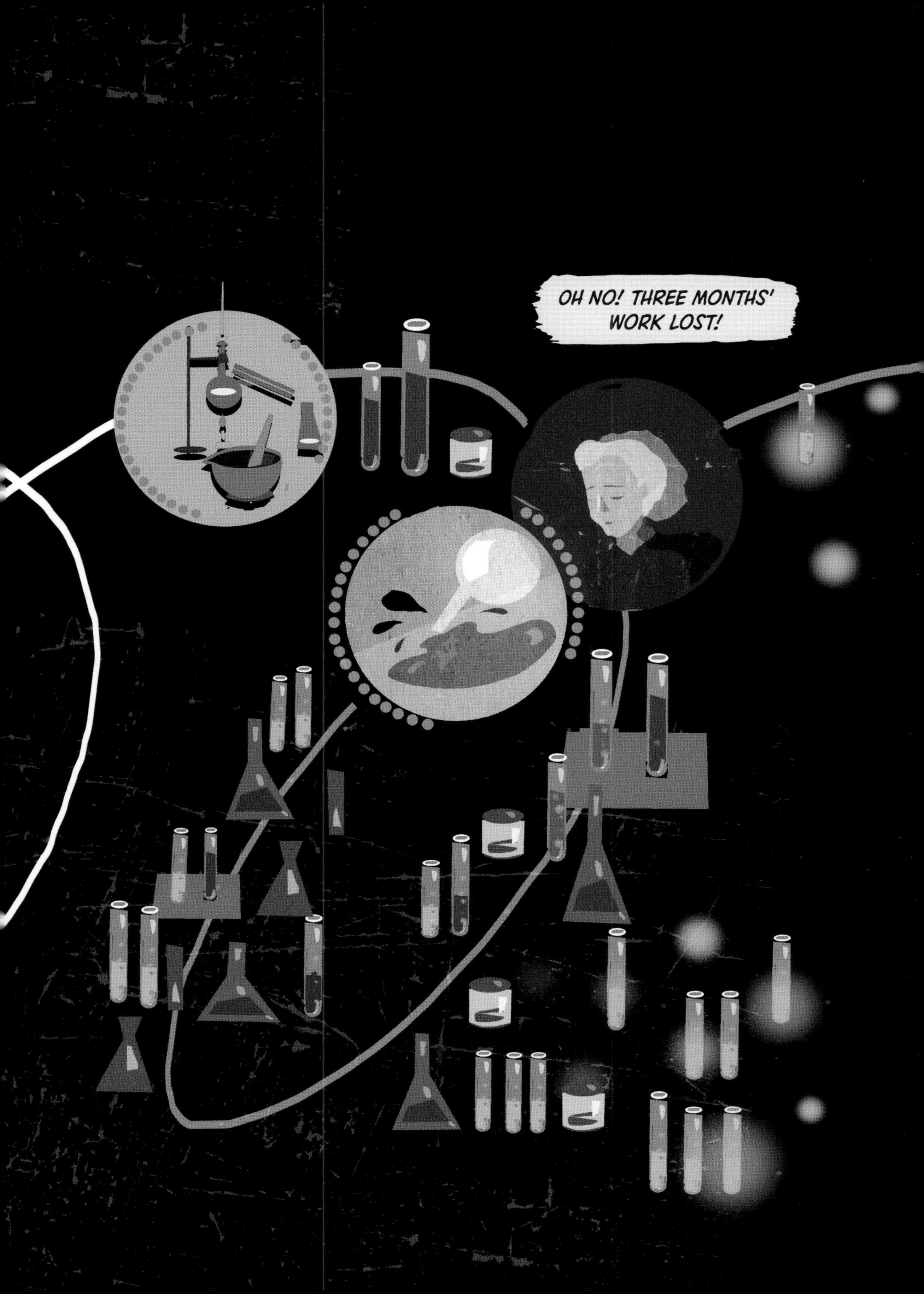
OH NO! THREE MONTHS' WORK LOST!

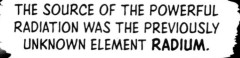

THE SOURCE OF THE POWERFUL RADIATION WAS THE PREVIOUSLY UNKNOWN ELEMENT **RADIUM**.

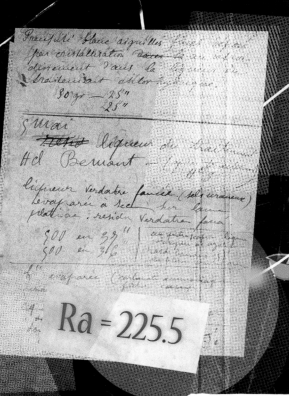

FROM MARIE'S NOTEBOOK.

PROCESSING THE PITCHBLENDE WAS NOT EASY. IT TOOK OVER *ONE TON* OF THE RAW MATERIAL FOR MARIE TO ESTABLISH HER METHOD AND PROVE RADIUM'S EXISTENCE.

BUT SHE WOULD NEED TO ISOLATE IT IN ITS PURE STATE. A COLOSSAL TASK, AS RADIUM IS HARD TO DISTINGUISH FROM **BARIUM**. THEY HAVE REMARKABLY SIMILAR PROPERTIES.

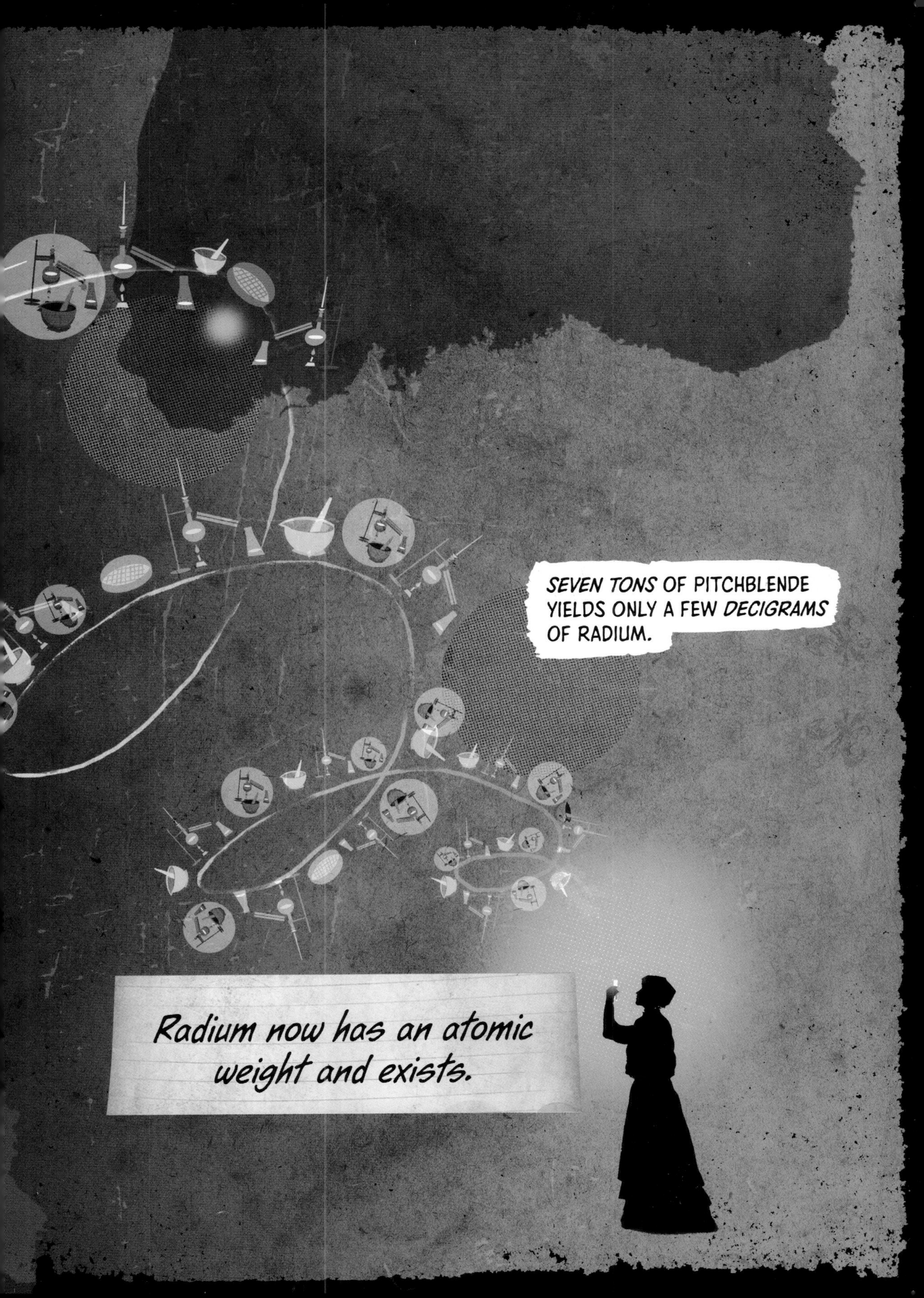
SEVEN TONS OF PITCHBLENDE YIELDS ONLY A FEW DECIGRAMS OF RADIUM.
Radium now has an atomic weight and exists.

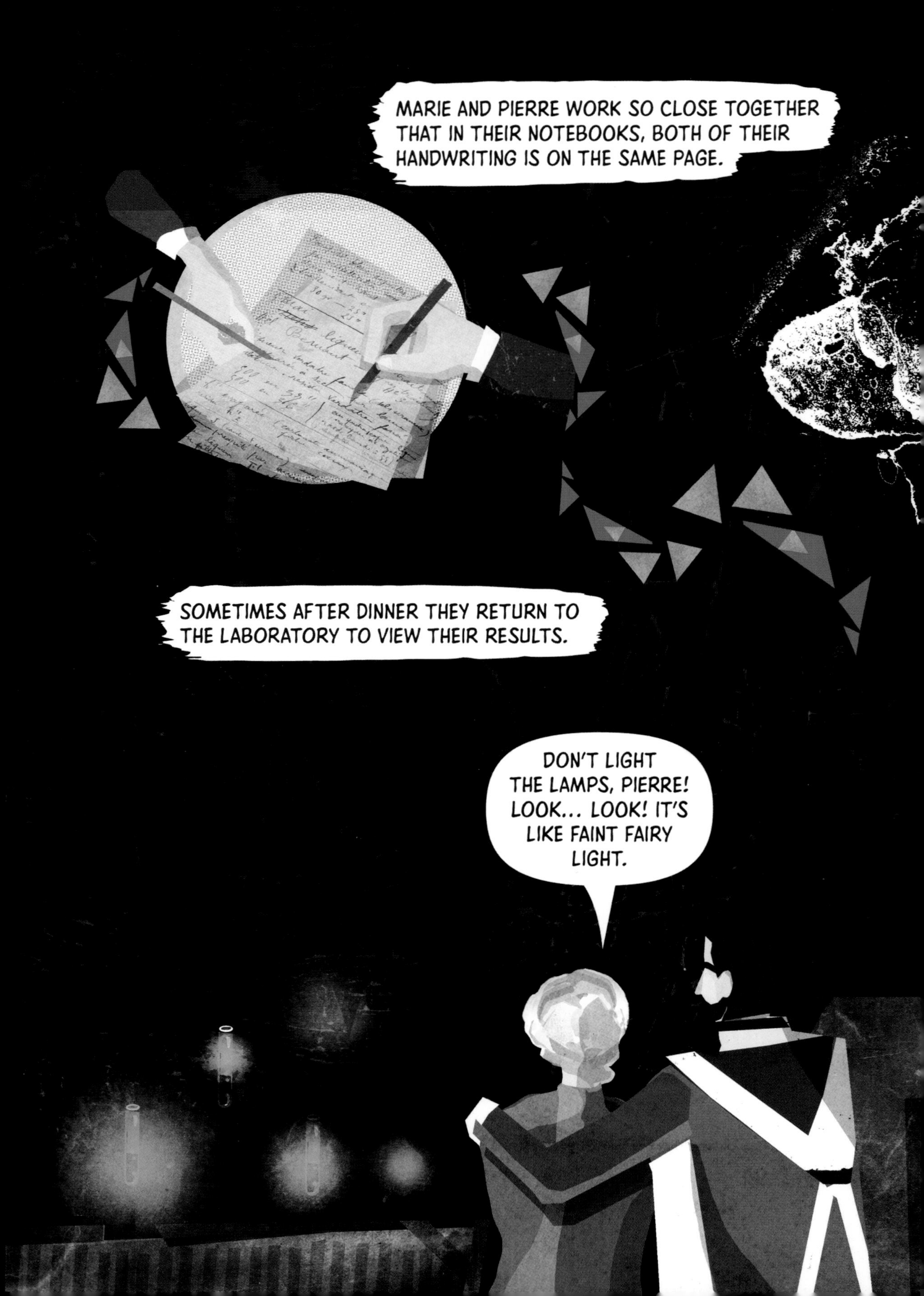
MARIE AND PIERRE WORK SO CLOSE TOGETHER THAT IN THEIR NOTEBOOKS, BOTH OF THEIR HANDWRITING IS ON THE SAME PAGE.
SOMETIMES AFTER DINNER THEY RETURN TO THE LABORATORY TO VIEW THEIR RESULTS.
DON'T LIGHT THE LAMPS, PIERRE! LOOK... LOOK! IT'S LIKE FAINT FAIRY LIGHT.

IN THEIR LABORATORY THREE NEW RADIOACTIVE ELEMENTS ARE FOUND: **RADIUM, POLONIUM,** AND **ACTINIUM.**
PIERRE ANNOUNCES THE FIRST DISCOVERY AT THE **FRENCH ACADEMY OF SCIENCE** IN JULY 1898.
WE BELIEVE THE SUBSTANCE WE HAVE EXTRACTED FROM PITCHBLENDE CONTAINS A METAL NOT PREVIOUSLY OBSERVED...
WE PROPOSE TO NAME IT POLONIUM* AFTER THE COUNTRY IN WHICH ONE OF US WAS BORN.
* FROM *POLONIA*, LATIN FOR POLAND.

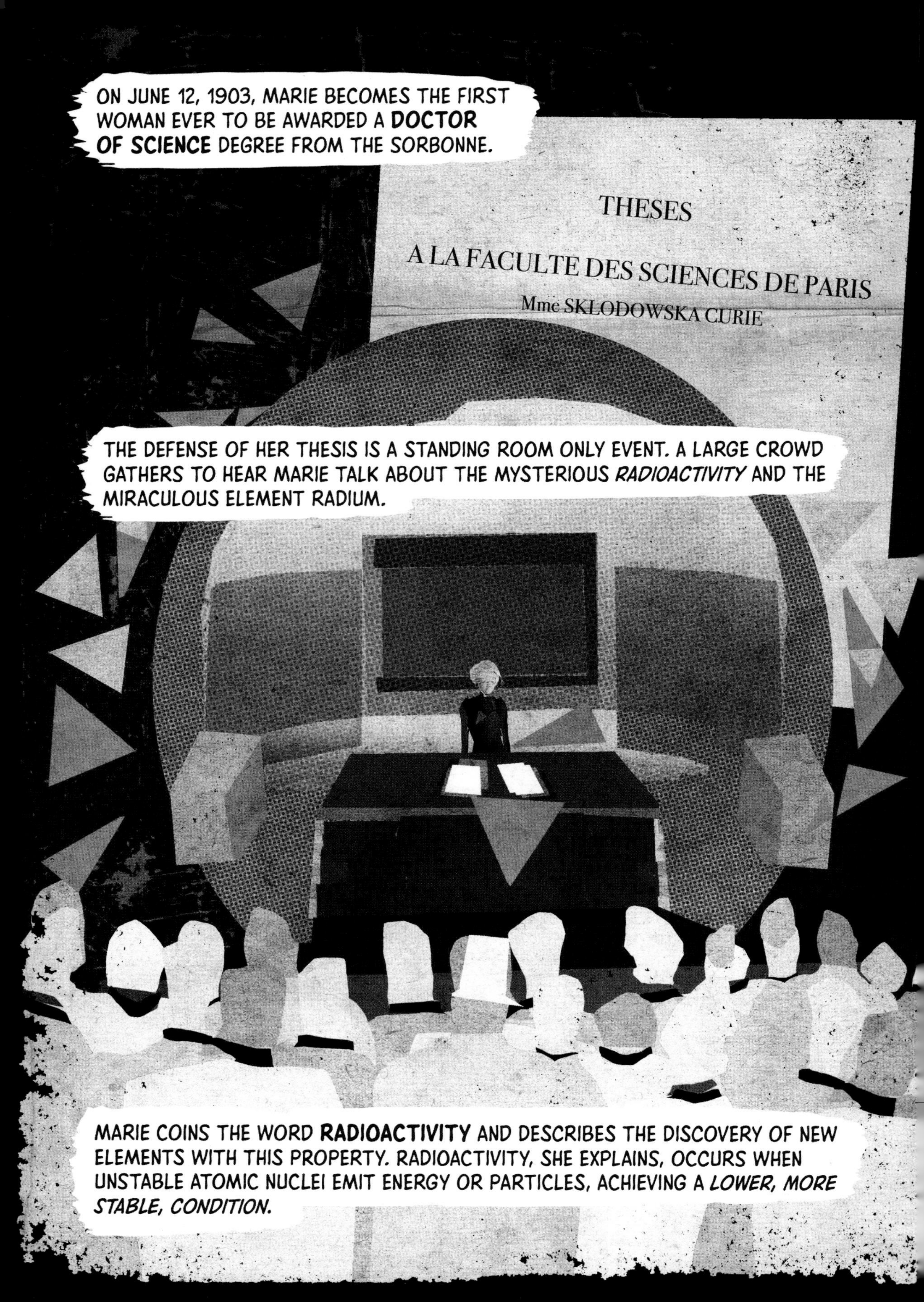
ON JUNE 12, 1903, MARIE BECOMES THE FIRST WOMAN EVER TO BE AWARDED A **DOCTOR OF SCIENCE** DEGREE FROM THE SORBONNE.
THESES
A LA FACULTE DES SCIENCES DE PARIS
Mme SKLODOWSKA CURIE
THE DEFENSE OF HER THESIS IS A STANDING ROOM ONLY EVENT. A LARGE CROWD GATHERS TO HEAR MARIE TALK ABOUT THE MYSTERIOUS *RADIOACTIVITY* AND THE MIRACULOUS ELEMENT RADIUM.
MARIE COINS THE WORD **RADIOACTIVITY** AND DESCRIBES THE DISCOVERY OF NEW ELEMENTS WITH THIS PROPERTY. RADIOACTIVITY, SHE EXPLAINS, OCCURS WHEN UNSTABLE ATOMIC NUCLEI EMIT ENERGY OR PARTICLES, ACHIEVING A *LOWER, MORE STABLE, CONDITION.*

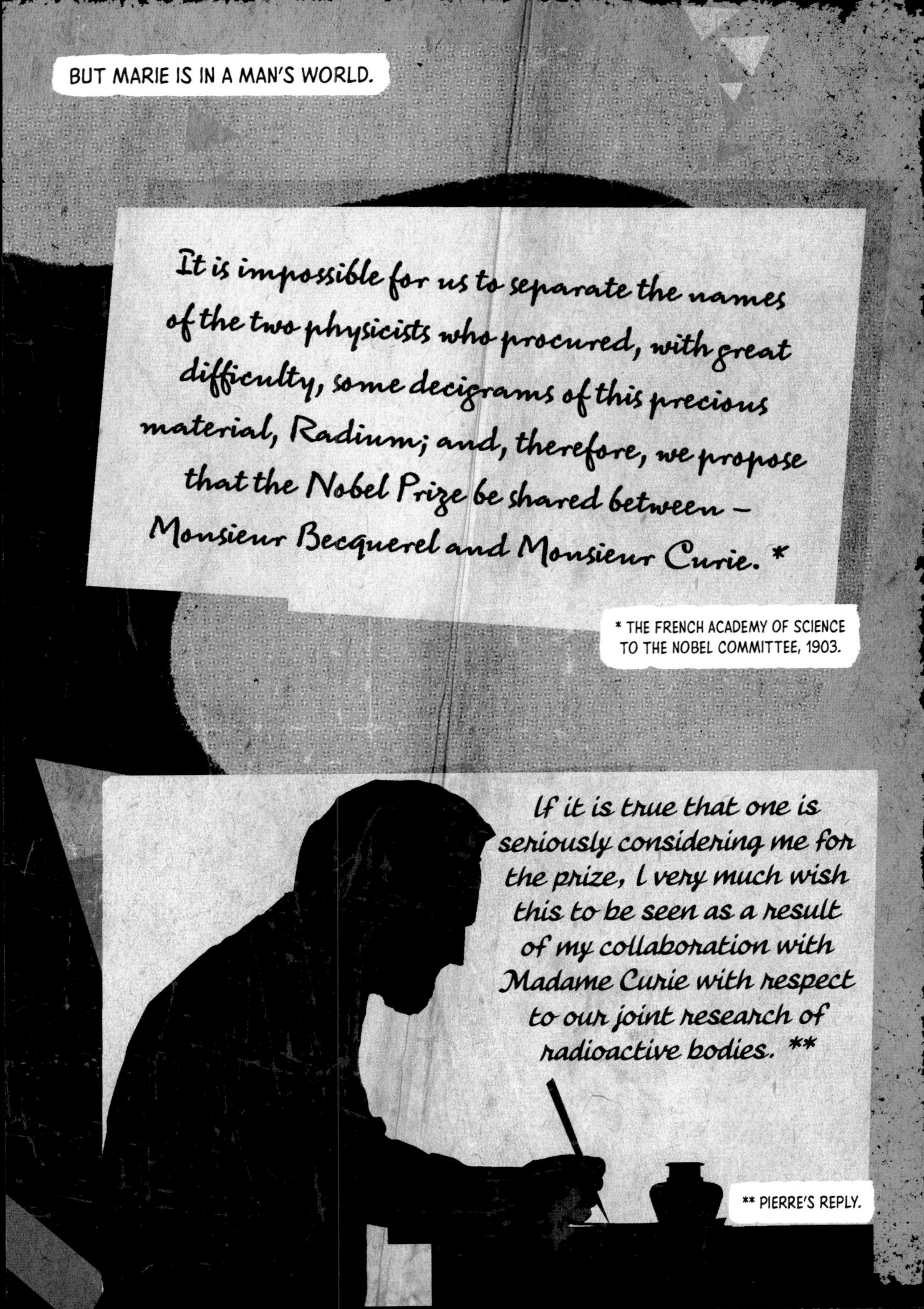
BUT MARIE IS IN A MAN'S WORLD.
It is impossible for us to separate the names of the two physicists who procured, with great difficulty, some decigrams of this precious material, Radium; and, therefore, we propose that the Nobel Prize be shared between – Monsieur Becquerel and Monsieur Curie. *
* THE FRENCH ACADEMY OF SCIENCE TO THE NOBEL COMMITTEE, 1903.
If it is true that one is seriously considering me for the prize, I very much wish this to be seen as a result of my collaboration with Madame Curie with respect to our joint research of radioactive bodies. **
** PIERRE'S REPLY.

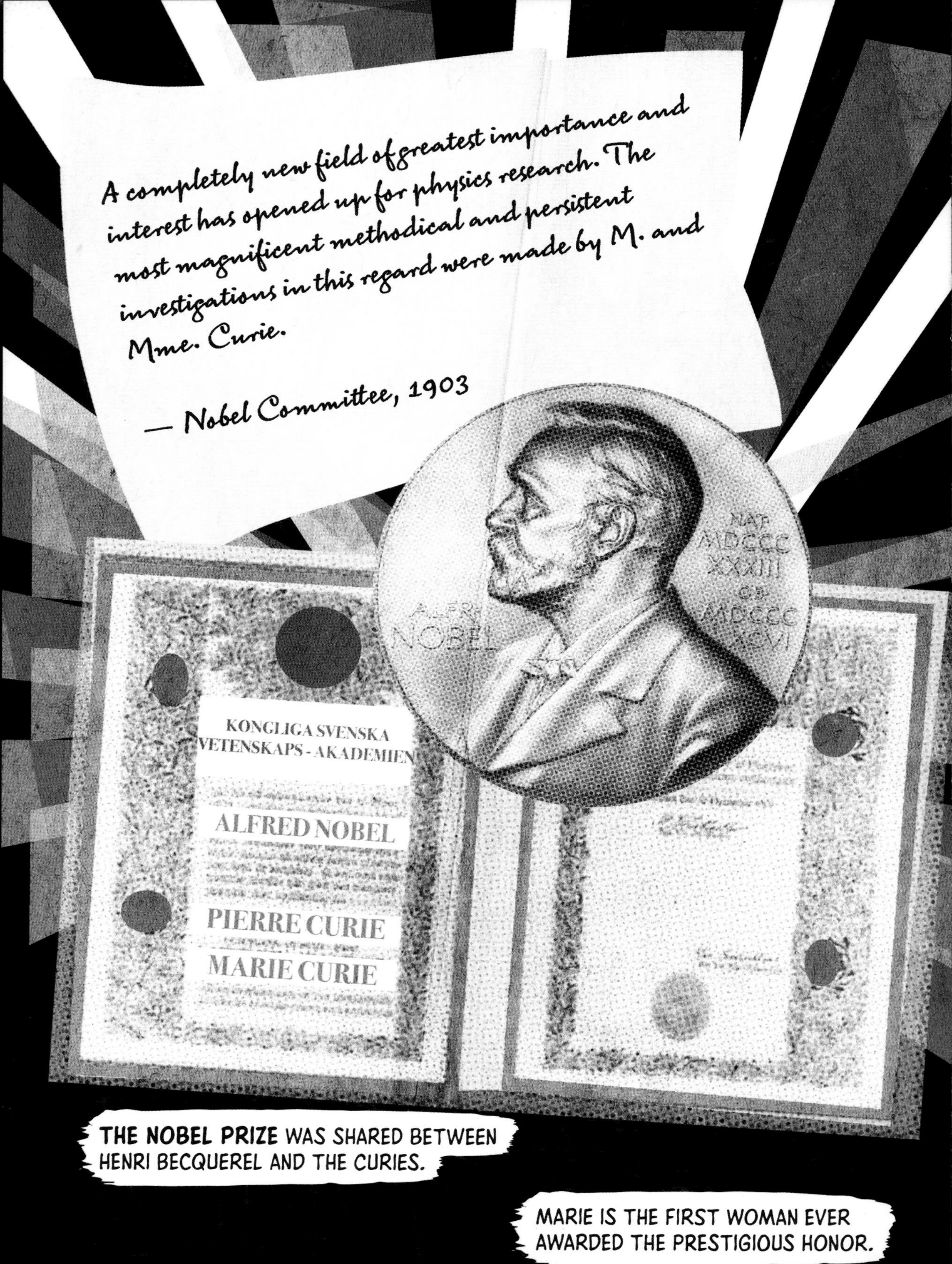

A completely new field of greatest importance and interest has opened up for physics research. The most magnificent methodical and persistent investigations in this regard were made by M. and Mme. Curie.
— Nobel Committee, 1903
NAT MDCCC XXXIII OB MDCCC XCVI
ALFR NOBEL
KONGLIGA SVENSKA VETENSKAPS - AKADEMIEN
ALFRED NOBEL
PIERRE CURIE
MARIE CURIE
THE NOBEL PRIZE WAS SHARED BETWEEN HENRI BECQUEREL AND THE CURIES.
MARIE IS THE FIRST WOMAN EVER AWARDED THE PRESTIGIOUS HONOR.

Chapter 5

1903-1911

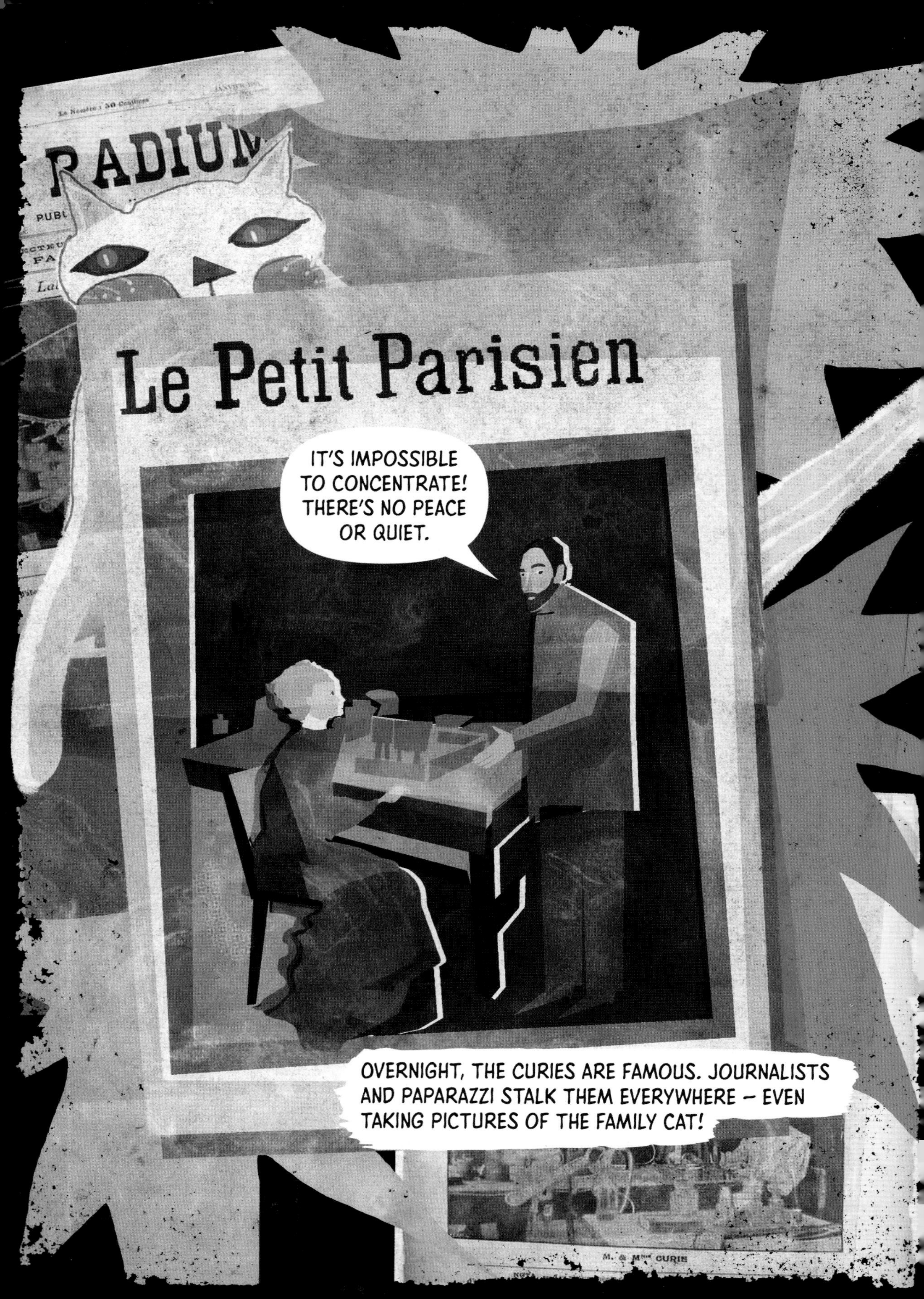
RADIUM
Le Petit Parisien
IT'S IMPOSSIBLE TO CONCENTRATE! THERE'S NO PEACE OR QUIET.
OVERNIGHT, THE CURIES ARE FAMOUS. JOURNALISTS AND PAPARAZZI STALK THEM EVERYWHERE – EVEN TAKING PICTURES OF THE FAMILY CAT!

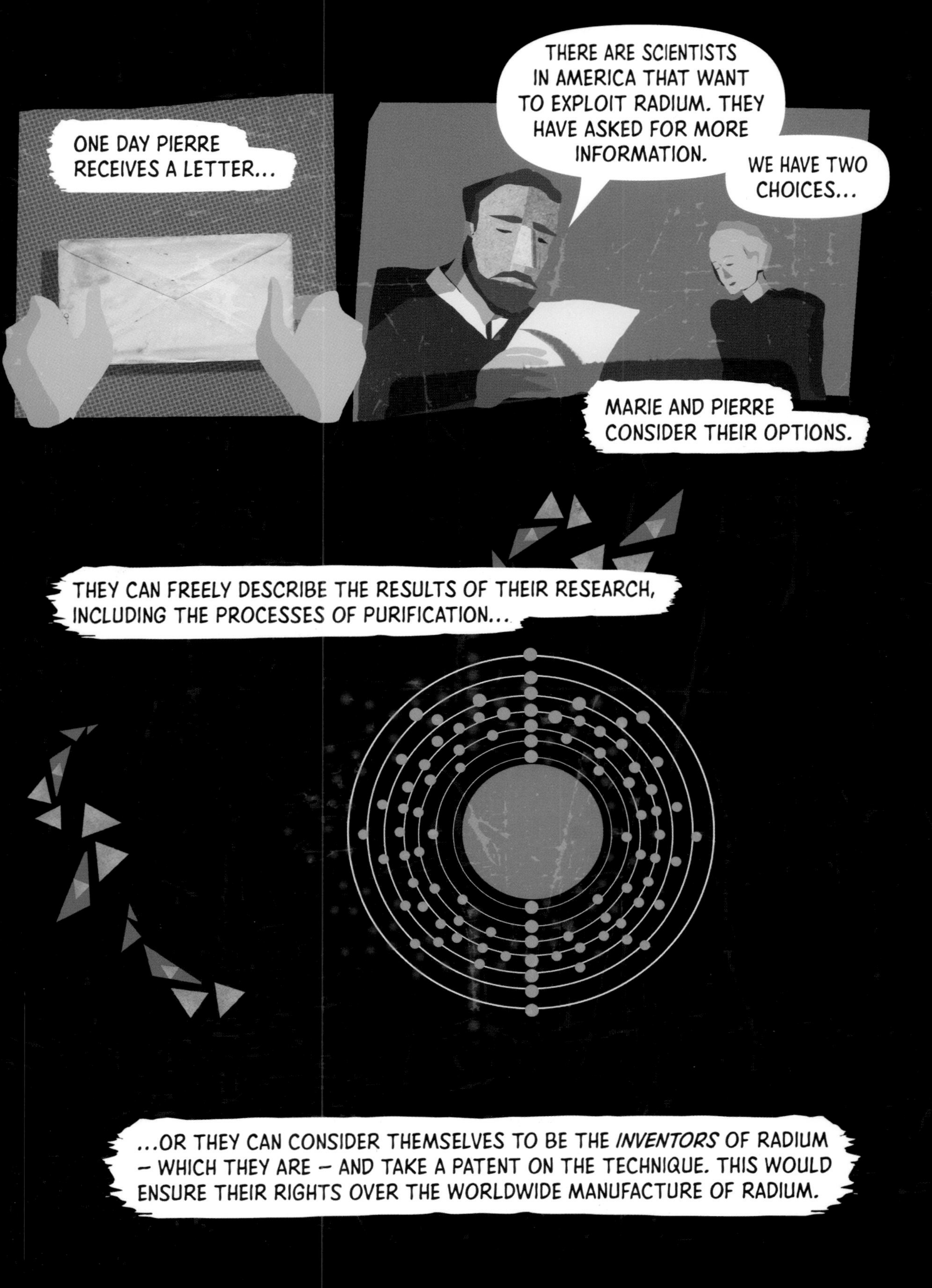

ONE DAY PIERRE RECEIVES A LETTER...
THERE ARE SCIENTISTS IN AMERICA THAT WANT TO EXPLOIT RADIUM. THEY HAVE ASKED FOR MORE INFORMATION.
WE HAVE TWO CHOICES...
MARIE AND PIERRE CONSIDER THEIR OPTIONS.
THEY CAN FREELY DESCRIBE THE RESULTS OF THEIR RESEARCH, INCLUDING THE PROCESSES OF PURIFICATION...
...OR THEY CAN CONSIDER THEMSELVES TO BE THE *INVENTORS* OF RADIUM – WHICH THEY ARE – AND TAKE A PATENT ON THE TECHNIQUE. THIS WOULD ENSURE THEIR RIGHTS OVER THE WORLDWIDE MANUFACTURE OF RADIUM.

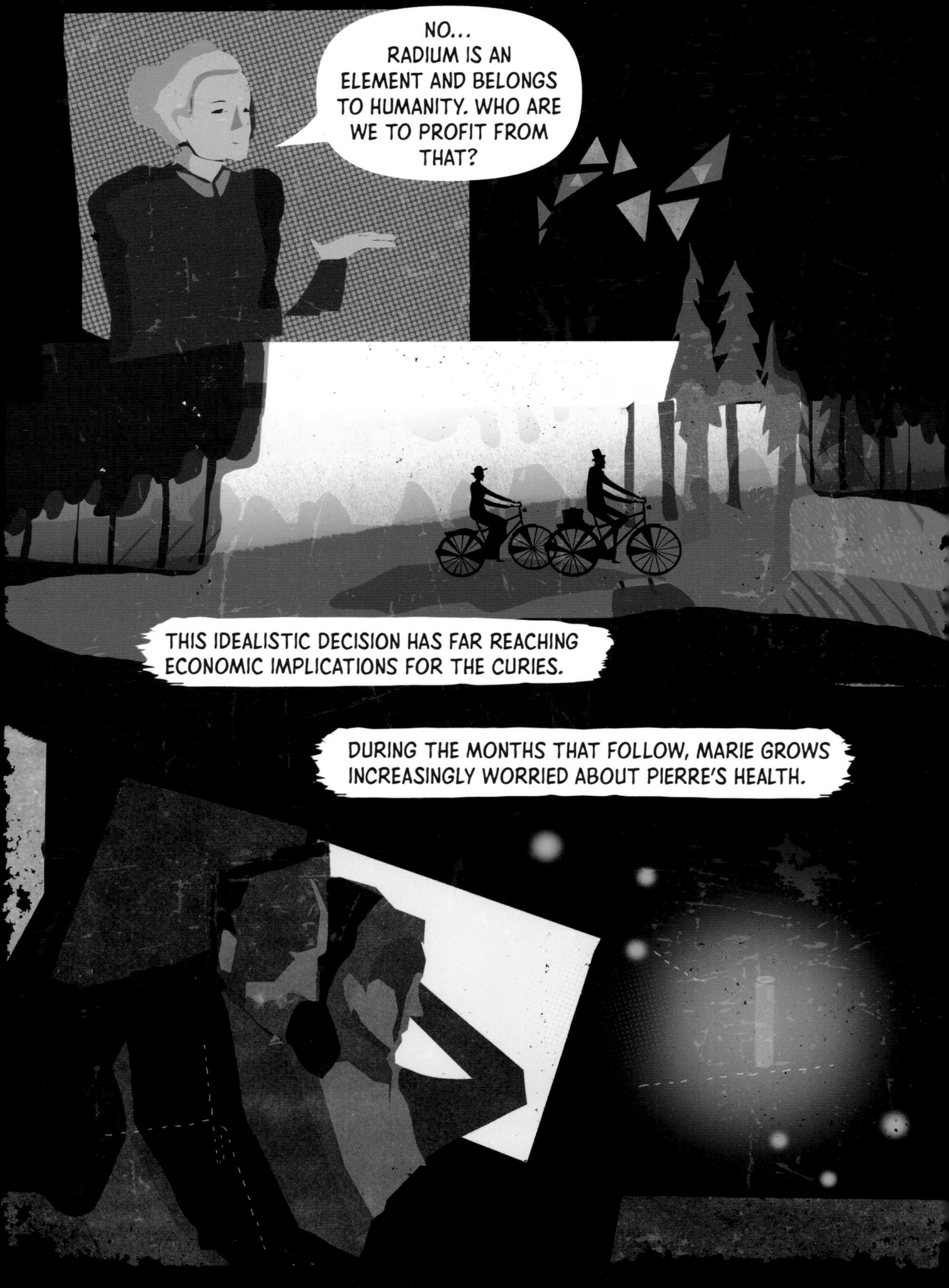
NO... RADIUM IS AN ELEMENT AND BELONGS TO HUMANITY. WHO ARE WE TO PROFIT FROM THAT?
THIS IDEALISTIC DECISION HAS FAR REACHING ECONOMIC IMPLICATIONS FOR THE CURIES.
DURING THE MONTHS THAT FOLLOW, MARIE GROWS INCREASINGLY WORRIED ABOUT PIERRE'S HEALTH.

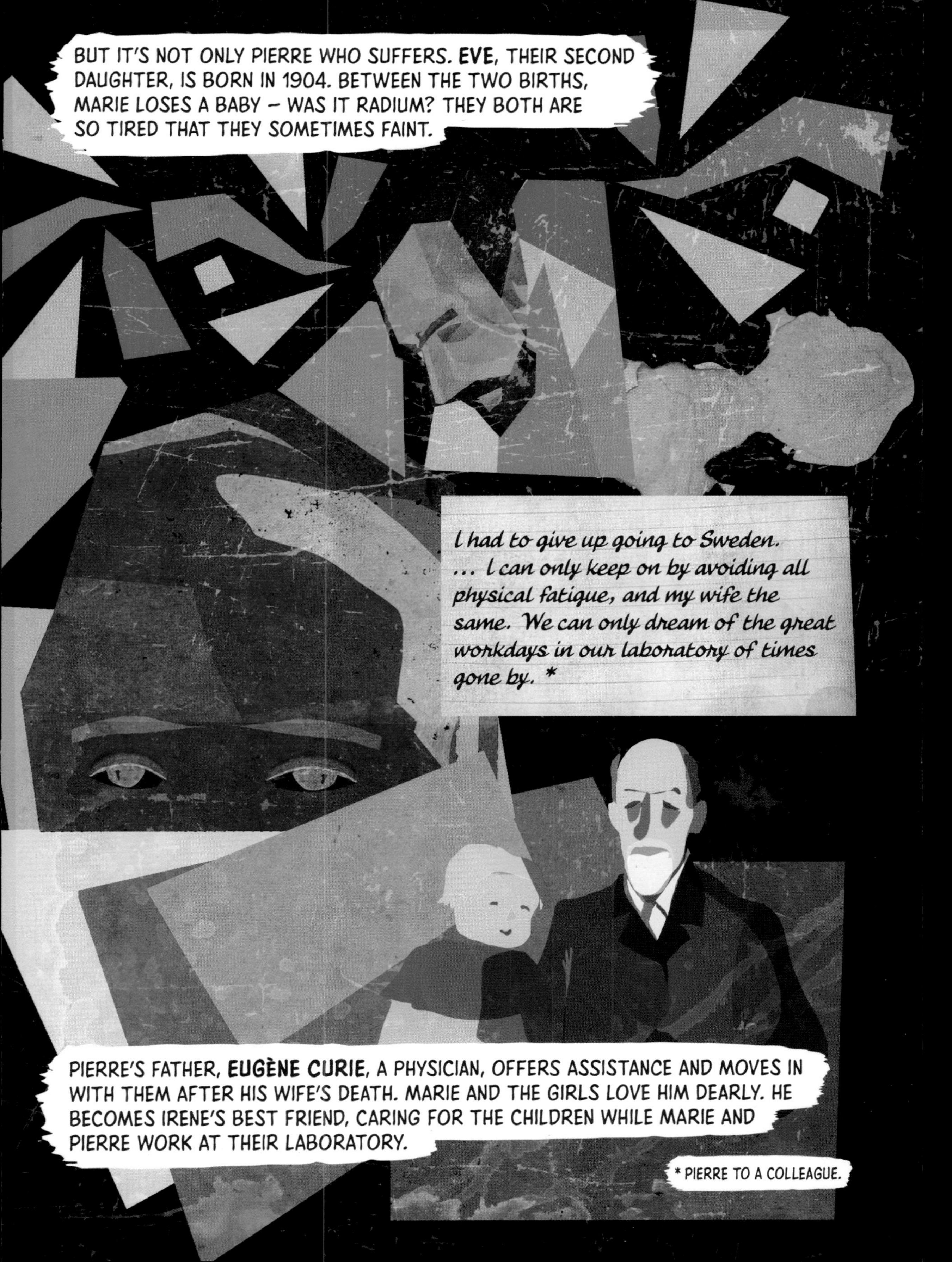

BUT IT'S NOT ONLY PIERRE WHO SUFFERS. EVE, THEIR SECOND DAUGHTER, IS BORN IN 1904. BETWEEN THE TWO BIRTHS, MARIE LOSES A BABY – WAS IT RADIUM? THEY BOTH ARE SO TIRED THAT THEY SOMETIMES FAINT.
I had to give up going to Sweden. ... I can only keep on by avoiding all physical fatigue, and my wife the same. We can only dream of the great workdays in our laboratory of times gone by. *
PIERRE'S FATHER, EUGÈNE CURIE, A PHYSICIAN, OFFERS ASSISTANCE AND MOVES IN WITH THEM AFTER HIS WIFE'S DEATH. MARIE AND THE GIRLS LOVE HIM DEARLY. HE BECOMES IRENE'S BEST FRIEND, CARING FOR THE CHILDREN WHILE MARIE AND PIERRE WORK AT THEIR LABORATORY.
* PIERRE TO A COLLEAGUE.

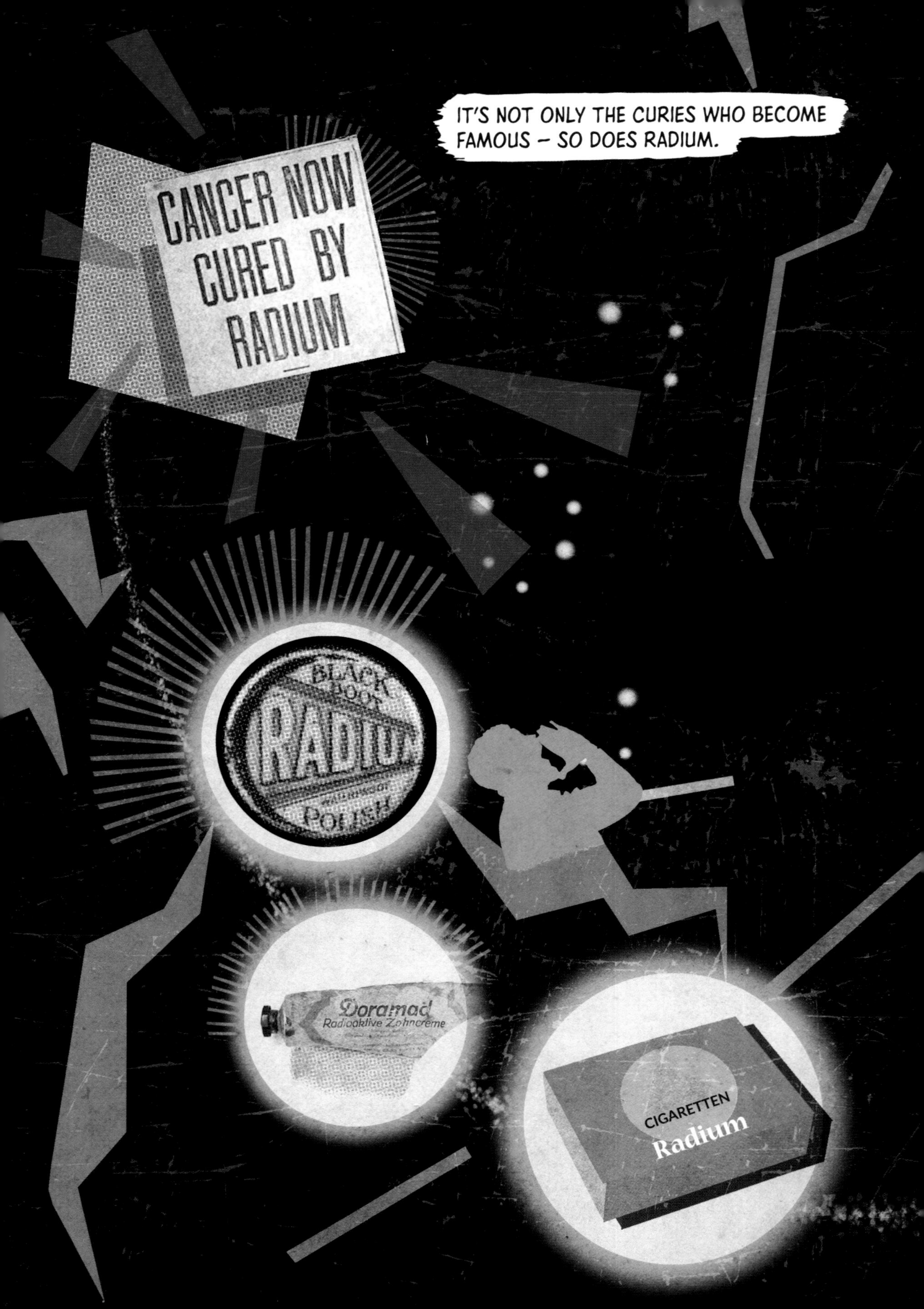
IT'S NOT ONLY THE CURIES WHO BECOME FAMOUS – SO DOES RADIUM.
CANCER NOW CURED BY RADIUM
BLACK
POLISH
Doramad
Radioaktive Zahncreme
CIGARETTEN
Radium

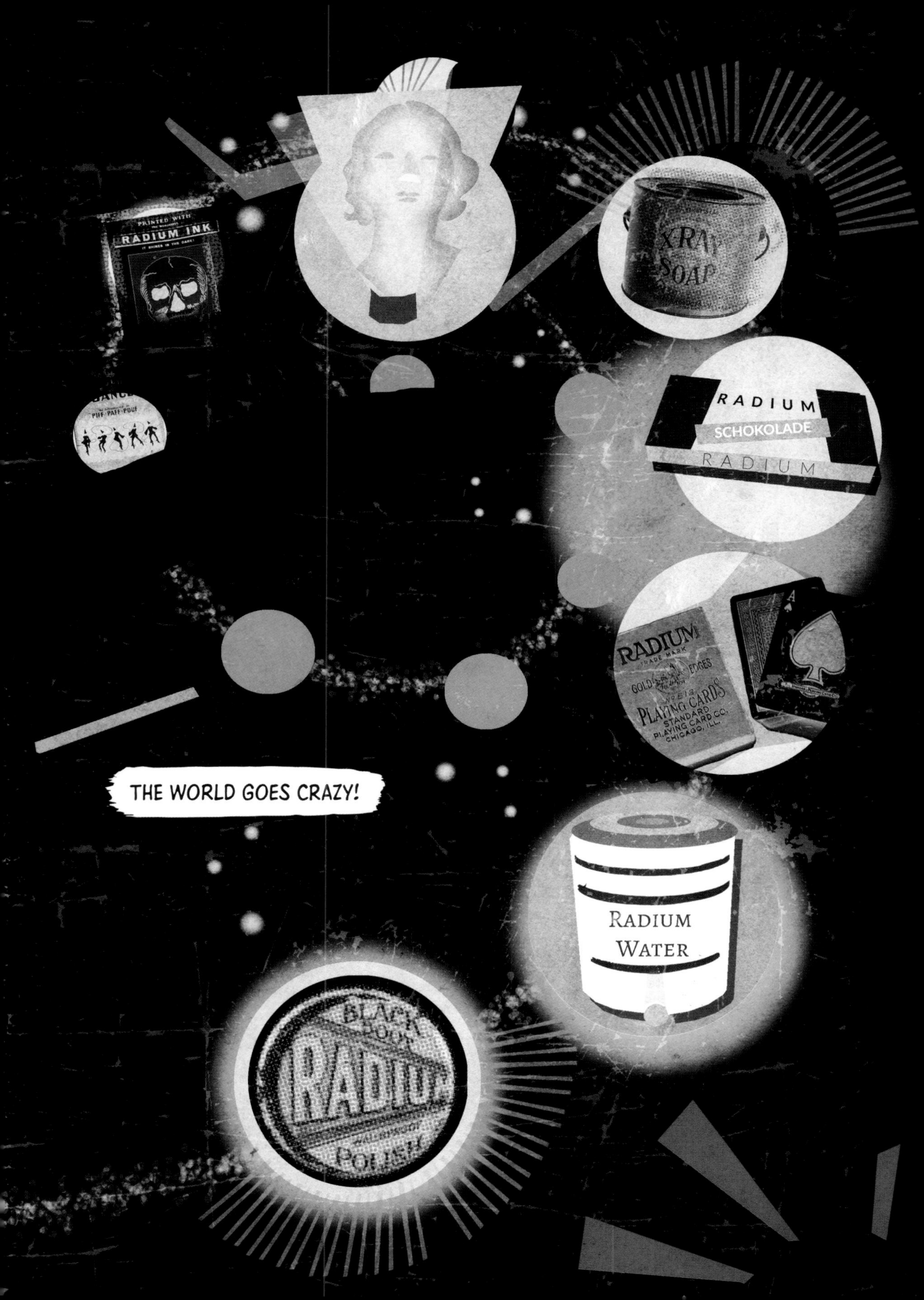
PRINTED WITH
RADIUM INK
IT SHINES IN THE DARK!
X-RAY SOAP
RADIUM
SCHOKOLADE
RADIUM
RADIUM
TRADE MARK
GOLD EDGES
PLAYING CARDS
STANDARD PLAYING CARD CO.
CHICAGO, ILL.
THE WORLD GOES CRAZY!
RADIUM
WATER
POLISH

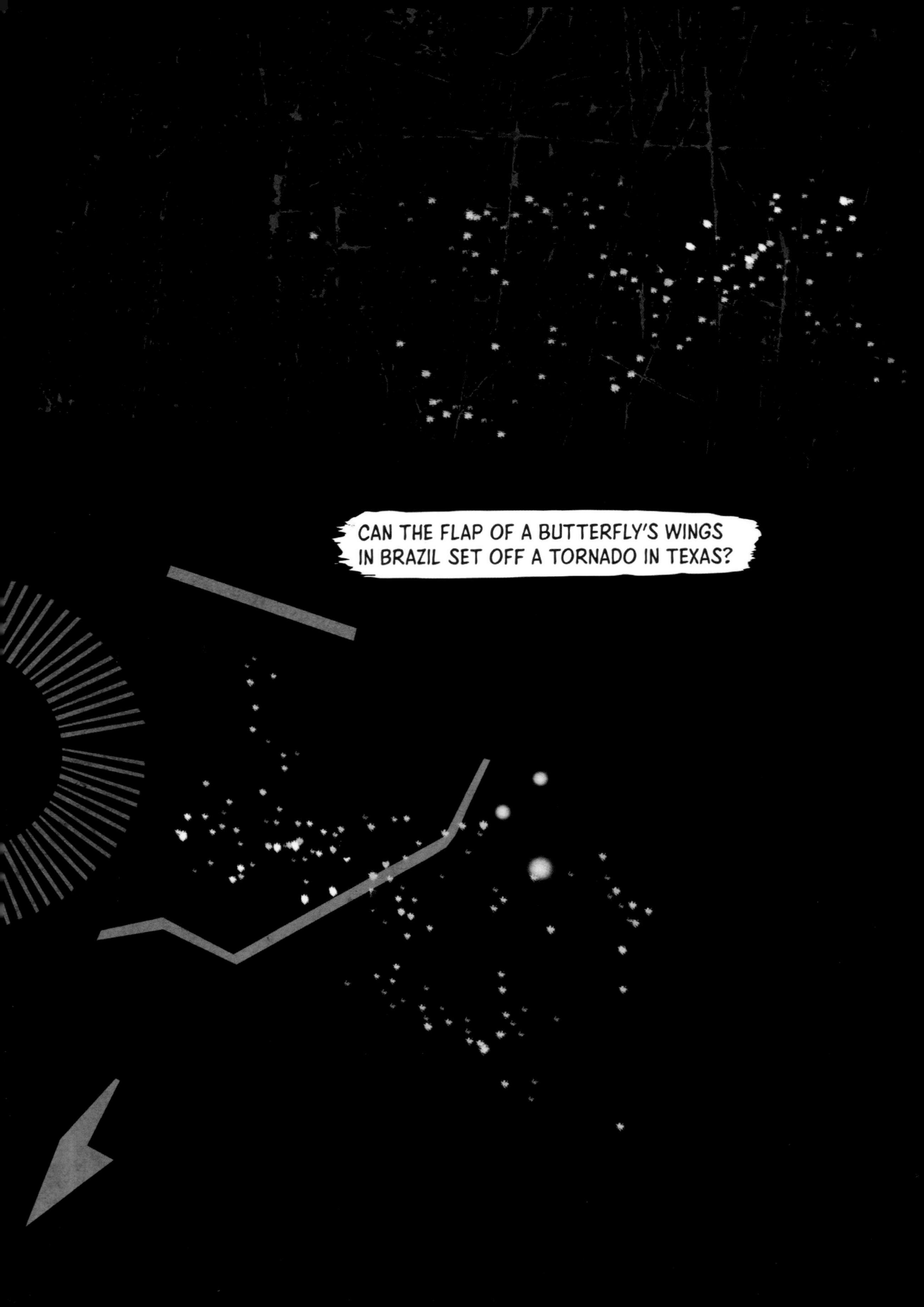
CAN THE FLAP OF A BUTTERFLY'S WINGS IN BRAZIL SET OFF A TORNADO IN TEXAS?

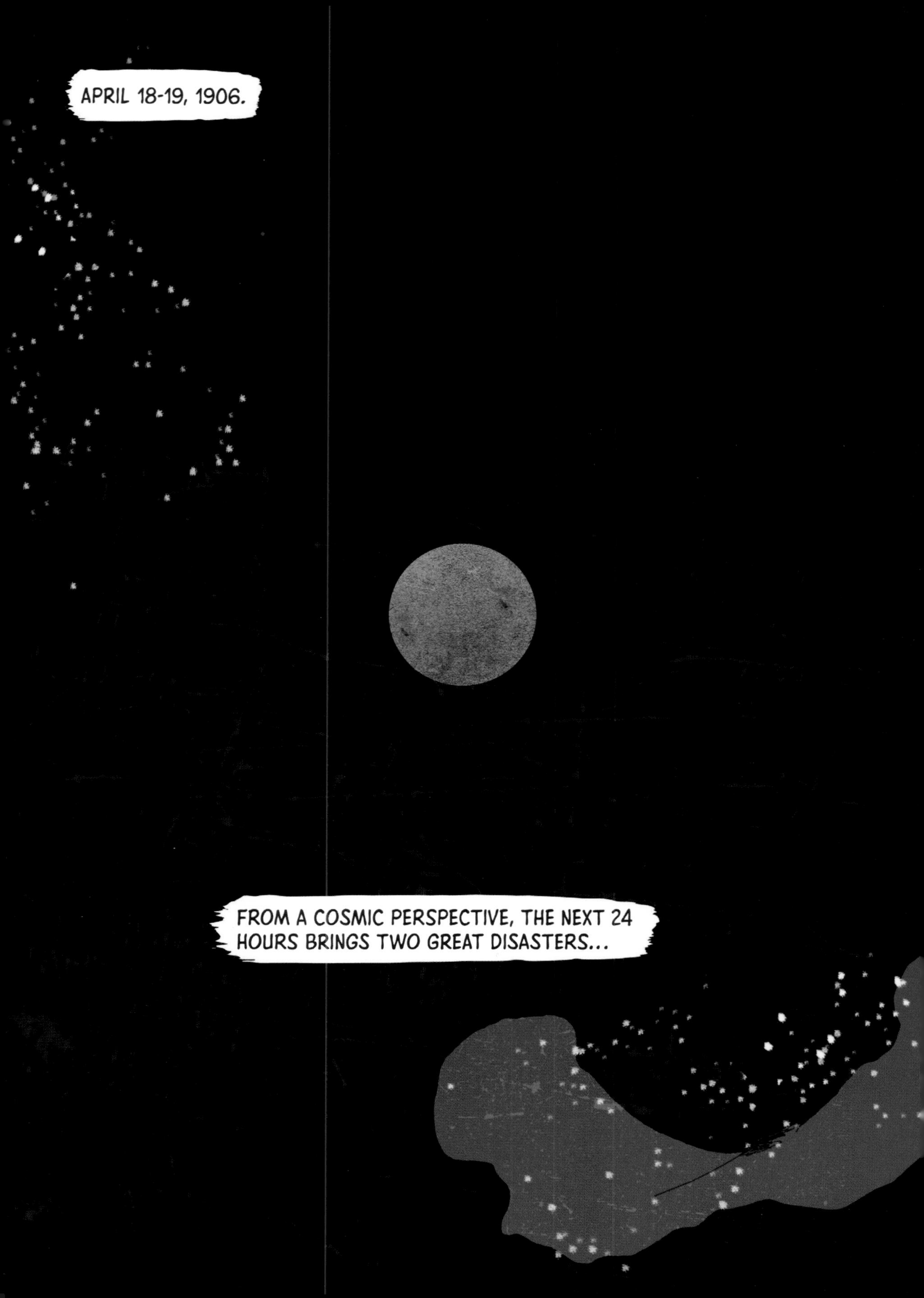
APRIL 18-19, 1906.
FROM A COSMIC PERSPECTIVE, THE NEXT 24 HOURS BRINGS TWO GREAT DISASTERS...

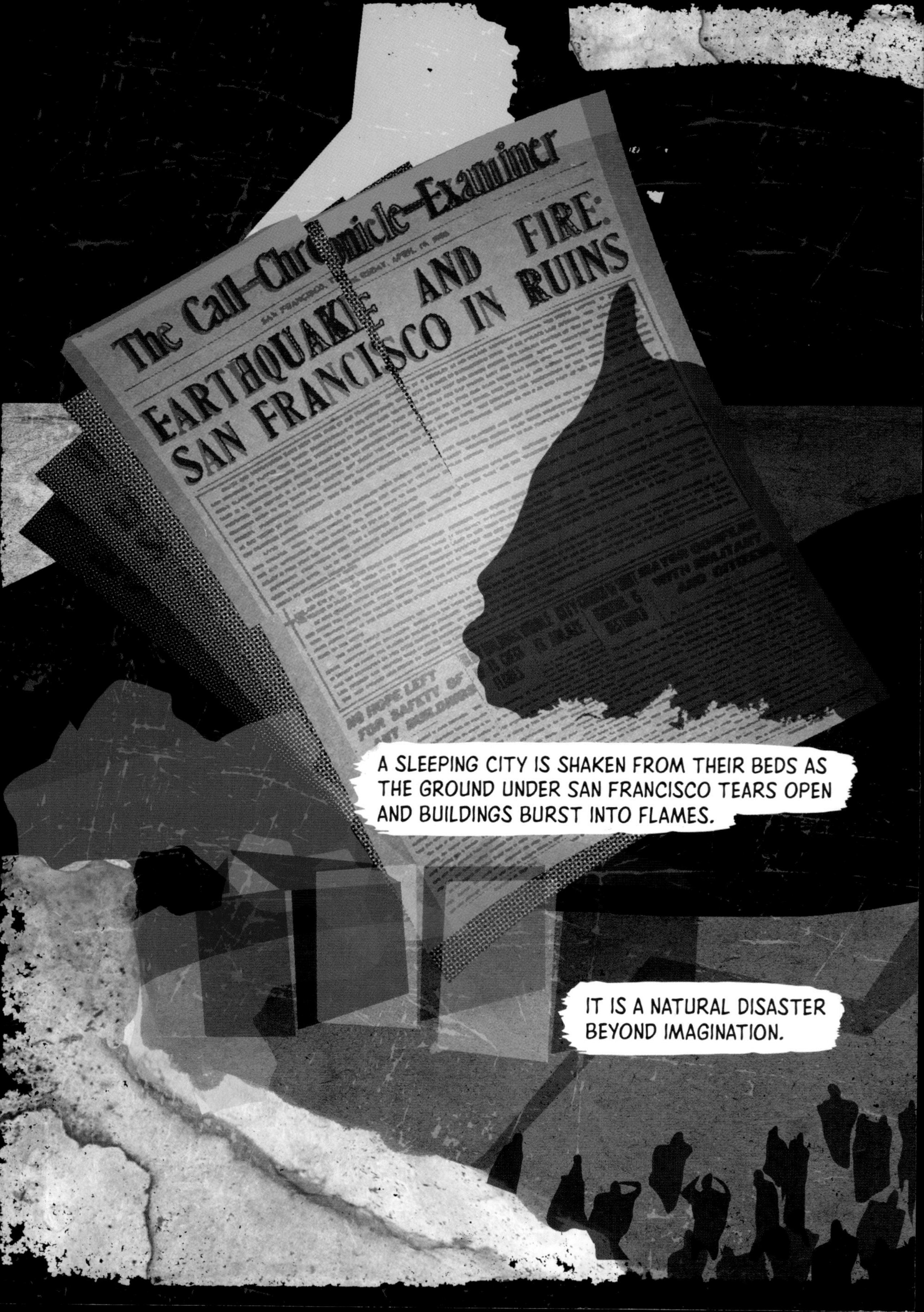
The Call-Chronicle-Examiner
EARTHQUAKE AND FIRE: SAN FRANCISCO IN RUINS
NO HOPE LEFT FOR SAFETY OF ANY BUILDINGS
A SLEEPING CITY IS SHAKEN FROM THEIR BEDS AS THE GROUND UNDER SAN FRANCISCO TEARS OPEN AND BUILDINGS BURST INTO FLAMES.
IT IS A NATURAL DISASTER BEYOND IMAGINATION.

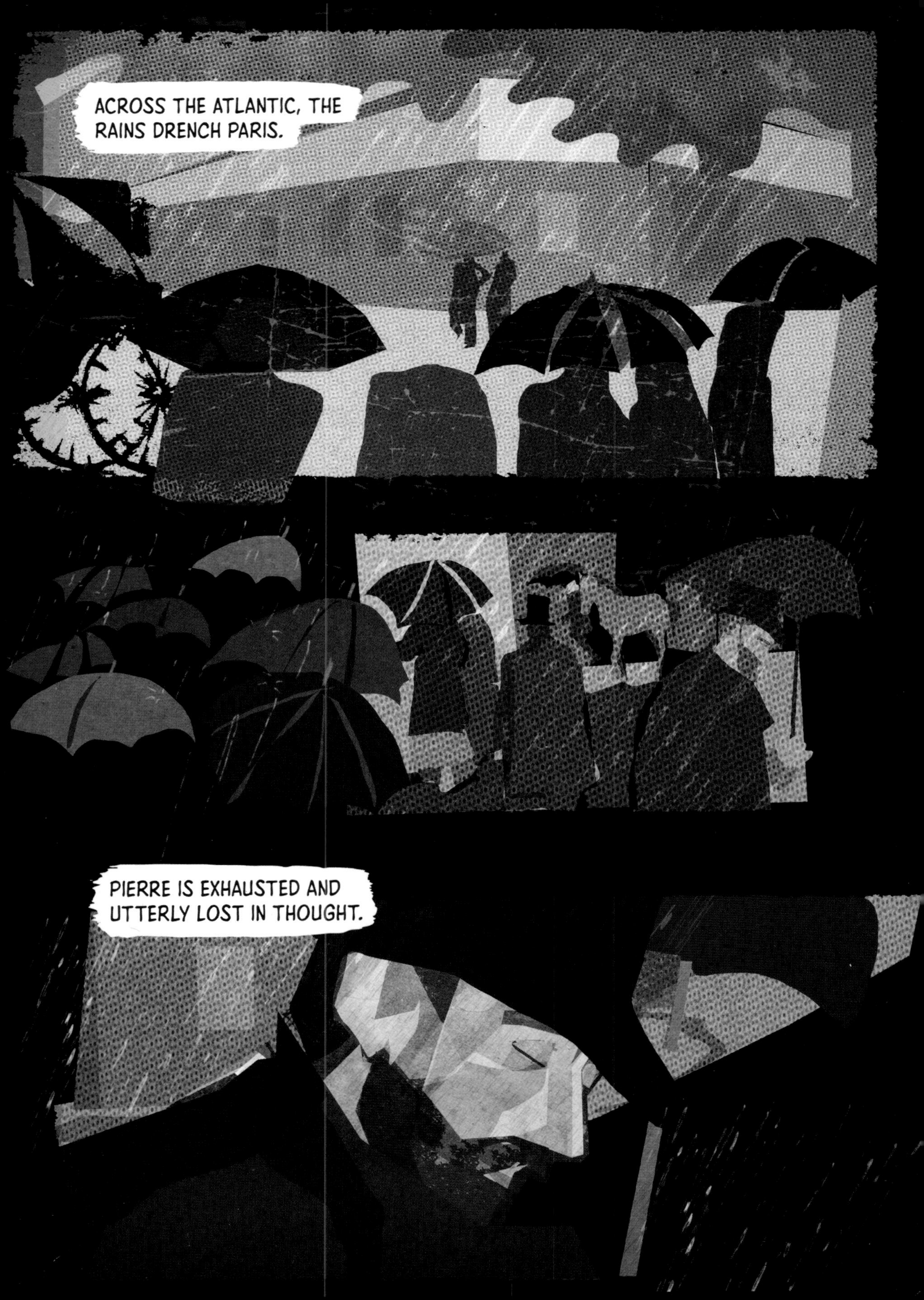
ACROSS THE ATLANTIC, THE RAINS DRENCH PARIS.
PIERRE IS EXHAUSTED AND UTTERLY LOST IN THOUGHT.

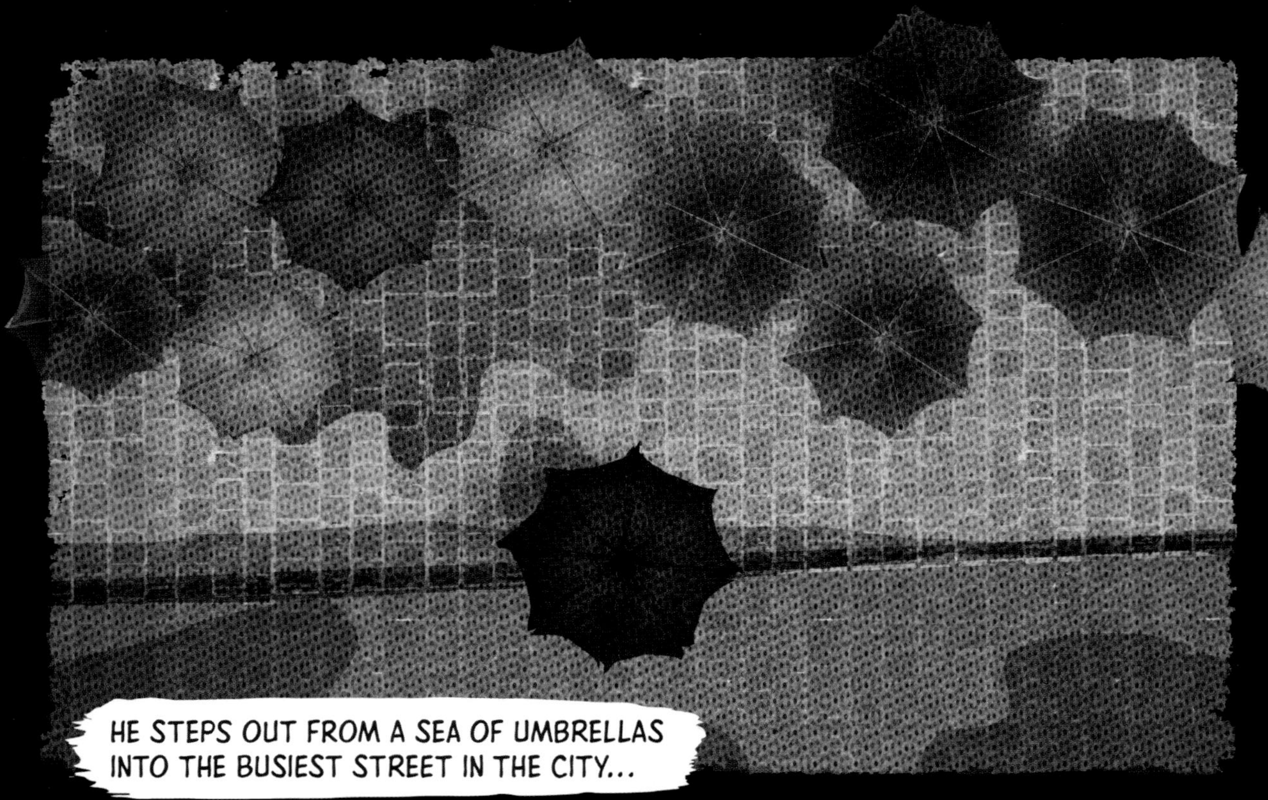
HE STEPS OUT FROM A SEA OF UMBRELLAS INTO THE BUSIEST STREET IN THE CITY...

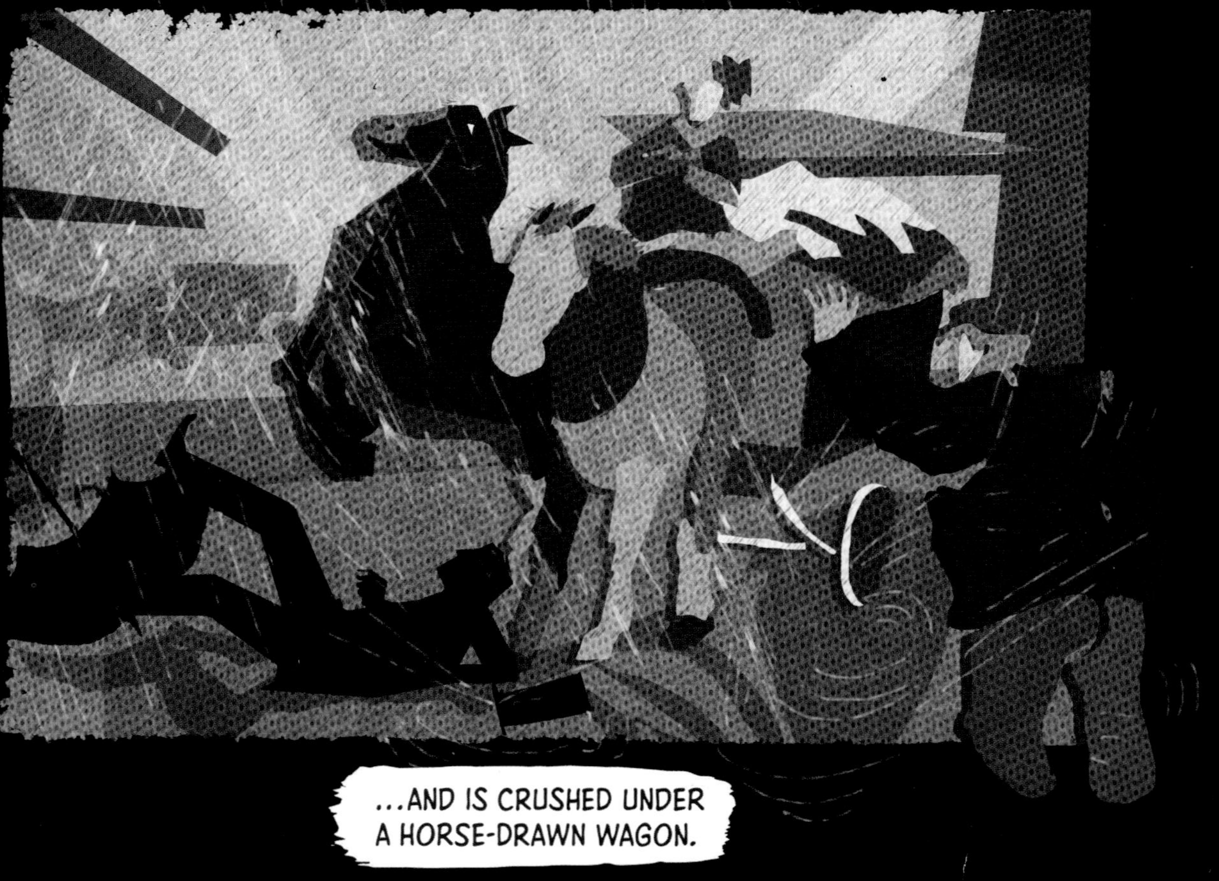
...AND IS CRUSHED UNDER A HORSE-DRAWN WAGON.

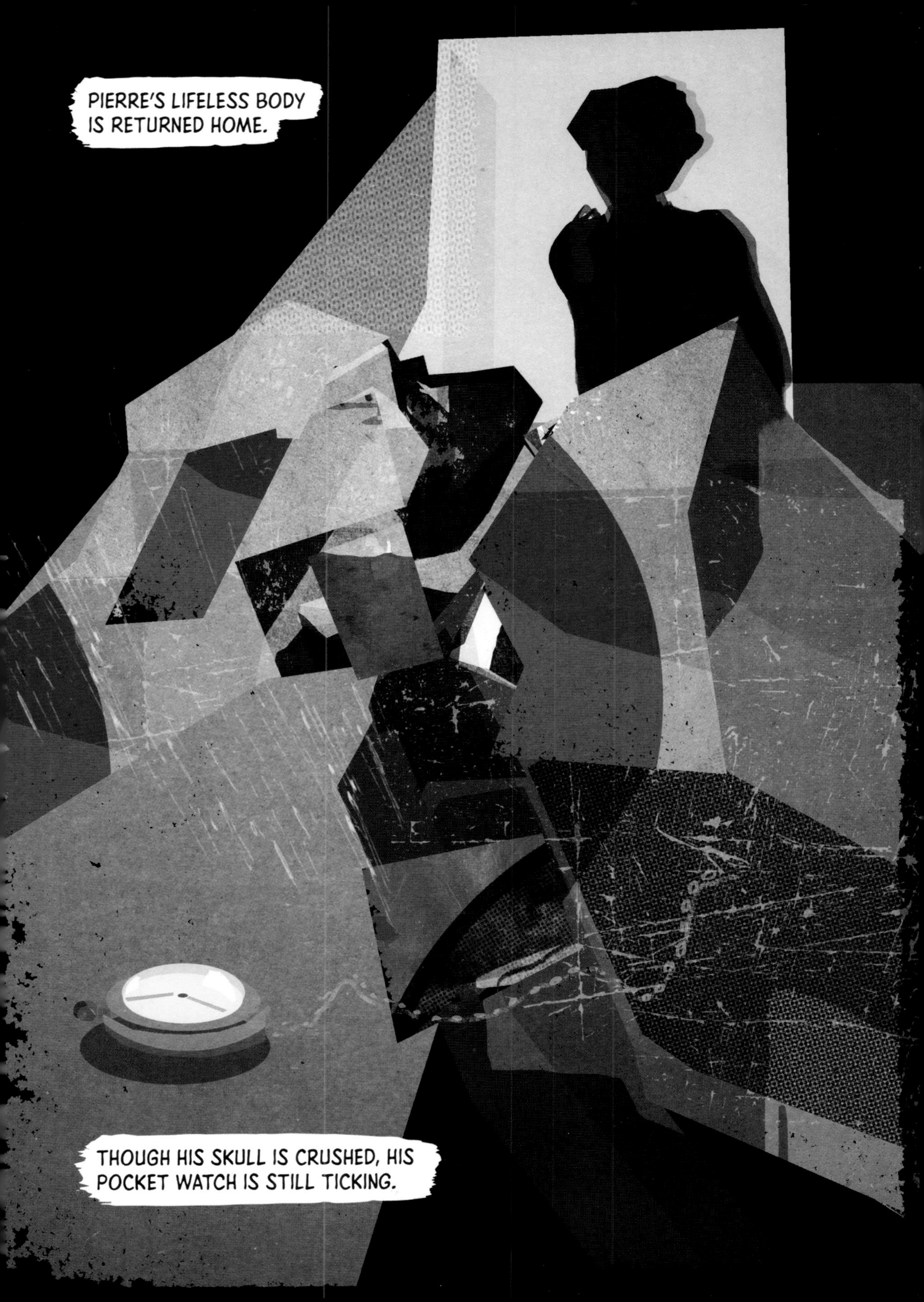
PIERRE'S LIFELESS BODY IS RETURNED HOME.
THOUGH HIS SKULL IS CRUSHED, HIS POCKET WATCH IS STILL TICKING.

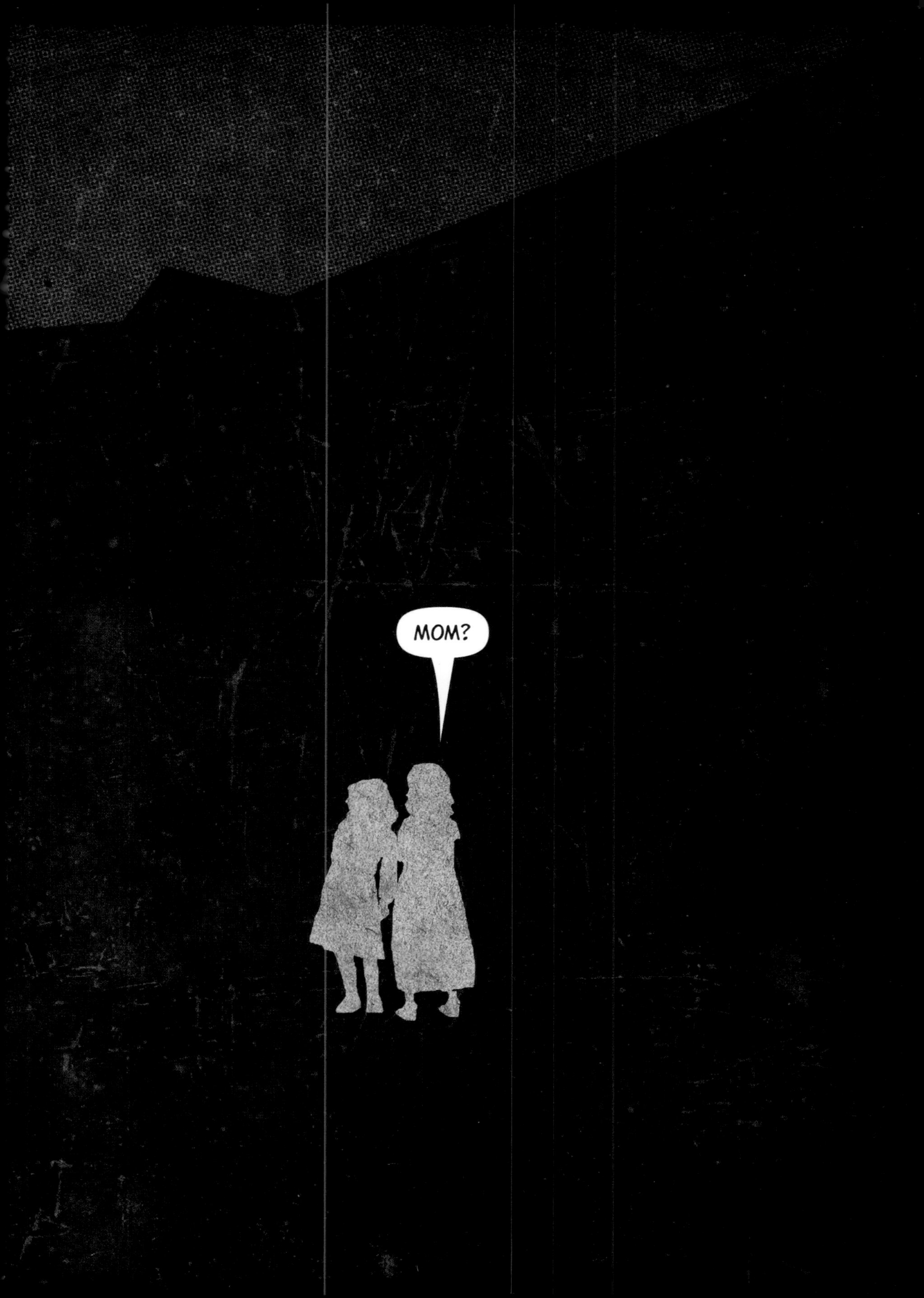
MOM?

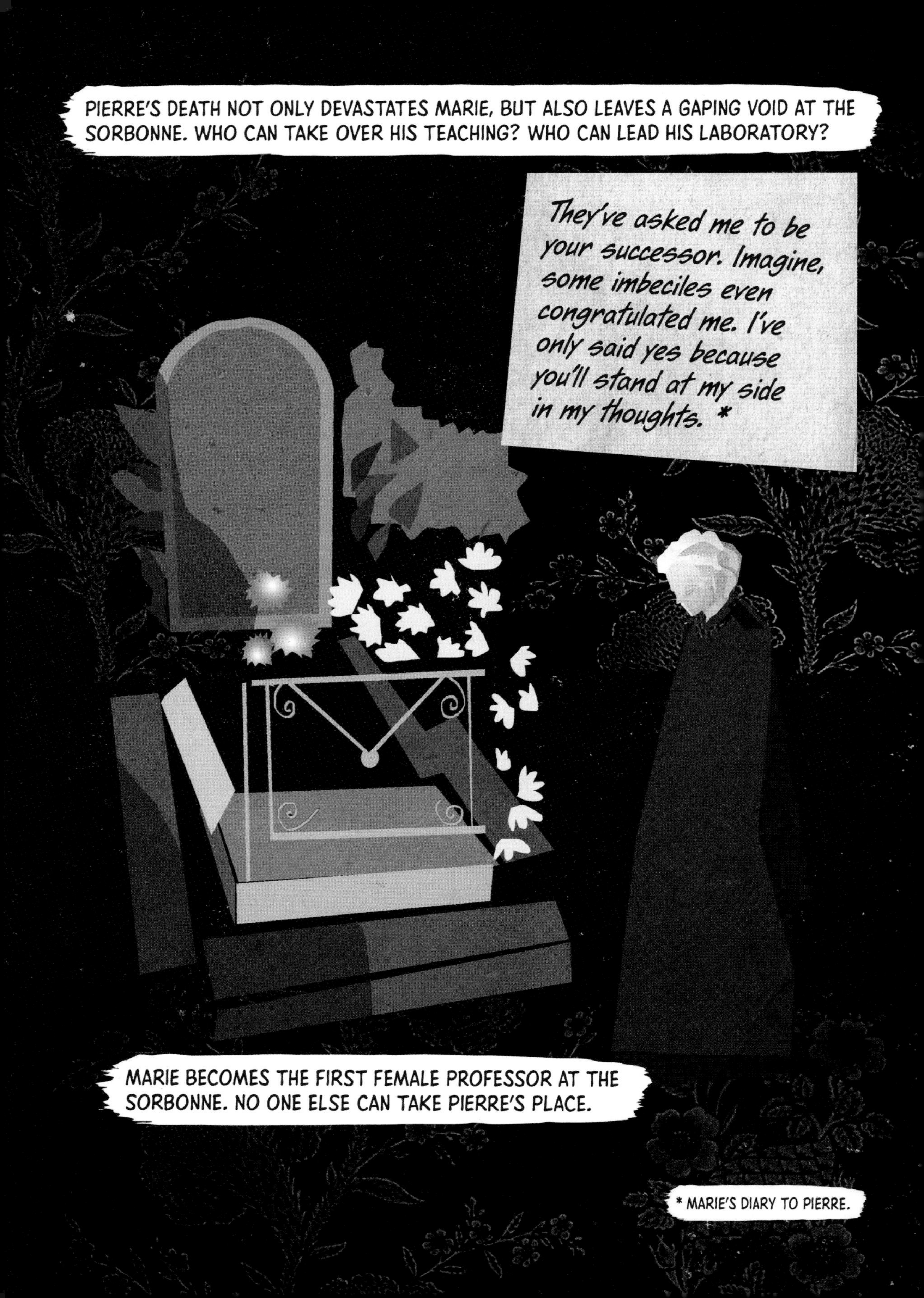
PIERRE'S DEATH NOT ONLY DEVASTATES MARIE, BUT ALSO LEAVES A GAPING VOID AT THE SORBONNE. WHO CAN TAKE OVER HIS TEACHING? WHO CAN LEAD HIS LABORATORY?
They've asked me to be your successor. Imagine, some imbeciles even congratulated me. I've only said yes because you'll stand at my side in my thoughts. *
MARIE BECOMES THE FIRST FEMALE PROFESSOR AT THE SORBONNE. NO ONE ELSE CAN TAKE PIERRE'S PLACE.
* MARIE'S DIARY TO PIERRE.

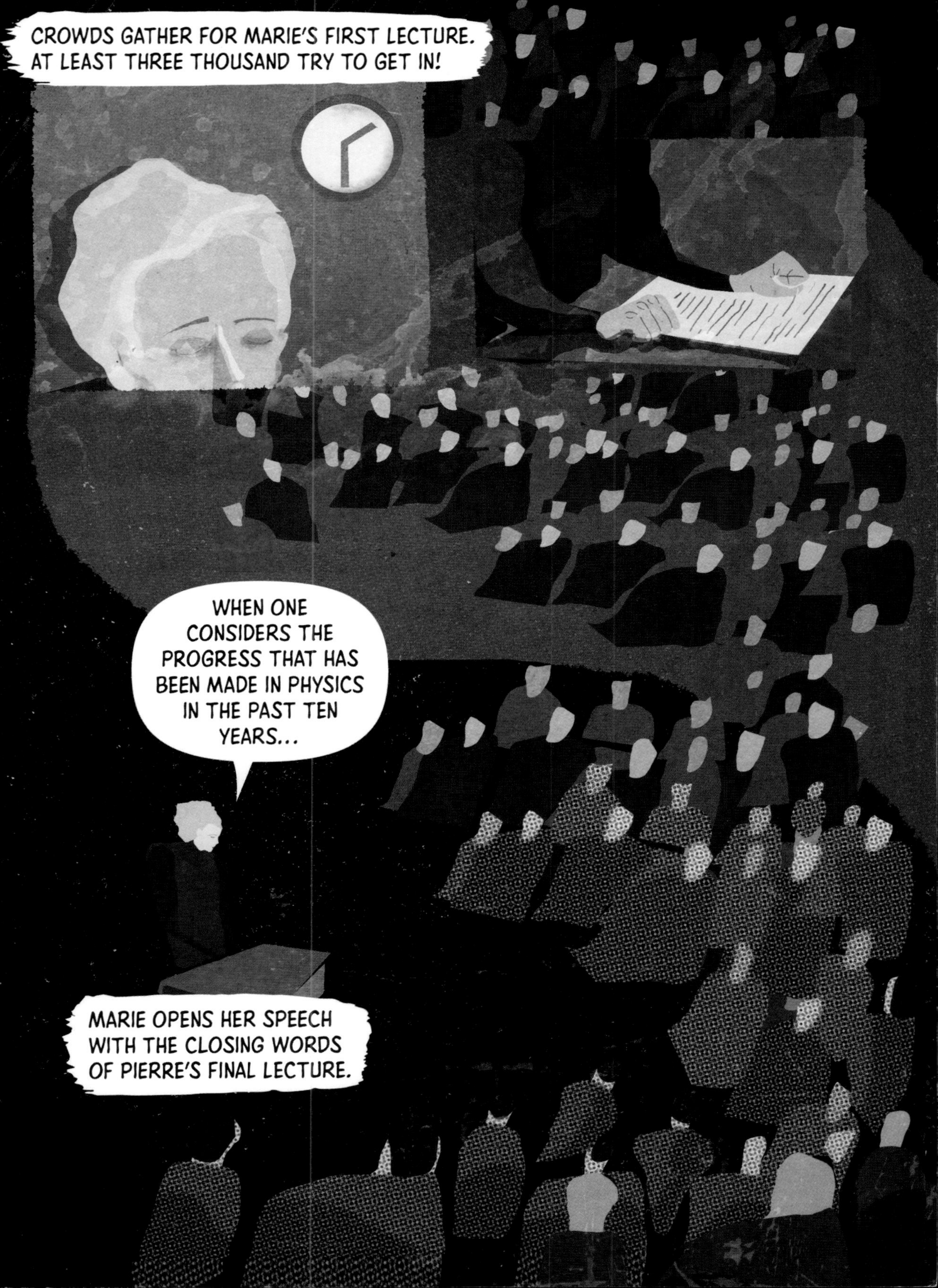
CROWDS GATHER FOR MARIE'S FIRST LECTURE. AT LEAST THREE THOUSAND TRY TO GET IN!
WHEN ONE CONSIDERS THE PROGRESS THAT HAS BEEN MADE IN PHYSICS IN THE PAST TEN YEARS...
MARIE OPENS HER SPEECH WITH THE CLOSING WORDS OF PIERRE'S FINAL LECTURE.

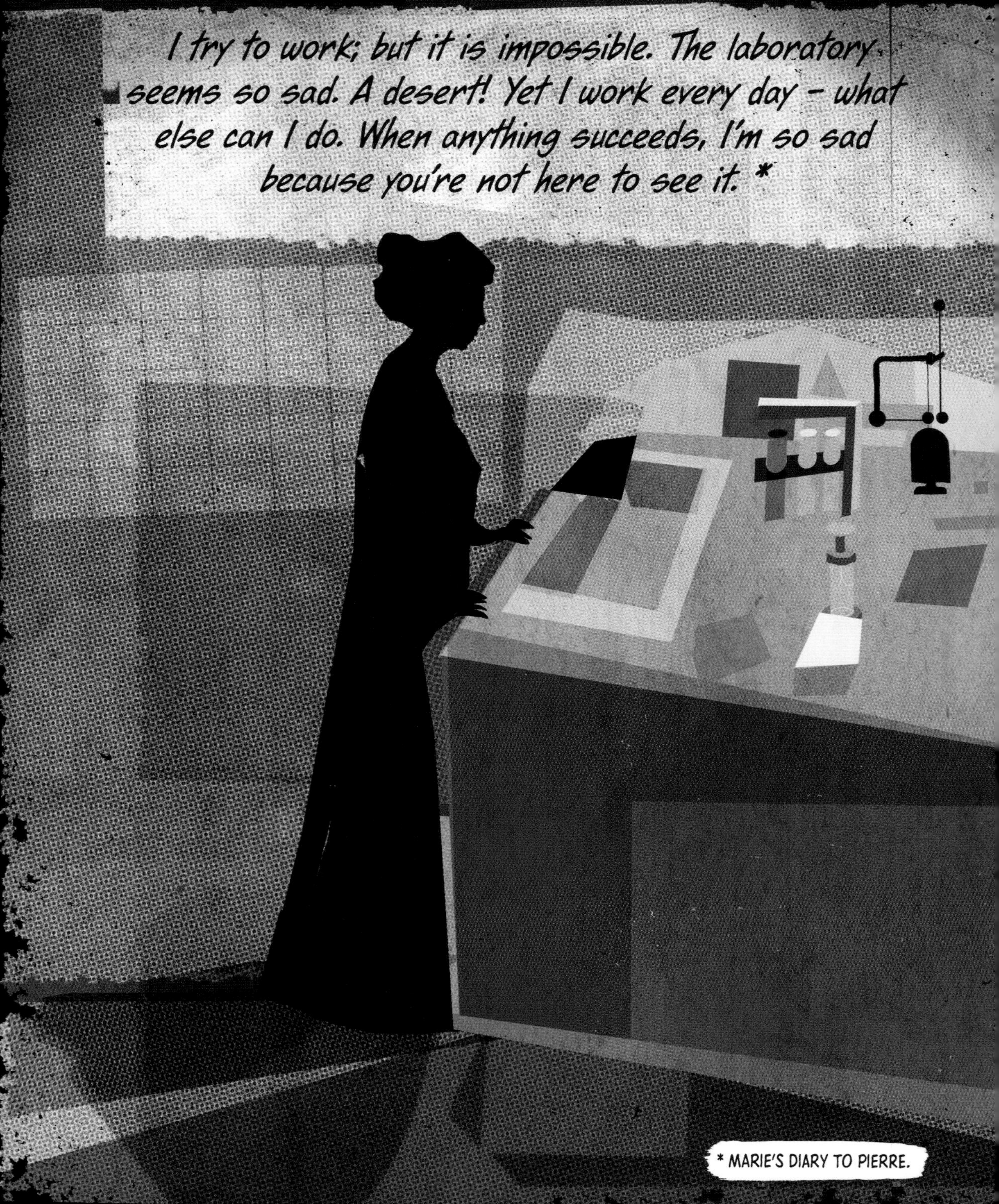
I try to work; but it is impossible. The laboratory seems so sad. A desert! Yet I work every day - what else can I do. When anything succeeds, I'm so sad because you're not here to see it. *
* MARIE'S DIARY TO PIERRE.

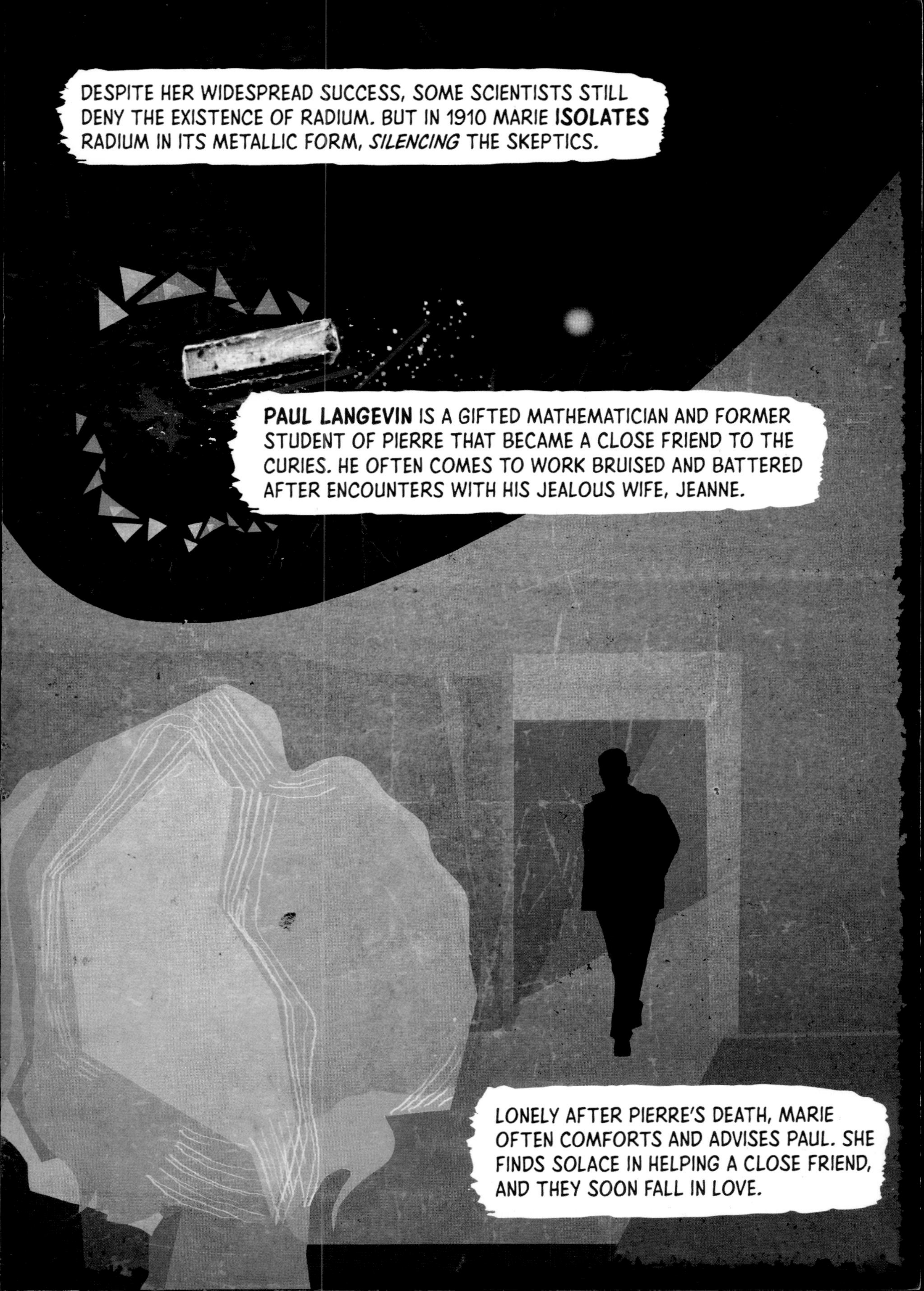
DESPITE HER WIDESPREAD SUCCESS, SOME SCIENTISTS STILL DENY THE EXISTENCE OF RADIUM. BUT IN 1910 MARIE **ISOLATES** RADIUM IN ITS METALLIC FORM, *SILENCING* THE SKEPTICS.
PAUL LANGEVIN IS A GIFTED MATHEMATICIAN AND FORMER STUDENT OF PIERRE THAT BECAME A CLOSE FRIEND TO THE CURIES. HE OFTEN COMES TO WORK BRUISED AND BATTERED AFTER ENCOUNTERS WITH HIS JEALOUS WIFE, JEANNE.
LONELY AFTER PIERRE'S DEATH, MARIE OFTEN COMFORTS AND ADVISES PAUL. SHE FINDS SOLACE IN HELPING A CLOSE FRIEND, AND THEY SOON FALL IN LOVE.

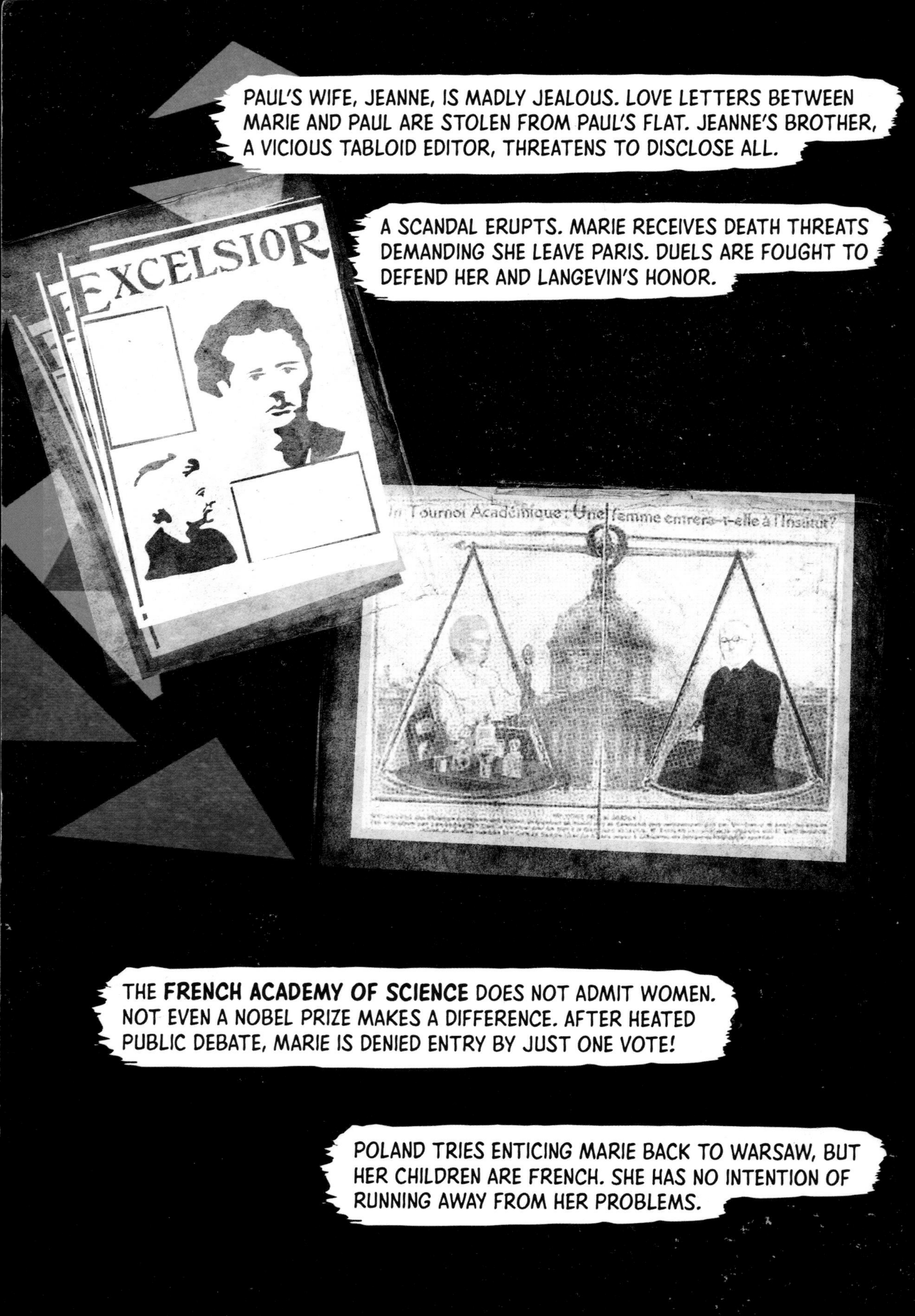
PAUL'S WIFE, JEANNE, IS MADLY JEALOUS. LOVE LETTERS BETWEEN MARIE AND PAUL ARE STOLEN FROM PAUL'S FLAT. JEANNE'S BROTHER, A VICIOUS TABLOID EDITOR, THREATENS TO DISCLOSE ALL.
A SCANDAL ERUPTS. MARIE RECEIVES DEATH THREATS DEMANDING SHE LEAVE PARIS. DUELS ARE FOUGHT TO DEFEND HER AND LANGEVIN'S HONOR.
EXCELSIOR
Un Tournoi Académique : Une femme entrera-t-elle à l'Institut?
THE **FRENCH ACADEMY OF SCIENCE** DOES NOT ADMIT WOMEN. NOT EVEN A NOBEL PRIZE MAKES A DIFFERENCE. AFTER HEATED PUBLIC DEBATE, MARIE IS DENIED ENTRY BY JUST ONE VOTE!
POLAND TRIES ENTICING MARIE BACK TO WARSAW, BUT HER CHILDREN ARE FRENCH. SHE HAS NO INTENTION OF RUNNING AWAY FROM HER PROBLEMS.

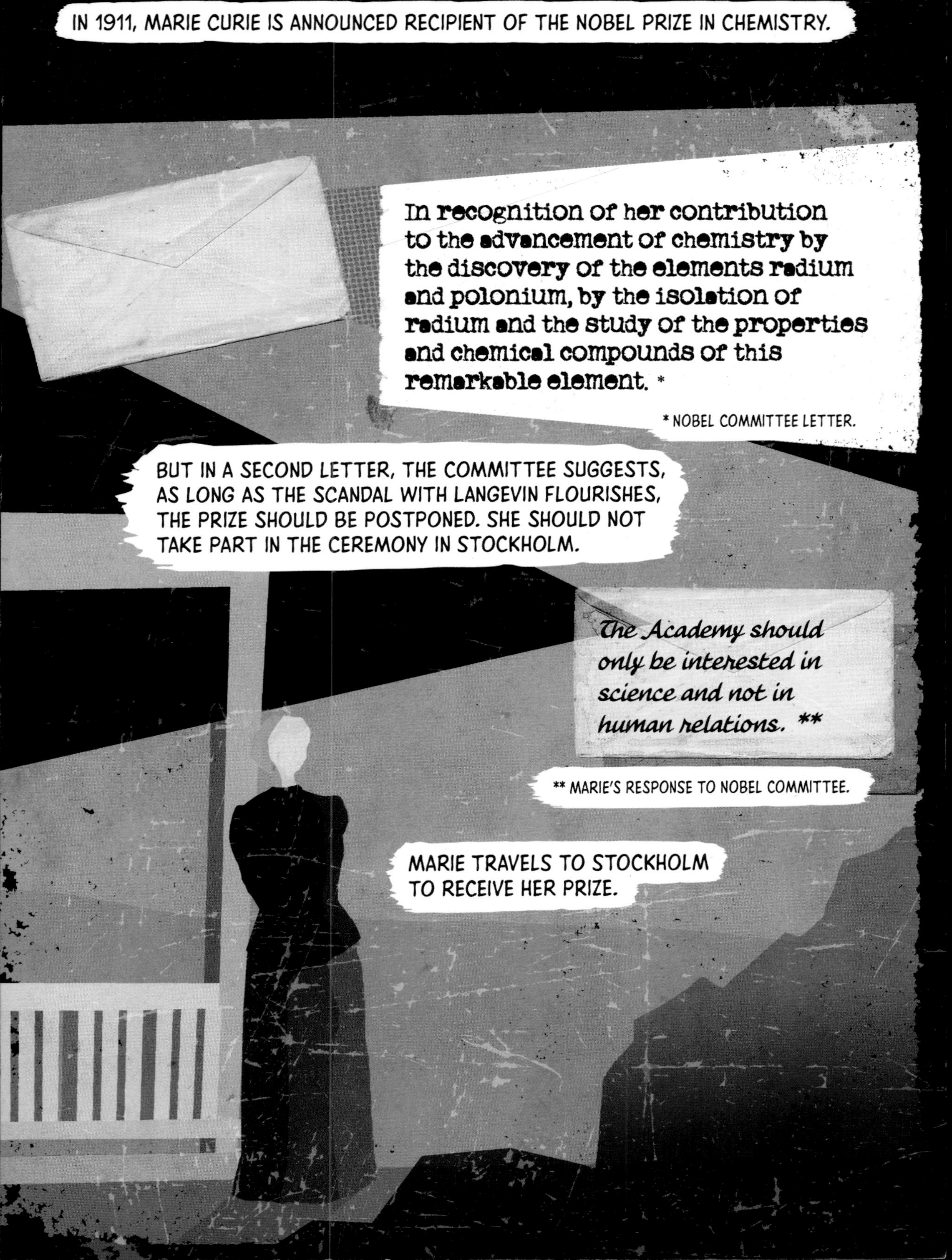
IN 1911, MARIE CURIE IS ANNOUNCED RECIPIENT OF THE NOBEL PRIZE IN CHEMISTRY.
In recognition of her contribution to the advancement of chemistry by the discovery of the elements radium and polonium, by the isolation of radium and the study of the properties and chemical compounds of this remarkable element. *
* NOBEL COMMITTEE LETTER.
BUT IN A SECOND LETTER, THE COMMITTEE SUGGESTS, AS LONG AS THE SCANDAL WITH LANGEVIN FLOURISHES, THE PRIZE SHOULD BE POSTPONED. SHE SHOULD NOT TAKE PART IN THE CEREMONY IN STOCKHOLM.
The Academy should only be interested in science and not in human relations. **
** MARIE'S RESPONSE TO NOBEL COMMITTEE.
MARIE TRAVELS TO STOCKHOLM TO RECEIVE HER PRIZE.

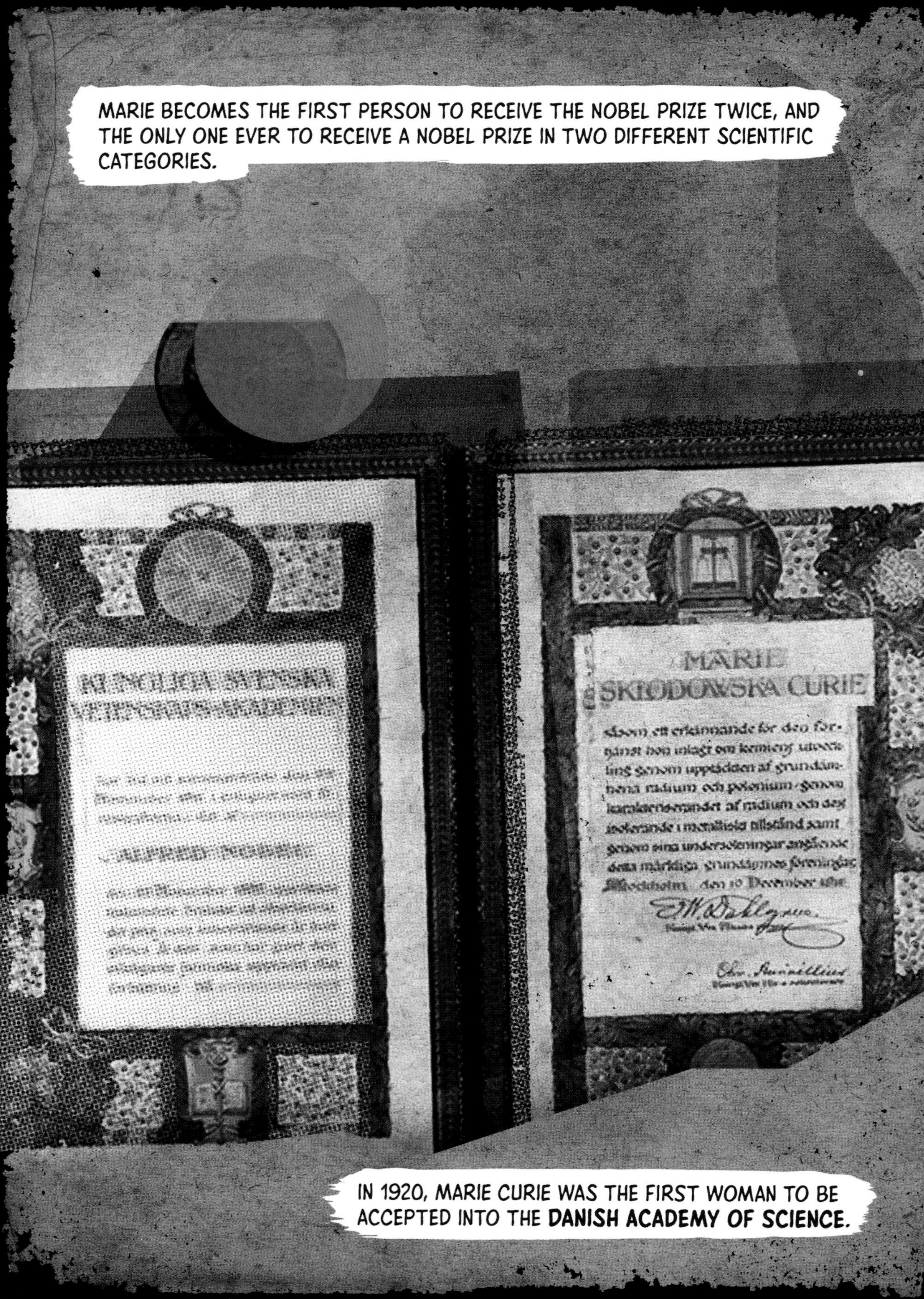
MARIE BECOMES THE FIRST PERSON TO RECEIVE THE NOBEL PRIZE TWICE, AND THE ONLY ONE EVER TO RECEIVE A NOBEL PRIZE IN TWO DIFFERENT SCIENTIFIC CATEGORIES.
IN 1920, MARIE CURIE WAS THE FIRST WOMAN TO BE ACCEPTED INTO THE **DANISH ACADEMY OF SCIENCE.**

Epilogue

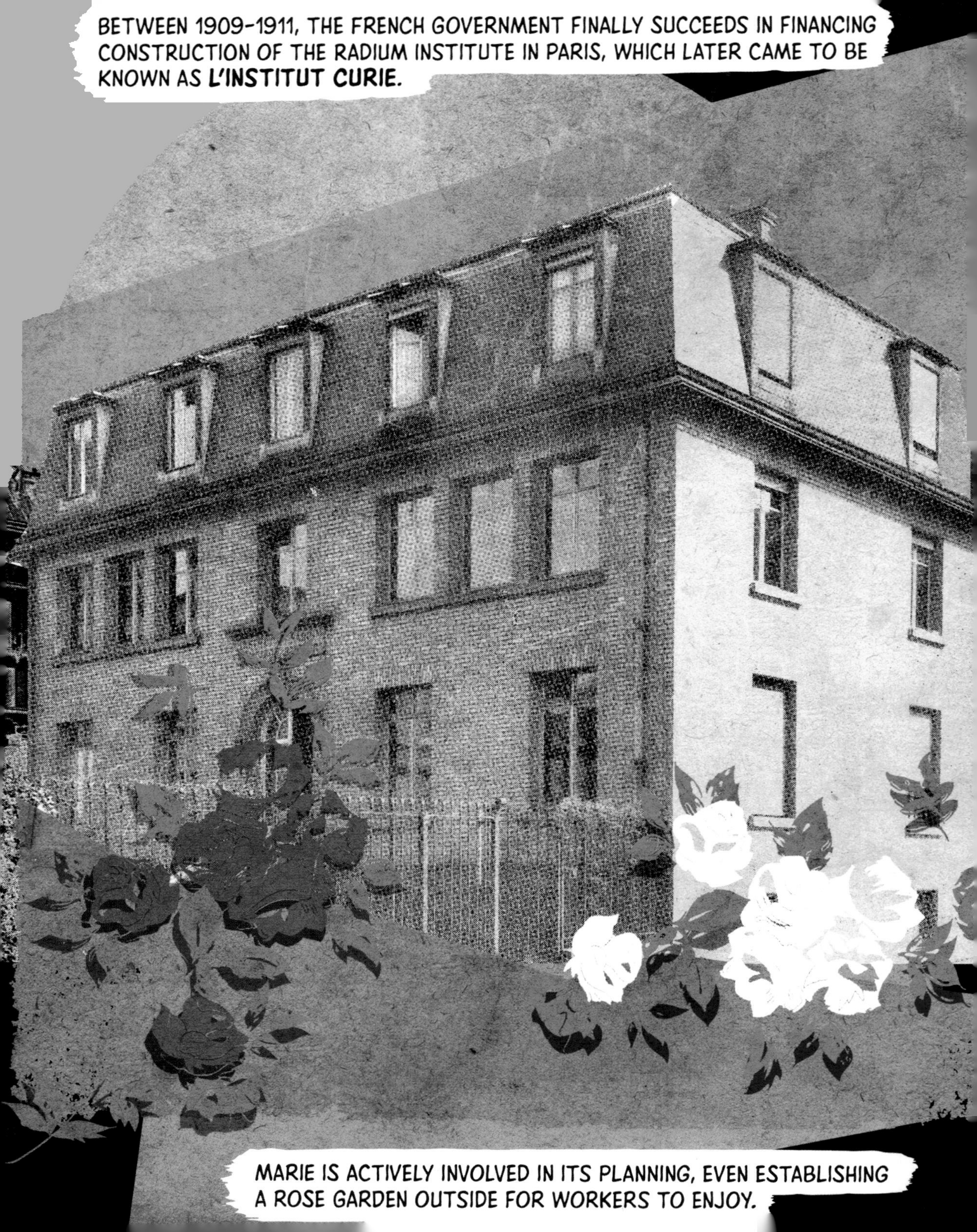
BETWEEN 1909-1911, THE FRENCH GOVERNMENT FINALLY SUCCEEDS IN FINANCING CONSTRUCTION OF THE RADIUM INSTITUTE IN PARIS, WHICH LATER CAME TO BE KNOWN AS **L'INSTITUT CURIE.**
MARIE IS ACTIVELY INVOLVED IN ITS PLANNING, EVEN ESTABLISHING A ROSE GARDEN OUTSIDE FOR WORKERS TO ENJOY.

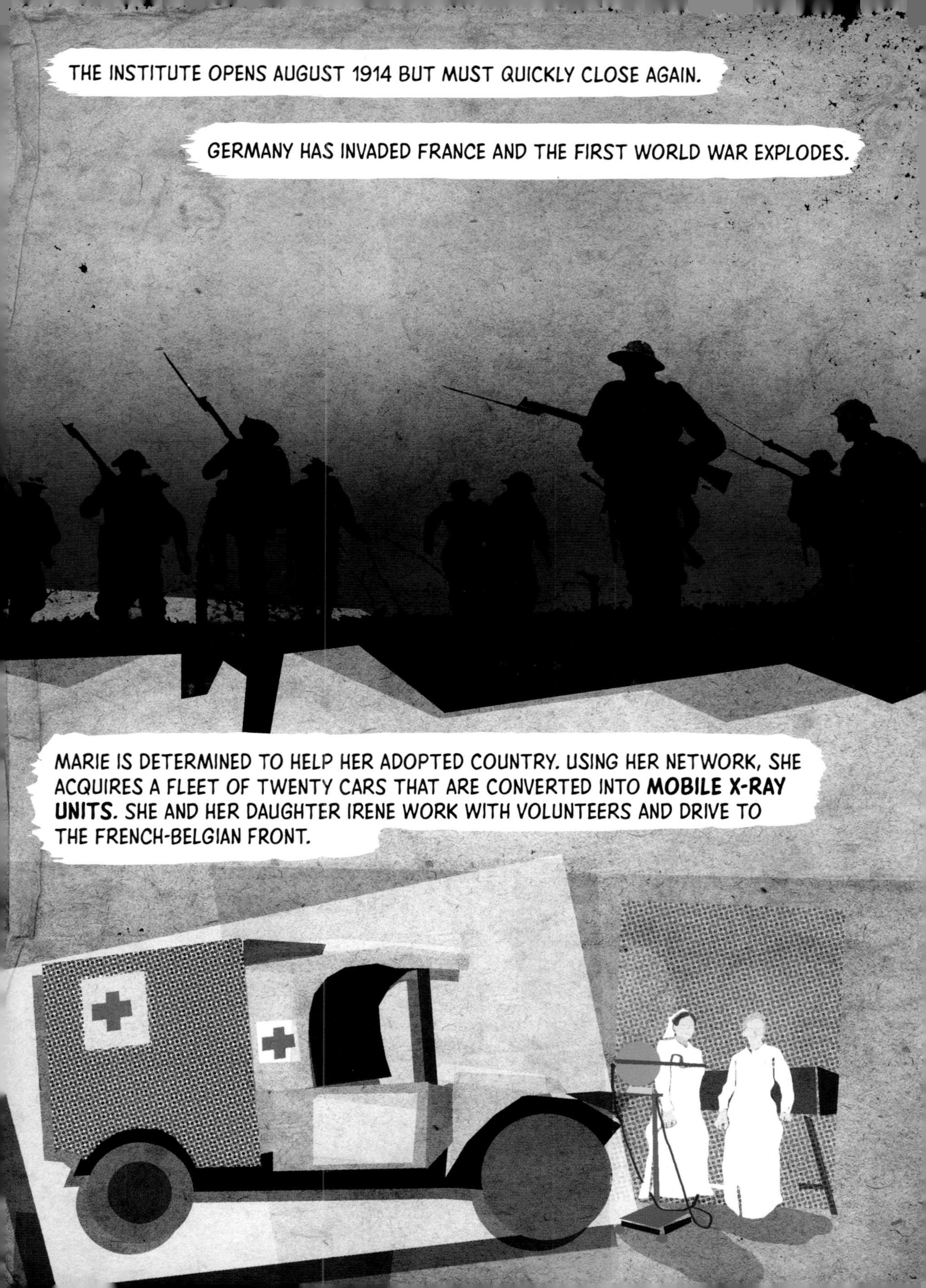
THE INSTITUTE OPENS AUGUST 1914 BUT MUST QUICKLY CLOSE AGAIN.
GERMANY HAS INVADED FRANCE AND THE FIRST WORLD WAR EXPLODES.
MARIE IS DETERMINED TO HELP HER ADOPTED COUNTRY. USING HER NETWORK, SHE ACQUIRES A FLEET OF TWENTY CARS THAT ARE CONVERTED INTO **MOBILE X-RAY UNITS.** SHE AND HER DAUGHTER IRENE WORK WITH VOLUNTEERS AND DRIVE TO THE FRENCH-BELGIAN FRONT.

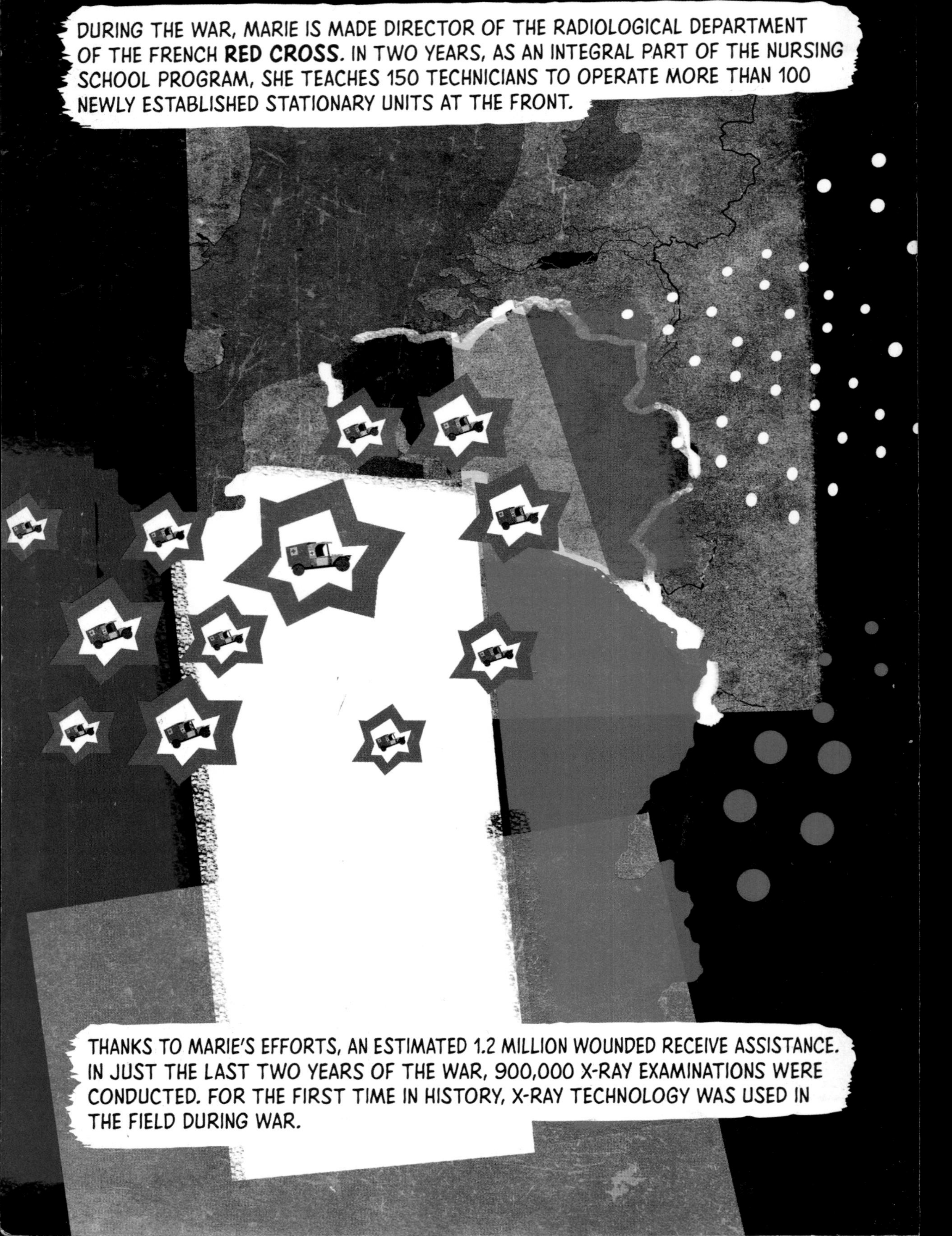
DURING THE WAR, MARIE IS MADE DIRECTOR OF THE RADIOLOGICAL DEPARTMENT OF THE FRENCH **RED CROSS**. IN TWO YEARS, AS AN INTEGRAL PART OF THE NURSING SCHOOL PROGRAM, SHE TEACHES 150 TECHNICIANS TO OPERATE MORE THAN 100 NEWLY ESTABLISHED STATIONARY UNITS AT THE FRONT.
THANKS TO MARIE'S EFFORTS, AN ESTIMATED 1.2 MILLION WOUNDED RECEIVE ASSISTANCE. IN JUST THE LAST TWO YEARS OF THE WAR, 900,000 X-RAY EXAMINATIONS WERE CONDUCTED. FOR THE FIRST TIME IN HISTORY, X-RAY TECHNOLOGY WAS USED IN THE FIELD DURING WAR.